Federal Fiscal Policy

in the

Postwar Recessions

Federal Fiscal Policy

in the

Postwar Recessions

WILFRED LEWIS, (JR.)

Studies of Government Finance

THE BROOKINGS INSTITUTION

WASHINGTON, D.C.

THE BROOKINGS INSTITUTION is an independent organization devoted to nonpartisan research, education, and publication in economics, government, foreign policy, and the social sciences generally. Its principal purposes are to aid in the development of sound public policies and to promote public understanding of issues of national importance.

The Institution was founded December 8, 1927, to merge the activities of the Institute for Government Research, founded in 1916, the Institute of Economics, founded in 1922, and the Robert Brookings Graduate School of Economics and Government, founded in 1924.

The general administration of the Institution is the responsibility of a self-perpetuating Board of Trustees. The Trustees are likewise charged with maintaining the independence of the staff and fostering the most favorable conditions for creative research and education. The immediate direction of the policies, program, and staff of the Institution is vested in the President, assisted by the division directors and an advisory council, chosen from the professional staff of the Institution.

In publishing a study, the Institution presents it as a competent treatment of a subject worthy of public consideration. The interpretations and conclusions in such publications are those of the author or authors and do not necessarily reflect the views of other members of the Brookings staff or of the administrative officers of the Institution.

Foreword

THIS VOLUME ON FEDERAL fiscal policy in the postwar recessions represents the first publication of the series of Studies of Government Finance sponsored by the National Committee on Government Finance. The Committee was appointed by the Trustees of the Brookings Institution to develop and supervise a comprehensive program of research and education on taxation and expenditures at all levels of government in the United States. The program is being carried out by scholars at Brookings and various other research organizations and universities. The activities of the National Committee are financed by a special grant from the Ford Foundation.

Federal taxes and expenditures greatly influence the economy at all times and may become particularly important in recession and recovery periods. This study analyzes federal government fiscal activity in the recessions and recoveries of 1948-50, 1953-55, 1957-59, and 1960-62. Emphasis is placed on deliberate countercyclical fiscal policy and the automatic responses of taxes and government expenditures to fluctuations in economic activity. But attention is also given to other aspects of the debate and actions on fiscal matters that continued during recessions and recoveries, often with little apparent relation to the current economic situation. The statements of public officials and others about what the government did and discussions of actions that were proposed but not carried out are reviewed in some detail because of their influence on public opinion and the development of a consensus concerning federal fiscal policy.

The objective of the study is to identify past sources of weakness and strength of fiscal policy and to suggest ways in which improvements can be made. As the author makes clear, however, fiscal policy operates under many constraints and is shaped by many circumstances other than the current economic situation. It may well be that the path toward improved fiscal policy for stabilization involves better understanding of and adaptation to these constraints, rather than the adoption of simple rules for economic stabilization.

When this study was completed in the spring of 1962, recovery from the fourth postwar recession was still under way. Statistics and other information included are the items available in March 1962.

Wilfred Lewis, Jr., who carried out the study while on leave from the staff of the U. S. Bureau of the Budget, is now a member of the staff of Robert R. Nathan Associates, Inc., economic advisers to the government of Afghanistan. The study was under the general direction of Richard Goode of the Brookings staff. The manuscript was reviewed by Joseph A. Pechman, Director of Economic Studies at Brookings and Executive Director of the National Committee on Government Finance, and by an advisory committee consisting of E. Cary Brown, Massachusetts Institute of Technology; Samuel M. Cohn, U. S. Bureau of the Budget; Bert G. Hickman, Brookings Institution; and Melvin I. White, Brooklyn College. Others who read sections of the manuscript and offered helpful suggestions were Arthur F. Burns, Benjamin Caplan, Franz Gehrels, A. E. Holmans, Leon Keyserling, Thomas Lusk, Louis Shere, Naomi Sweeney, and James Witte. David Lusher and Norman Ture were helpful to the author in the discussion of both historical and analytical questions. Lyndall McCloud facilitated the study by making available the computing equipment of the Board of Governors of the Federal Reserve System for processing some of the income tax data. The encouragement and assistance of Samuel M. Cohn were especially helpful to the author. Virginia Parker edited the manuscript. Ernst Reichl produced the design for the book. Sunder Dass assisted in checking statistical data. The author's wife, Joan Lewis, assisted in typing and proofing. The author and the Institution are grateful to all of these persons for their help.

The interpretations and opinions are those of the author and do not necessarily reflect the views of the members of the National Committee on Government Finance or those of the advisory committee; staff members, officers, or trustees of the Brookings Institution; or the Ford Foundation.

ROBERT D. CALKINS

President

October 1962

Studies of Government Finance

Studies of Government Finance is a special program of research and education in taxation and government expenditures at the federal, state, and local levels. These studies are under the supervision of the National Committee on Government Finance appointed by the Trustees of the Brookings Institution, and are supported by a special grant from the Ford Foundation.

Contents

Text Tables

Charts

Appendix Tables

CHAPTER I

Introduction

SINCE WORLD WAR II, the growth of the American economy has been interrupted four times—in 1948, in 1953, in 1957, and again in 1960—by temporary recessions in the general level of economic activity.[1] The federal government, since the Employment Act of 1946, has had a commitment to try to maintain high levels of income, employment, and purchasing power. Most economists and many other people have expected the government to use fiscal policy to help fulfill this pledge. They have expected the government to raise aggregate demand and national income by lowering tax collections or increasing government expenditures during recessions.

The postwar recessions have been brief and mild by standards of the 1930's. The contractions lasted from two to four calendar-year quarters, and involved declines in the gross national product (GNP) of from 2 to 4 percent. Nevertheless, all four recessions brought expressions of alarm from economists and—with varying degrees of timeliness and effectiveness—attempts by the federal government to take corrective fiscal action.

[1] The immediate postwar drop in gross national product when defense spending was cut back in 1945-46 was not a decline of the kind usually embraced by the term "recession," and is excluded from the present study. Consumer and business purchases rose in that period, and reduced employment was reflected in a smaller labor force rather than increased unemployment.

1

Scope and Methods

This study attempts to describe, measure, and evaluate the planned and unplanned fiscal actions of the federal government—changes in government receipts and expenditures—in the postwar recessions and recoveries.[2] That the government, in theory, can counteract recession by suitably chosen fiscal policies has been demonstrated too well in a voluminous literature to require discussion here. Similarly, this study presumes agreement with, and does not undertake to defend, the general proposition that the federal government should try to use its fiscal powers to combat unemployment and promote stable growth. However, particular antirecession fiscal actions can be better or worse with respect to effectiveness, timing, efficiency, and compatibility with other goals, and some of the policies pursued in the past have been worse rather than better. It is hoped that, by examining these past actions in some detail, the choice of fiscal weapons for future recessions and the strategy used in applying them may be improved.

How the postwar recessions came to be, and how likely they are to recur in the future, for the most part, are beyond the field of inquiry. However, the federal government's actions affecting receipts and expenditures in the postwar economy have not been confined to counteracting declines in private spending. In fact, on more than one occasion, federal fiscal actions have initiated or aggravated the recession. To the extent that such occasions are examined, the present study becomes involved in causes as well as corrections.

It is impossible to completely ignore some of the monetary, credit, and public debt actions that were closely related to the development of fiscal policy or to the financing of recession-induced deficits. But, for the most part, the study is limited to fiscal policy and actions. This obviously will give an incomplete picture of total federal government activity affecting the economy. While monetary and credit activities are perhaps the major omission in this respect, there are others. These include federal guarantees or insurance of private loans, price and wage controls, minimum wage legislation, actions of regulatory agencies, and exhortations, from time to time, by public officials about private behavior of various kinds.

[2] See Appendix D for "Notes on Sources and Data."

Periods Covered

This study is concerned with two kinds of periods. First are those periods in which economic activity fell noticeably below levels reached earlier. Second are those immediately afterwards during which the economy still was below its previous rate in using the available labor force and other factors of production. To focus on periods during which rates of factor utilization are below "normal" does not deny the importance of economic stabilization problems associated with inflation at other phases of the cycle or, perhaps, to some extent, even during the recession and recovery periods themselves. But it does carry a strong implication that, during periods of recession and recovery, the major stabilization problem is the level of unemployment, and that such inflationary pressures as may be present are not due in significant degree to the pressure of demand against capacity.

More specifically, the recession and recovery periods studied here were selected by considering two basic statistical measures. One of these is the gross national product (GNP) as estimated by the U.S. Department of Commerce—the best single measure of the level of economic activity. The other is the seasonally adjusted rate of unemployment of the civilian labor force as reported by the U.S. Department of Labor. The recession, or contraction, phase covers the period from the prerecession peak in GNP to the subsequent low point in GNP two to four quarters later. In theory, the real (deflated) GNP was used in designating peaks and troughs; in practice, for the four postwar recessions, these were identical with peaks and troughs as identified by the GNP in current dollars. So defined, the four postwar recessions are summarized in Table 1.

Quarterly peaks and troughs in GNP usually, but do not necessarily, coincide with the more widely used business cycle peaks and troughs identified by the National Bureau of Economic Research (NBER), which are established by considering the movement of a large number of economic indicators. The NBER quarterly and monthly cyclical peaks and troughs are given for comparison in Table 2. The main difference, when the NBER method is used, is a somewhat later dating of recession troughs.

The phase designated as "recovery" is intended to represent the

TABLE 1. Postwar Recessions and Recoveries[a]

Recession and Recovery Calendar Years	Prerecession Peak Quarter in GNP	Trough Quarter in GNP	Number Quarters of Decline	Percent Change in Real GNP, Peak to Trough	Terminal Quarter of Recovery
1948-50	1948-IV	1949-II	2	−2.3	1950-II
1953-55	1953-II	1954-II	4	−3.7	1955-II
1957-59	1957-III	1958-I	2	−4.3	1959-II
1960-62	1960-II	1961-I	3	−2.2	1962-II

[a] Source, U.S. Department of Commerce. See text for explanation of terminal quarters.

period from the trough quarter in GNP to the time the economy returns to high employment. The percentage of the labor force employed is used as the primary means of indicating recovery, not because labor is the only underused resource during recession and recovery, but because this is probably the best single statistic available to indicate the extent to which production resources in general are being utilized.

It will be recognized that the "recovery" period described above is only the first phase of the "expansion" period used in the NBER chronologies of business cycles. The expansion period as defined by NBER covers the whole period from the trough to the following peak. However, it appears consistent with the observed behavior of public officials, as well as useful analytically, to attempt a distinction between periods in which the economy is moving along a reasonably

TABLE 2. Postwar Business Cycle Peaks and Troughs, Dated by the National Bureau of Economic Research[a]

MONTHS		QUARTERS	
Peak	Trough	Peak	Trough
Nov. 1948	Oct. 1949	1948-IV	1949-IV
July 1953	Aug. 1954	1953-II	1954-III
July 1957	Apr. 1958	1957-III	1958-II
May 1960	Feb. 1961	1960-II	1961-I

[a] Sources, Geoffrey Moore (ed.), *Business Cycle Indicators* (Princeton University Press for NBER, 1961); Julius Shiskin, *Signals of Recession and Recovery* (NBER, 1961); and U.S. Bureau of the Census, *Business Cycle Developments*, January 1962, p. 57.

satisfactory growth path and periods in which it is returning to such a path after contraction.

While the GNP trough is an unambiguous means of identifying the start of a recovery, selecting a point in time to mark its completion is necessarily somewhat arbitrary. For example, the outbreak of the Korean War in mid-1950, which occurred while the economy was still recovering from the first postwar recession, pushed up price levels spectacularly, although the rate of unemployment for another half year or so remained substantially higher than it had been before the recession. After both the 1954 and 1958 recessions, the unemployment rate never dropped as low as it had been previously. However, for setting various quantitative benchmarks and other measurements, it is convenient to designate specific calendar quarters as marking the termination of recovery, even though this does not conform neatly to the actual behavior of the economy. The quarters selected for this purpose are referred to as "terminal quarters." The second quarter of 1950 was selected as the terminal quarter of recovery from the first postwar recession because the course of the economy after that time was governed largely by activities associated with the outbreak of hostilities in Korea. The second quarters of 1955 and 1959 were designated terminal quarters because the unemployment rate declined little or no farther after those points. The second quarter of 1962 was tentatively projected as the terminal quarter for the fourth postwar recession because the unemployment ratio was expected (in March 1962) to be down by then almost to the prerecession level.[3]

Measuring Federal Receipts and Expenditures

A definition of fiscal activities as those involving government receipts and expenditures is not as precise as it sounds, because receipts and expenditures can be, and have been, measured in different ways. Of the alternative tabulations of federal government receipts and expenditures which have been developed over the

[3] The validity of the analysis does not depend significantly on the selection of 1962-II as the terminal quarter or on the accuracy of the projections of the unemployment rate and GNP in that quarter. These projections are used mainly as benchmarks for high employment estimates. See Appendixes A and B.

years for various purposes, three are of central interest in studying fiscal policy:

1. *The Budget of the United States Government,* which is the focal point of the President's annual Budget Message to Congress, and—until recently—"the" budget in the parlance of most government officials. This version is usually referred to by economists as the "administrative," "regular," or "conventional" budget.

2. *Federal Government Receipts from and Payments to the Public,* which is known to economists as the "cash" or "consolidated cash" budget. This version includes, in addition to the administrative budget transactions, such important transactions as those of the social security, unemployment, and highway trust funds, which are excluded from the administrative budget.

3. *The National Income Budget,* which reflects federal receipts and expenditures as recorded in the national income accounts of the U.S. Department of Commerce. This budget, like the consolidated cash budget, is comprehensive with respect to trust fund transactions. However, there are important differences, aimed at measuring the direct effects of federal activity on aggregate private income. Perhaps the major differences in this respect are (a) the inclusion of corporate profits taxes in the national income budget when the liability accrues, rather than when the government receives payment, and (b) the exclusion from national income account expenditures of loans, mortgage purchases, purchases of land, and similar transactions which are exchanges of existing assets rather than additions to current private incomes.[4]

The President's annual administrative budget—because it omits so many important transactions of the government and because of the timing with which it reflects others—is seriously deficient as an index of the government's impact on the economy. However, the

[4] The differences between the three measures are explained in more detail in *The Budget of the United States Government for the Fiscal Year Ending June 30, 1963* (January 1962), Special Analysis B, pp. 279-82, and Special Analysis C, pp. 283-89; and in U.S. Department of Commerce, *U.S. Income and Output* (1958), Table III-10, pp. 178-79.

formulation and discussion of fiscal policy by public officials traditionally has been conducted within its framework, and it will be necessary to refer to totals in the administrative budget at a number of points in this study.

The superiority of the national income tabulation of receipts and expenditures as measures of the impact of federal activity on national income is widely accepted by economists, and the focus in this analysis will be those activities summed up in the federal surplus or deficit in the national income accounts. In fact, a good definition of "fiscal"—pragmatically as well as theoretically—is in terms of those receipts and expenditures reflected in the national income accounts. Differences between the national income budget and the consolidated cash budget, for example, can almost all be reduced to differences between transactions having direct income effects on the private economy, and those which affect the supply or liquidity of assets but not directly the incomes of the private sector.[5] It is convenient to regard the former as fiscal actions, and the latter as monetary-credit-debt actions. This does not imply a difference in importance, but it does imply a difference in function. It goes without saying that no single measure of federal activity is best for all purposes. Because the national income budget deliberately excludes loans, mortgage purchases, and similar transactions in existing assets, for example, it is undoubtedly less informative for purposes of analyzing interest rates and capital markets than either the consolidated cash budget or federal transactions as recorded by the Federal Reserve in its flow-of-funds statistics.

High Employment Benchmarks

Hypothetical high employment norms are used at several points in this study as benchmarks against which to compare the actual performance of the federal budget and the economy during the recession and recovery periods. One reason for attention to these high employment norms during recession and recovery in a growing economy is that actual data measured from peak to trough may

[5] See the article "Federal Receipts and Expenditures—Alternative Measures," *Monthly Review* of the Federal Reserve Bank of Kansas City, August 1961. See also Michael E. Levy, "Federal Budget: Deficit or Surplus," *Business Record* of the National Industrial Conference Board, February 1962.

understate the magnitude of the problem. For example, if the GNP remained unchanged for several quarters—neither rising nor falling—unemployment would grow because of the normal increase in the labor force, and corrective fiscal action probably would be called for. Here these benchmarks purposely have been made as simple as possible; and they have been made conservative by understating, in case of doubt, the potential performance of the economy and any failure to achieve it. The method of constructing the benchmarks, and the results in terms of gross national product are given in Appendix A. Basically, the method consists of making a linear interpolation between the actual observed value of GNP (or whatever series is being considered) at the prerecession peak and the value at the terminal quarter of recovery, after adjusting the latter for any remaining shortfall from the prerecession peak in the percentage of labor force employed.

This procedure requires a brief explanation. There is no attempt to adjust for any amount by which the economy may have been below its potential at the prerecession peak.[6] Taking the actual unemployment rate at each prerecession peak as a norm for measurement purposes does not imply that the question of whether that rate was too high or too low does not warrant public discussion or policy attention. But changes in the unemployment rate over a period of years can be logically separated from the short-term changes in unemployment caused by recessions or cyclical instability of the economy.

Changes in unemployment over longer periods may be viewed as matters of "trend." These trends may reflect long-run change in the basic structure of the economy, transition from a wartime to a peacetime economy, changes in the composition of the labor force, or perhaps secular change in political and social attitudes toward what constitutes acceptable performance of the economy. Even when long-term trends in unemployment are viewed as indications of secular stagnation in the economy—and, there-

---

[6] This distinguishes the high employment estimates used in this study from most "full employment" estimates of the gross national product and the implicit budget surplus, such as those used by the Council of Economic Advisers in the *Economic Report of the President, January 1962*, pp. 49 ff.

TABLE 3. Unemployment as Percent of Civilian Labor Force in the Postwar Recessions and Recoveries[a]

Recession and Recovery	Peak Quarter[b]	Trough Quarter[b]	Terminal Quarter of Recovery
1948-50	3.7	5.9	5.7
1953-55	2.6	5.8	4.3
1957-59	4.3	6.3	5.1
1960-62	5.2	6.8	...

[a] From U.S. Department of Labor, *Monthly Report on the Labor Force*, February 1960 and January 1962.
[b] The GNP peaks, troughs, and terminal quarters of recovery are as in Table 1. Maximum unemployment rates generally came sometime later than the GNP trough. (See Table 15.)

fore, like recession, a problem of inadequate aggregate demand—a distinction is still appropriate. Egle, writing on the need to distinguish between the problems of cyclical economic instability and of secular stagnation, which he calls a "pseudo" stabilization problem, points out that for stabilization policies speed and flexibility are of the utmost importance, while for economic growth (anti-stagnation) policies, such characteristics are distinctly subordinate to stamina.[7] Of course, it is often hard to distinguish in practice between "inadequate recovery from recession" and "inadequate growth." Moreover, the particular secular setting of each recession will, or at least should, influence the stabilization policies adopted. Accordingly, the framework outlined above will have to be stretched somewhat in evaluating such policies.

The method of adjusting terminal quarter statistics for any remaining shortfall from the prerecession rate of factor utilization is conservative, in that only the difference in the employment rate of the labor force is taken into account. Actually, in each of the four terminal quarters, the economy was below potential (or expected to be below potential), not merely because of unutilized labor force (as shown in Table 3), but also because productivity, hours of work, and the size of the labor force itself probably were all below potential.

[7] Walter P. Egle, *Economic Stabilization: Objectives, Rules and Mechanisms* (Princeton University Press for the University of Cincinnati, 1952).

Meaning of a Budget Surplus

The use of fiscal policy to stabilize the economy calls for either increasing federal expenditures or reducing federal receipts during recessions, or both. Any of these categories of action means decreasing the surplus in the federal budget or increasing its deficit. Thus, a question naturally arises—even among those who accept the idea that the budget does not have to be balanced every fiscal year—as to what size the federal budget surplus should be "normally." And "normally" means to some an average over the business cycle, while to others it means high employment. Popular folklore about the propriety of "balanced" federal budgets to the contrary, it is not possible—at least on economic criteria—to specify in the abstract the proper absolute "normal" size of the federal surplus or deficit.

For one thing, a budget surplus or deficit of a particular size represents a greater or smaller economic impact, depending on the level and composition of the receipts and expenditures which enter into its calculation. For example, taxes are paid at least in part from private saving, without correspondingly decreasing investment, whereas government purchases of goods directly add to GNP by the full amount. Therefore, equal amounts of taxes and of government purchases will ordinarily mean that the government is adding to aggregate demand; an increase in the size of the budget will be expansionary even if the surplus or deficit remains unchanged.[8] However, this statement does not hold for government transfer payments,[9] since transfer payments add to GNP only indirectly—when the payments are spent by their recipients. And federal grants may cause an increase in total government spending by more than the amount included in the federal budget if states are required to put up matching funds which they otherwise would not have spent.

[8] This is the implication of the famous "balanced budget multiplier" theorem, of which the classic statement is by Trygve Haavelmo, "Multiplier Effects of a Balanced Budget," *Econometrica,* Vol. 13 (October 1945), pp. 311-18. See also Richard A. Musgrave, *The Theory of Public Finance* (McGraw-Hill, 1959), pp. 429-32.

[9] "Government transfer payments" are expenditures which add to private incomes, but for which no currently produced goods or services are rendered to the government in exchange.

Contrariwise, there may be little, if any, change if federal grants are substituted for amounts states would have spent from their own funds anyway.

Aside from the effects of composition, a surplus of a particular size cannot be taken as a measure of the total economic impact of government activity. Private demand will also be affected by the issuance of new government orders, federal guarantee and insurance activity, wage legislation, direct price and wage controls, monetary policy, debt management, action by regulatory agencies, and similar government activities.

Moreover, the economic effects of a surplus of any given size depend on the private response to changes in income or assets—reactions which can, and do, change over time. In short, the effects of a budget surplus of a given size will vary with its composition, with trends in federal activity which affect the economy but are not reflected in the budget, and with the strength of private income-expenditure relationships. Stated differently, a zero balance—or even a deficit at one point of time—may be no more inflationary than a surplus equal to several percentage points of GNP at another, even assuming full employment in both cases.

Since it is not possible generally to state on economic grounds the appropriate size of a federal surplus at high employment, it is fortunate that an answer to this abstract question is not really needed in order to conduct fiscal policy intelligently. Rather, the question which typically confronts the policy official is: Given the existing state of the budget, what change in budget surplus or deficit would accord with present and prospective levels of private economic activity? Economic analysis is better able to answer a question of this kind for two reasons: First, while determination of the precise amount may be impossible, the direction of the economic effect of an increase in expenditures or decrease in tax rates is unambiguously expansionary. Second, for short intervals of time, the impact of a budget surplus of a given size often can be assumed approximately unchanged. This follows from the facts that private income-expenditure relations and the composition of the budget usually change slowly, and because the unbudgeted federal activities usually also change little in the short run.

To sum up, it is often possible to assert that, because private economic activity is falling, or is below desired levels, a decrease in the federal surplus is called for—without even attempting to answer the question of what absolute level of surplus or deficit would be appropriate under "normal" conditions. In other circumstances, similar reasoning may indicate an increase in the surplus.

The Implicit Federal Surplus at Hypothetical High Employment

Because the level of national income determines the amount of revenue collected from given tax rates, the size of the actual budget surplus at any particular time depends passively on the level of economic activity as well as actively on discretionary tax and expenditure actions. In using the budget surplus to indicate whether discretionary fiscal behavior has neutral, expansionary, or contractionary effects on the economy, it is essential to distinguish between active and passive changes in the surplus. The distinction is made at several places in this study by the use of an analytical tool of fairly recent development—the implicit federal surplus.

The implicit federal surplus, as used in this study, is the difference between federal receipts and expenditures calculated for existing programs and tax rates, but assuming the economy is at high employment so far as the fiscal effects of the built-in stabilizers are concerned. The basic idea underlying this concept of implicit federal surplus is not new. It bears a close kinship, for example, to the "stabilizing budget" policy which has been recommended by the Committee for Economic Development (CED) since early in the postwar period.[10] The CED's suggested policy would set discretionary taxes and expenditures so as to yield some surplus at high employment and would tolerate deficits caused by induced declines in tax collections if economic activity fell below high employment. However, until recently there have been few attempts to draw fiscal policy conclusions or recommendations from quantitative estimates or judgments about the size of the federal surplus at hypothetical high employment.[11]

[10] See *Taxes and the Budget* (Committee for Economic Development, 1947).
[11] See statement of Charles L. Schultze in *Current Economic Situation and*

If a decrease in the *actual* federal surplus in recession represents nothing more than the automatic drop in revenues or increase in unemployment compensation caused by the drop in economic activity below a high employment trend, the *implicit* federal surplus will remain unchanged in size. With tax rates and government expenditure programs unchanged, fiscal policy can be regarded as neutral in an important sense, rather than compensatory or expansionary. This does not mean that the income-generating effects of a deficit caused by built-in stabilizers are any less than if the deficit were the result of discretionary factors. Rather, it refers to the fact that a purely passive federal offset to private expenditure reductions would be self-reversing with the start of recovery and self-terminating with the return of the economy to high employment. A budget policy which is neutral in this sense is consistent with a return to high employment and recovery of the pre-existing rate of utilization of other factors of production only if the original cause of decline in private spending is removed, or if it is offset by increases in other categories of private spending.[12] A decrease in the size of the implicit federal surplus, on the other hand, can be taken as indicating that the income-generating effects of the budget have increased relative to high employment GNP.

A neutral budget policy can be successful only if the recession is caused by a temporary and self-correcting decline of private expenditures. Even more important, unless fiscal policy makes use of calculations on a fairly current basis of the size and effects of the implicit surplus, there is danger of perverse fiscal behavior which would aggravate the decline in private spending—or, more likely, slow or prevent complete recovery. This is because actual figures on the budget surplus may give misleading signals during recession about the income-generating effects of the budget. The passive drop in revenues can produce a decrease in actual surplus large enough to hide an increase in the implicit surplus.

Outlook, Joint Economic Committee Hearings, 86 Cong. 2 sess. (1961), pp. 120-22; statement of Herbert Stein in *Hearings on the Economic Report of the President,* Joint Economic Committee, 87 Cong. 1 sess. (1961), pp. 209 ff.; and CEA, *Economic Report of the President, January 1962,* pp. 79-84.

[12] "Neutral" in this sense can be viewed as short-run neutrality. In the long run, the degree of built-in flexibility in the budget must be viewed as a variable which can be changed as a matter of public policy.

The foregoing possibilities are not idle speculations. The record of discretionary fiscal policy during the postwar recessions and recoveries has left something to be desired. And misleading budget signals given off by actual, rather than implicit, surpluses and deficits are a part of this story.

The analytical tables which appear toward the end of Chapters IV through VII (Tables 20, 24, 28, and 30) show three different concepts of the federal surplus or deficit. These are (1) the implicit surplus as defined above; (2) the surplus at the prerecession peak, adjusted for factors not caused by the recession; and (3) the actual surplus as shown in national income accounts. While both of the first two concepts are based on the assumption of continuing high employment, the second concept differs from the implicit surplus in that it does not reflect any fiscal actions classified as discretionary antirecession measures. The surplus at the prerecession peak, adjusted for factors not induced by recession, approximately measures what the federal surplus would have been had no recession occurred. Inasmuch as both antirecession expenditures and changes in government expenditures and taxes undertaken for other reasons affect aggregate demand, the implicit surplus, which combines the two, should be used in deciding whether the federal government's fiscal actions were neutral, expansionary, or contractionary from one period to the next. The actual surplus or deficit shows the combined effects of discretionary actions and the built-in stabilizers.[13]

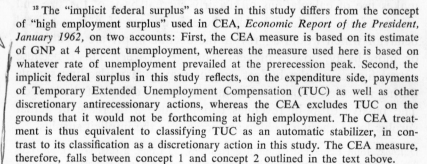

[13] The "implicit federal surplus" as used in this study differs from the concept of "high employment surplus" used in CEA, *Economic Report of the President, January 1962,* on two accounts: First, the CEA measure is based on its estimate of GNP at 4 percent unemployment, whereas the measure used here is based on whatever rate of unemployment prevailed at the prerecession peak. Second, the implicit federal surplus in this study reflects, on the expenditure side, payments of Temporary Extended Unemployment Compensation (TUC) as well as other discretionary antirecessionary actions, whereas the CEA excludes TUC on the grounds that it would not be forthcoming at high employment. The CEA treatment is thus equivalent to classifying TUC as an automatic stabilizer, in contrast to its classification as a discretionary action in this study. The CEA measure, therefore, falls between concept 1 and concept 2 outlined in the text above.

The Findings in Brief

Since the major focus of this study is on fiscal policy, much attention is given to distinguishing among and, to the extent possible, determining separate amounts involved in automatic built-in fiscal stabilizers, discretionary antirecessionary actions, and expenditure and tax changes occurring primarily for reasons other than recessions. An overall summary of federal receipts and expenditures during the four postwar recessions and recoveries, as shown in Table 4, provides a useful point of departure.

Automatic Stabilizers

The built-in fiscal stabilizers—automatic responses, under existing law, of tax receipts and certain governmental expenditures, particularly unemployment compensation—are treated for all four postwar recessions in Chapters II and III. Chapter II deals with the impact of these stabilizers on federal receipts, expenditures, and the budget surplus or deficit. The economic effects of the built-in stabilizers, which are not identical with their fiscal effects and which are not the same for each automatic stabilizer, are discussed in Chapter III.

The built-in fiscal stabilizers have made a substantial contribution to the stability of the postwar economy. They have pushed the federal budget strongly toward deficit when that was needed in each postwar recession, thus helping to slow the economic decline. The resulting change in the surplus has been large relative to the change in total output, ranging from 40 percent of the fall in GNP from peak to trough in 1948-50 to more than 100 percent in 1960-61. Moreover, in spite of a lagged impact on the federal cash budget, the economic effects of the built-in stabilizers have been timely with respect to contraction. It appears likely that the built-in stabilizers have limited the duration as well as the severity of postwar contractions. Of course, after the trough is passed and employment and output rise, the built-in stabilizers reverse direction. Then they increase the surplus or reduce the deficit, and thus retard recovery.

The built-in fiscal stabilizers are of two general types: some have direct effects; others, indirect effects. Those having a direct

TABLE 4. Summary of Federal Receipts and Expenditures, Postwar Recessions and Recoveries[a]

(In billions of current dollars)

Recession and Recovery	Peak Quarter	Trough Quarter	Terminal Quarter of Recovery	Change, Peak to Trough	Change, Trough to Recovery
1948-50	1948-IV	1949-II	1950-II		
Receipts	42.6	38.5	47.3	—4.1	8.8
Expenditures	38.8	42.4	39.0	3.6	—3.4
Surplus or deficit (—)	3.8	—3.9	8.3	—7.7	12.2
(Change in surplus due to built-in fiscal stabilizers)	...	...	...	(—3.7)	(6.1)
1953-55	1953-II	1954-II	1955-II		
Receipts	72.3	63.3	71.7	—9.0	8.4
Expenditures	79.4	68.7	68.1	—10.7	—0.6
Surplus or deficit (—)	—7.0	—5.4	3.5	1.6	8.9
(Change in surplus due to built-in fiscal stabilizers)	...	...	...	(—6.6)	(10.4)
1957-59	1957-III	1958-I	1959-II		
Receipts	82.5	75.4	91.6	—7.1	16.2
Expenditures	79.9	83.5	91.1	3.6	7.6
Surplus or deficit (—)	2.6	—8.1	0.5	—10.7	8.6
(Change in surplus due to built-in fiscal stabilizers)	...	...	...	(—8.7)	(17.4)
1960-61	1960-II	1961-I	1961-IV[b]		
Receipts	96.9	92.5	103.1	—4.4	10.6
Expenditures	92.5	98.0	105.2	5.5	7.2
Surplus or deficit (—)	4.5	—5.5	—2.1	—10.0	3.4
(Change in surplus due to built-in fiscal stabilizers)	...	...	...	(—6.8)	(10.8)

[a] On basis of national income accounts, seasonally adjusted annual rates. From Table 5 and U.S. Department of Commerce, *U.S. Income and Output* (1958) and *Survey of Current Business*, July 1961 and February 1962. Figures here and in subsequent tables may not add because of rounding.

[b] The last quarter for which data are available is 1961-IV, although 1962-II is considered the terminal quarter of recovery in this study.

effect on disposable personal income—individual income tax, unemployment compensation, and employment taxes—have become somewhat more important for several reasons. Increases in payroll tax rates, mainly for old-age and survivors insurance (OASI), have so promoted employment taxes as a built-in stabilizer that their effects on government receipts are now about a third as large as the variations in the yield of the individual income tax. At unchanged tax rates, the individual income tax grows faster than gross national product and seems to have acquired somewhat increased sensitivity to cyclical changes in GNP. Finally, there is some evidence that private consumption has become more responsive to cyclical changes in disposable personal income, and this promotes the importance of the stabilizers which directly cushion declines in such income.

The indirect stabilizers—corporation income tax and excises—account for larger portions of the change in federal surplus or deficit than the direct stabilizers. However, at least for minor recessions, they are inefficient because they probably add substantially less to private spending than they subtract from federal budget receipts. This effect might be a net disadvantage if the public and political response were so opposed to budget deficits that expansionary fiscal action of a discretionary nature were thereby inhibited. Moreover, concern about budget deficits is strengthened by the lag in the collection of corporation income taxes, which produces a cash budget deficit after recovery is under way.

Discretionary Fiscal Actions

Chapters IV through VII describe, chronologically for each of the four recessions, discretionary policies and actions. Compared to the automatic stabilizers, deliberate actions to counter recessions generally have been less helpful. Recession is never the only factor, and seldom the most important factor, shaping federal fiscal and budgetary policy. As a consequence, specific antirecession actions have been subject to numerous constraints which have limited their effectiveness from a stabilization standpoint.

As a rule, the government has favored countercyclical actions that could be justified, at least in part, on other than purely stabilization grounds. This is perhaps the major reason why countercyclical actions on the expenditure side of the budget have had more appeal than tax cuts, which would have required justification primarily on counterrecession grounds. Under this "mixed motives" approach, expenditures which would have been undertaken anyway sometimes have been labeled "counterrecession." The converse is probably also true—some redefinition of long-term program goals undoubtedly has taken place in the heat of battle against recession. As a consequence, it is frequently difficult—sometimes impossible —to decide definitely whether or not the motive in particular actions was primarily to counter recession. But, insofar as a distinction is possible, those actions which appear to have been primarily counterrecessionary have been on the expenditure side of the budget. A possible exception is the reduction of excise taxes in 1954, for which the recession was a frequently advanced but not the only argument.

Measured by changes in the implicit federal surplus at high employment during the recession phase, discretionary fiscal actions of the federal government were sharply contractionary during the recession of 1953-54, were mildly expansionary in 1948-49, and were approximately neutral during the other recessions. The story during the recovery phases is less favorable, even allowing for discretionary antirecession actions. In the 1949-50 and 1954-55 recoveries, the implicit surplus increased even though the economy was still below high employment. In both these cases, however, a net increase in the implicit surplus in the terminal quarter compared to the prerecession peak proved not to be too restrictive a budget policy in the light of later developments in the economy. In the 1958-59 recovery, the implicit surplus through the end of calendar 1959 was not much larger than it had been before the recession. However, a reaction to the very large fiscal 1959 deficit resulted in cutbacks in expenditures which, coupled with tax increases, caused a drastic increase in the rate of the implicit federal surplus in early 1960. The 1960-62 period of recession and recovery is the only one for which the implicit surplus declined from prerecession peak to terminal quarter (based on expectations in March 1962). However, the prospect in early 1962 was for a reversal of this behavior by the end of the year and prior to the achievement of what the administration had declared was its full employment target of 4 percent unemployed.

Interestingly, the general magnitude of counterrecessionary increases in expenditures has been roughly the same for the three recessions in which such actions took place, in spite of different mixtures of actions. (Compare, for example, Tables 24, 28, and 30.)

The 1954 recession featured an administrative speed-up which leaned heavily on the Department of Defense. In 1958, Congress was considerably more aggressive, but the administrative speed-up that year exempted the Department of Defense. The 1961 administrative actions included activities of the Department of Defense, and featured congressional action also, but less than in 1958. Although the President proposed some steps in 1949, no significant counterrecession actions were actually undertaken in that recession.

A direct comparison of the relative contributions of deliberate counterrecession actions and built-in stabilizers is somewhat misleading because of different timing. Discretionary actions have not been in effect before the trough month so that, except for possible anticipatory effects, they have not been a factor in cushioning the decline or in causing turning points. On the other hand, discretionary actions have made a contribution during the recovery phase, which is a time when the built-in stabilizers reverse direction and operate to slow recovery. However, the fiscal effects (and reasonable estimates of economic effects) of discretionary actions during the recovery phase have been considerably smaller than the contribution of the automatic stabilizers during the recession phase.

It has not been difficult to reverse discretionary actions, at least for those identified as primarily counterrecessionary. Such actions generally have been self-terminating, or were terminated by discretionary action prior to full recovery. Actions that might be more difficult to reverse, such as new public works starts (as distinguished from speeding work in progress) generally have been avoided.

While expenditures could be, and were, justified in part on other than stabilization grounds, tax cuts would have required (or at least were so viewed) an admission by public officials that a recession was serious enough to call for corrective action not otherwise justifiable. This made the expenditure side more attractive to public officials, particularly in the early stages of recession when the extent of need for corrective action was still uncertain. In addition, tax cuts faced a serious obstacle on those occasions when they were considered or recommended because they involved controversial questions of equity and the distribution of tax burdens by income groups.

Constraints on Antirecession Policy

Some of the constraints under which discretionary actions have operated recur with enough frequency to command more attention than they generally get from economic analysts.

A major category of constraints on counterrecession policy can be described as "prior commitments and long-range goals." It would have been most difficult for President Truman, just re-elected in a campaign featuring charges of Republican "fiscal irresponsibility" for having cut taxes in 1948, to have proposed tax cuts in January 1949. Similarly, it would have been difficult for the newly installed Eisenhower administration, pledged to reduce spending and the budget deficit, to propose expenditure increases in 1953-54; or for newly elected President Kennedy, having pledged expenditure increases and possibly tax increases to meet the Soviet threat, to ask for tax cuts in 1961. Such commitments are not necessarily inconsistent with counterrecession action, but certainly limit the range of policy alternatives.

Short-run uncertainty about whether the economy was or was not in recession, or about to be in recession, has been a limitation on counterrecession action, but not so serious as public statements and appearances might suggest. Concern over the need to maintain public and business confidence has sometimes limited public acknowledgment of recession and delayed the initiation of corrective actions. As a rule, administrations have delayed public acknowledgment of recession until the evidence was overwhelming —well into the period of decline—but have called the turn promptly, and started to reimpose fiscal restraints, as soon as the trough was passed and recovery started. Uncertainty about whether the economy might not a year or so hence be faced with the problem of inflation has been a greater limitation than inability to make short-term forecasts. Lack of certainty about the government's own requirements for defense expenditures has been a factor in this. In at least three of the four postwar recessions, there were, at times which were critical for purposes of antirecession decisions, strong feelings that defense expenditures might have to be increased by unknown, but potentially inflationary, amounts. As a consequence, there has been a high—probably too high—premium on reversibility, and often actions that were judged not reversible were avoided. The feeling that tax cuts might prove irreversible, for example, was a definite factor against their use.

Concern over balanced budgets in one form or another has been an active constraint in each postwar recession. There have been only brief interludes around the trough when the desire for balanced budgets has been suspended temporarily in favor of deliberate additions to the budget deficit. The 1946 Employment Act probably stimulated more aggressive antirecession actions than might otherwise have been forthcoming. However, there is little in the record to support the contention sometimes voiced that this legislation has biased public policy toward inflation by promoting more aggressive action to combat unemployment than inflation. Sentiments for balanced budgets and fiscal responsibility are still strong; discretionary antirecession actions have been reversed sharply during recovery. And it can be argued that any strengthening by the Employment Act of the linkage in public attitudes between the budget and the state of the economy applies to inflation as well as unemployment. Neither major party has shown a monopoly on "fiscal responsibility," and it has not been the exclusive property of either the executive or legislative branches. Anxiety over rising prices during some of the contractions and some of the recoveries has also operated as a constraint on expansionary fiscal actions, and balance of payments difficulties also played this role at the time of the 1959 recovery and the 1960-62 recession and recovery.

Recurring attention to the geographical distribution of expenditures by surplus labor areas has not enhanced overall stabilization goals, and the attention given to such attempts may have delayed action on other more effective measures. There have also been repeated suggestions to raise minimum wages—an ambiguous antirecession action at best.

Concern with "efficiency" aspects of budgeting by both the executive branch and Congress has sometimes served as a constraint on counterrecession expenditures. For example, the Department of Defense was left out of the 1958 procurement speed-up partly because it was felt that this was inconsistent with program objectives. In 1961, when consideration was being given to a list of public

works projects which agencies could start within six months and
complete within two years if additional funds became available,
the point was made that several of the projects on the list were
needed less than other larger and slower projects. Further, the
starting of additional military public works for purely counterrecession purposes was questioned as possibly inconsistent with defense goals.

Other constraints have been present in the principle of trust
fund financing and earmarked revenues for highways, social security, and unemployment. There is evidence that expenditures for
highways have more potential flexibility than most other federally
financed public works. However, under present arrangements, highway expenditures are closely geared to earmarked highway-user
charges, so that any speed-up requires offsetting increases of tax
rates immediately or within a short period. (In 1958, highway expenditures were accelerated, but the condition of the trust fund at
that time was fortuitous and temporary.) This forestalled using
highways as an antirecession action in 1961. Similarly, social security and unemployment expenditure proposals often have had
to be matched by early payroll tax rate increases, the timing of
which has not been helpful from a stabilization standpoint. There
has been at least one increase in OASI payroll tax rates—in support
of the trust fund principle—in each of the four recession-recovery
periods.

Considering their timing and generally modest proportions, it
seems doubtful that the discretionary counterrecession actions can
be assigned much importance in limiting the duration or severity of
the postwar recessions. The fact that accomplishments were as great
as they were suggests that equity, national needs, or other arguments
than recession could be marshalled in behalf of the actions that were
taken.

Given the many constraints that have been operative, and the
general absence of detailed contingency plans, it is somewhat prob-
lematical whether fiscal programs which were more expansionary
could have been put together on short notice if, in fact, they had
been needed. The variety of *ad hoc* expenditure proposals, and the
ingenuity with which these were defended, suggest that the government may have come close to reaching the full potential of the

flexibility that exists on the expenditure side of the budget. Also the political sensitivity of equity aspects of tax cuts, and the failure to reach advance political consensus on which tax cuts would have been most desirable in recession, make it unlikely that quick action could have been taken on the tax side.

Federal fiscal actions undertaken primarily for reasons other than the recession on some occasions have been perverse; on other occasions, they have been more helpful in stimulating the economy than actions taken primarily to counter recession. Drastic tightening of federal fiscal activity for budgetary reasons or long-run program goals was a major initiating factor in the 1953-54 and the 1960-61 recessions, and an aggravating factor during the early stages of the 1957-58 decline. A large well-timed tax cut in 1948 helped greatly to cushion the 1948-49 decline, but was undertaken for quite different reasons. Increases in defense outlays at one stage or another of the 1949, 1958, and 1961 recessions were fortuitous since they reduced the need for discretionary counter recession actions that might not so easily have won approval.

By concentrating on the effectiveness or ineffectiveness of particular fiscal proposals and actions, and on cataloging the constraints which have operated on public officials, it is hoped that this study will help to define the policy problems which are likely to be faced in future recessions. However, this approach makes it easy to lose sight of the real progress that has been made over the postwar period in improving the fiscal response to recession. In 1948-49, both the Congress and the executive branch initially had appeared so opposed to unbalanced budgets as to pose a threat of quite perverse fiscal actions. By the middle of 1949, at least a passive budget deficit was accepted and even defended by President Truman as the proper policy. In 1954, President Eisenhower's administration was willing to accept a limited number of discretionary increases in public spending. By 1958, Congress and Eisenhower's second administration both undertook a wide range of antirecession actions, although with some reluctance on the part of the administration and some regret on the part of both branches afterwards. And in 1961, the Kennedy administration proposed promptly and publicly a coordinated attack on recession—still, however, with signs of regret about the deficit financing this entailed, and a rather hasty reversal after the initiation of recovery was assured.

There are many remaining constraints, however, and a great
deal of work is needed to sharpen the fiscal tools to be used in combating recession, and in improving the skill and timing with which
they are used. It is especially important that the deficits generated
automatically during recession shall not be allowed to provoke fiscal
reactions that impede the return of the economy to high employment.

CHAPTER II

Fiscal Effects
of the Built-in Stabilizers

UNLESS POLICY ACTIONS are taken to prevent it, the federal budget automatically tends to move toward deficit—or toward a smaller surplus—during recessions. When private incomes turn down in recession, tax receipts based on these incomes also decline, assuming no change in tax rates. Similarly, the rise in unemployment that takes place during economic contraction causes increased government expenditures for unemployment compensation under existing laws and rules. These automatic changes in the federal budget, not involving policy decision or action, have helped limit the severity of postwar recessions.

While the federal budget responds automatically to changes in the level of economic activity, the magnitude of this response is not best described in terms of some simple percentage of gross national product. First, the sensitivity of the budget to cyclical changes in income is ordinarily much higher than its sensitivity to growth of income over a period of years. Second, the structures of the tax system and the unemployment insurance system, which can be, and have been, changed, determine the size of the automatic budgetary response to recession. For example, other things being equal, high

25

tax rates mean a large response of automatic stabilizers for a given change in GNP. Third, the magnitude of the response depends on a number of factors determined by the behavior of the private economy. For example, the response of both unemployment compensation payments and individual income tax collections in recession will be smaller if a given drop in aggregate income represents reduced hours of work rather than layoffs. And because the tax rates on corporate and individual income differ, the budgetary response to a drop in GNP depends on the distribution of the decline between corporate and personal incomes—a factor determined in the private economy. Finally, the magnitude of response depends on the rate and duration of the decline in economic activity. It is not true, as is sometimes stated, that an actual decline in GNP is required to push the budget automatically toward deficit. In fact, the three major built-in stabilizers—individual income tax, corporation income tax, and unemployment compensation—would all change in the direction of a budget deficit if the GNP remained unchanged for a few quarters. As a result, the budgetary response is relatively larger in a shallow decline in GNP than in a steep one.

General Framework

Built-in fiscal stabilizers are defined for purposes of this study as those federal receipts and expenditures which, in response to contraction, operate in the direction of increasing the federal deficit, or decreasing the surplus, without the need for policy decision or action. The major stabilizers fitting this definition are the individual and corporation income taxes, excise taxes, employment taxes, and unemployment compensation benefit payments. The elements of the federal budget which have automatic stabilizing effects with respect to fluctuations in the economy did not come into existence for this purpose. Rather, built-in stabilizer effects are an incidental benefit of legislation enacted for other purposes.

The built-in fiscal stabilizers help support the economy in recession mainly by reducing the rate at which an initial decrease in aggregate demand and in earned income before tax tends to have a magnified or "multiplier" effect on the economy by inducing further declines in expenditures for personal consumption. For example, because a drop in income reduces tax liability, after-tax incomes (and private expenditures based on after-tax incomes) drop by less than if there were no decline in tax liability. Similarly, the rise in unemployment compensation in recession cushions the decline in consumption by keeping the drop in disposable personal incomes less than the drop in incomes earned in current production. In addition to these effects on consumption, the built-in stabilizers also cushion potential declines in private investment. This is done indirectly to the extent that inventory or fixed investment is influenced by private consumption expenditures which, as a result of the stabilizers, are more stable than otherwise. It is done directly to the extent that investment is influenced by current after-tax business receipts. These influences, which vary from stabilizer to stabilizer and from one phase of recession to the next, are considered in some detail in Chapter III. Here, the concern is with measuring, and explaining the source of, the impact of built-in stabilizers on the federal surplus or deficit. However, a few points dealing with coverage and method need clarification first.

Actual Changes Compared to High Employment Shortfalls

While the four recessions covered in this study were periods in which the GNP declined, an actual decline in GNP is not required for the built-in stabilizers to come into play. With a growing economy, the three largest fiscal stabilizers—corporation and individual income taxes, and unemployment compensation—all operate so as to push the federal budget toward actual deficit in response to a slowing of the rate of increase in GNP. The fact that a recession in which GNP does not actually recede is not inconceivable is one reason why, in the following estimates, measurement of the fiscal effects of the stabilizers is made both in terms of shortfalls from high employment, and in terms of actual changes, peak to trough and trough to recovery.[1]

---

[1] A more basic reason for recording shortfall estimates will appear in Chapters IV through VII, where they are used to help appraise the effectiveness of discretionary fiscal policy.

Automaticity of Stabilizers

The definition given above confines built-in stabilizers to those receipts or expenditures which operate in response to recession. The temptation to regard any expenditure which helps maintain aggregate income as a "stabilizer" should be avoided. While it is tempting to consider any government expenditure—indeed any private expenditure—which does not fall to zero in recession as a stabilizer, this category is too large to be meaningful. For reasons given later in this chapter federal farm price supports—although often regarded as a built-in fiscal stabilizer—do not really qualify as such, at least for moderate recessions.

Since this part of the study is concerned with the automatic aspects of fiscal response, measurement of the contribution of the built-in stabilizers requires estimates of that part of the change in actual recorded data which results from discretionary rather than automatic actions. For example, the data on tax collections during the 1953-54 recession reflect not only automatic response to changing income, but the termination on January 1, 1954, of certain tax increases enacted during the Korean conflict. For present purposes, the concern is not whether the motives of the discretionary changes were counterrecessionary—merely whether the changes were discretionary or automatic.

Flexibility of Tax Base and Tax Yield

The tax response to a change in the gross national product logically divides itself into two stages: first, the response of the particular component of GNP on which the tax is based to changes in GNP, and second, the response of tax yield to a change in tax base. More specifically, the ratio of change in tax to change in GNP can be represented as the product of the ratios of (1) change in tax base to change in GNP, and (2) change in tax to change in tax base.[2] The first ratio is determined by the way in which the private econ-

[2] If Y stands for gross national product, B for the tax base, and T for the tax yield,

$$\frac{\Delta T}{\Delta Y} = \frac{\Delta B}{\Delta Y} \cdot \frac{\Delta T}{\Delta B}$$

omy works during contraction as well as the tax code, while the second depends primarily only on the specific provisions of the tax code. In the discussion in this chapter, these ratios will be considered separately where possible.

Cash Payments and Tax Accruals

The point in time at which federal taxes have their principal impact on private spending decisions probably varies from one tax to another. In the case of corporations, the time at which income tax liability accrues is probably more significant than the later time when payment is made to the government. In the case of individuals, most of whom do not keep records of accrued income and outgo, the time of cash payment may be more significant. But in either case, it seems logical—in trying to relate change in tax to change in income—to first examine the behavior of tax accruals in relation to the income on which they are based, and to consider separately the effects of payment lags.

Fiscal effects in this chapter are measured by tax accruals. In general, this means using federal receipts and expenditures as reflected in the national income accounts, rather than the administrative or cash budgets which record collections. However, for a major portion of one of the principal built-in stabilizers—the individual income tax—the national income accounts are on a cash flow rather than an accrual basis. Moreover, they do not allow separation of the effects of changes in the tax code. An alternative, more nearly accrued, measure of the individual income tax is used in this study (see Appendix B).

Fiscal Response of the Built-in Stabilizers

The behavior of the built-in fiscal stabilizers during postwar recessions is summarized in Table 5. As seen there, the fiscal stabilizers have changed by from roughly 40 percent to over 120 percent of the decline in GNP during contractions, and have regularly offset only about one-third or less of the subsequent rise in GNP during recovery.

Actual receipts have been adjusted for changes in tax law, so that the amounts shown represent the estimated change in tax accruals at constant prerecession rates. The adjustments were made

TABLE 5. Summary of Fiscal Effects of Major Built-in Stabilizers, Postwar Recessions and Recoveries[a]

(Amounts in billions of current dollars)

RECESSION AND RECOVERY	AMOUNT OF CHANGE		PERCENT OF CHANGE IN GNP	
	Peak to Trough[b]	Trough to Terminal Quarter of Recovery[c]	Peak to Trough[b]	Trough to Terminal Quarter of Recovery[c]
1948-50 recession and recovery				
Corporate profits tax accruals	—2.4	3.8	25.3	21.1
Excise taxes	—	0.6	—	3.3
Employment taxes	—0.1	0.2	1.3	1.0
Individual income tax accruals	—0.2	1.3	2.3	7.4
Unemployment compensation payments	1.0	—0.2	10.5	1.1
Total effect on federal surplus	—3.7	6.1	39.4	33.9
1953-55 recession and recovery				
Corporate profits tax accruals	—3.6	4.5	36.4	13.2
Excise taxes	—0.7	1.7	7.1	5.0
Employment taxes	—0.1	0.5	1.4	1.3
Individual income tax accruals	—0.7	2.8	7.5	8.2
Unemployment compensation payments	1.4	—0.9	14.1	2.6
Total effect on federal surplus	—6.6	10.4	66.5	30.4
1957-59 recession and recovery				
Corporate profits tax accruals	—4.6	8.7	29.9	15.6
Excise taxes	—0.6	1.5	3.9	2.7
Employment taxes	—0.3	1.1	2.2	2.0
Individual income tax accruals	—1.7	5.0	11.1	8.9
Unemployment compensation payments	1.4	—1.1	9.1	2.0
Total effect on federal surplus	—8.7	17.4	56.2	31.2
1960-61 recession				
Corporate profits tax accruals	—3.2	5.9	57.1	14.3
Excise taxes	—0.9	1.0	16.1	2.4
Employment taxes	—0.3	1.0	6.1	2.5
Individual income taxes	—1.0	2.3	17.9	5.5
Unemployment compensation payments	1.4	—0.6	25.0	1.4
Total effect on federal surplus	—6.8	10.8	122.2	26.1

[a] National income and product account basis (except for individual income tax in the first three recessions, which is on the full accrual basis explained in Appendix B). All are seasonally adjusted annual rates, adjusted to eliminate the effects of discretionary actions, such as changes in tax rates and temporary extensions of unemployment benefit duration.

[b] Peaks and troughs of GNP, as identified in Table I.

[c] Change, trough to terminal quarter for first three recoveries as in Table I; for 1960-61, first three quarters of recovery only (1961-I to 1961-IV).

30

by simply multiplying actual recorded accruals by the ratio of pre-recession to actual tax rates. For example, if tax rates at the pre-recession peak were 10 percent greater than they were at the trough of the recession (this was actually the case in 1954), actual accruals at the trough were increased by 10 percent to place them on a comparable basis. It can be argued that, in the absence of a change in tax rates, the whole time-shape of recession and recovery might have differed, with repercussions on the response of the built-in stabilizers as well. Without a detailed model for tracing the various implications of alternative tax rates, this proposition cannot be thoroughly evaluated. Nevertheless, the figures shown probably reflect the correct general order of magnitude.

Measurements of unemployment compensation and taxes other than the individual income tax are based on the national income and product account statistics. Individual income tax data used in these measurements differ from the national income account data in two respects. First, the portion of the tax which is not withheld and refunds are estimated on an accrual basis, whereas these are reported in the national income accounts on the basis of collections. Second, tax attributable to individual capital gains income—which is excluded from national income statistics—is not included in the calculations, but is discussed separately.

Corporation Income Tax

The largest built-in stabilizer, at least in terms of dollar impact on the federal budget, is the corporation income tax. Receipts from this tax, in percentage terms, drop substantially more in recession than gross national product, and the volatility of the tax accounts for one-half or more of the automatic decline in federal receipts in the postwar recessions. The volatility of yield in this tax is caused by changes in the level of corporate profits over the cycle rather than progressivity or other features of the tax.

Cyclical Behavior of the
Corporation Tax Base

The extent to which before-tax corporate profits have declined relative to gross national product in recession years is shown in

TABLE 6. Relationship of Corporate Profits to Gross National Product, 1948-61[a]

(Amounts in billions of current dollars)

CALENDAR YEAR	CORPORATE PROFITS BEFORE TAX		CHANGE FROM PRECEDING YEAR	
	Amount	Percent of GNP	Before-Tax Profits	GNP
1948	33.0	12.7	3.5	25.1
1949 (Trough)	26.4	10.2	—6.6	—1.4
1950	40.6	14.3	14.3	26.5
1951	42.2	12.8	1.5	44.4
1952	36.7	10.6	—5.5	18.0
1953	38.3	10.5	1.6	18.4
1954 (Trough)	34.1	9.4	—4.2	—2.3
1955	44.9	11.3	10.8	34.4
1956	44.7	10.7	—0.2	21.7
1957	43.2	9.8	—1.5	23.6
1958 (Trough)	37.4	8.4	—5.8	1.8
1959	46.8	9.7	9.4	38.2
1960	45.0	8.9	—1.8	21.7
1961 (Trough)	46.1	8.8	1.1	16.9

[a] Trough year as given in Table 1. Source, U.S. Department of Commerce, *Survey of Current Business,* July 1961 and February 1962.

Table 6. While profits have averaged only about 10 percent of GNP, they have absorbed from 50 to 120 percent of the decline from peak to trough in GNP (on a quarterly basis) in the postwar recessions. Another cyclical phenomenon that stands out in Table 6 is the tendency of profits to reach levels the year after recession that are not maintained in subsequent years of high-level economic activity. In the construction of high employment benchmarks later in this study, it will be assumed that, in the absence of recession, profits would tend to maintain a stable relationship to GNP. This ignores what appears to be a downward drift in the profits share of GNP during the postwar period, perhaps because the levels associated with open inflation in the early postwar years were extraordinary. But the significance of "trend" in this respect is probably not great for the two-year stretches covered by the benchmarks.

The cyclical pattern of changes in corporate profits has several aspects. Total income originating in corporate business declines more sharply than GNP, partly as a result of the nature of a recession in which the demand for goods, produced mainly by corporations, falls more sharply than the demand for services.[3] In addition, within the corporate sector, profits decline more than other income shares. Chart 1 shows these relations graphically. There are several possible explanations for the rise in unit costs and the decline in the profits share of total output during contraction. A factor stressed by Schultze is the emergence of excess capacity which requires fixed costs such as depreciation to be spread over fewer units of output.[4] Another factor is stressed by Kuh;[5] this is the tendency of corporations to cut back on employment, particularly overhead employment, more slowly than output.

Also apparent from Chart 1 is the tendency for profits to recover rapidly after the trough. In three of the four recessions they reached levels during recovery higher than before the recession relative to GNP. It can be seen from the chart that the tendency of profits to over-recover is a characteristic of the profits share of corporate product rather than the corporate sector's share of GNP. If corporations have been slow in reducing employment during the contraction, the increases in demand during the early phases of expansion can be accommodated with declining unit costs by utilizing the available labor force more efficiently. This thesis is consistent with the well-known tendency of employment to lag behind output increases during recovery.

Cyclical variation in the profits share of income importantly affects the stability of the economy above and beyond its impact on the federal budget. The larger is the share of GNP decline borne by profits, the smaller will be the impact of recession on personal incomes and consumption expenditures. Spending propensities (rela-

---

[3] See preliminary paper by Charles L. Schultze, "Short-Run Movements of Income Shares," National Bureau of Economic Research, Conference on Research in Income and Wealth, April 28-29, 1961, mimeographed.

[4] However, see Bert G. Hickman's comments on the Schultze paper, *ibid.*

[5] Edwin Kuh, *Profits, Profit Markups, and Productivity,* Study Paper No. 15, Study of Employment, Growth, and Price Levels, Joint Economic Committee, 86 Cong. (1960).

Chart 1

Output, Corporate Income and Profits in Four Recessions
As percent of prerecession peak, in current dollars

Legend: ———— Gross National Product ········ Corporate Profits Before Tax
----- Income Originating in Corporate Sector

P, peak; T, trough; and R, terminal quarter of recovery

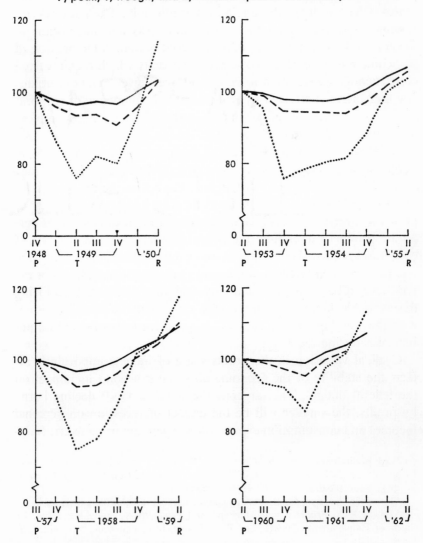

Sources: U.S. Department of Commerce, Survey of Current Business, July 1961, and U.S. Income and Output (1958); and Economic Report of the President, 1962.

34

tive to income) are probably much less for corporations than for individuals—a point which is discussed in Chapter III.

Cyclical Sensitivity of Yield

The rate structure adds little additional flexibility to the corporate tax. The corporation income tax now has rudimentary progressivity, in that net income under $25,000 is taxed at the normal rate
of 30 percent, while income above $25,000 is subject also to a sur-
tax of 22 percent. However, the proportion of income taxed at the
lower rate is relatively minor. In 1957, for example, while 82.3 percent of corporations reported taxable income of $25,000 or less,
they accounted for only 11.5 percent of total taxable income. The
next year, a recession year, the proportion of corporations in the
lower bracket increased to 82.8 percent and their share of taxable
income to 13 percent. This mild progressivity is not enough to significantly increase the cycle sensitivity of the tax. In fact, measured
in national income terms, the average rate of tax tends to rise in
recession years (Appendix Table C-2). The major reason for the
rise seems to be that the national income accounts figures on profits
offset the deficits of loss corporations against the income of other
corporations, although the corporations experiencing losses do not
have negative taxes. (Other differences between taxable profits and
profits as estimated in the national income accounts are discussed in
Appendix C.)

Although the average rate of tax relative to corporate income
on taxable returns is fairly constant, the tax falls relatively less in
recession, and increases relatively less during recovery, than profits
as recorded on a national income account basis. However, this factor is far less significant than the tendency of profits to rise and fall
more sharply than GNP, so that the tax has a GNP elasticity substantially greater than unity.

Summary, Corporation Income Tax

Table 7 summarizes on a quarterly basis the corporate profits
tax accruals in the postwar recessions and recoveries. For each, the
comparison with hypothetical high employment levels is given, together with the actual changes over the course of recession and

TABLE 7. Federal Corporate Profits Tax Accruals, Postwar Recessions and Recoveries[a]

(In billions of current dollars)

Calendar-Year Quarters, Including Peaks (P), Troughs (T), and Terminal Quarters of Recovery (R)

1948 recession and recovery

Item	1948			1949				1950	
	II	III	IV-P	I	II-T	III	IV	I	II-R
Actual accruals	..	..	11.6	10.5	9.2	9.8	9.6	12.6	15.5
Less estimated effect, tax code changes:									
Revenue Act of 1950	..	..	..	..	..	..	..	1.1	1.3
Excess profits tax	..	..	..	..	..	..	..	1.0	1.2
Adjusted accruals, prerecession tax rates	..	..	11.6	10.5	9.2	9.8	9.6	10.5	13.0
Change: peak to trough; trough to recovery	..	..	..	..	-2.4	..	..	..	3.8
Hypothetical accruals, high employment and prerecession tax rates	..	..	11.6	11.8	12.0	12.3	12.5	12.7	12.9
Shortfall: adjusted less hypothetical accruals	..	..	—	-1.3	-2.8	-2.5	-2.9	-2.2	0.1

1953-55 recession and recovery

Item	1953			1954				1955	
	II-P	III	IV	I	II-T	III	IV	I	II-R
Actual accruals	21.0	20.0	15.9	15.7	16.1	16.3	17.7	19.3	19.9
Less estimated effect, tax code changes:									
Revenue Code of 1954	..	..	..	-0.5	-0.5	-0.5	-0.5	-0.6	-0.6
Expiration, excess profits tax	..	..	..	-0.7	-0.8	-0.9	-1.1	-1.2	-1.4
Adjusted accruals, prerecession tax rates	21.0	20.0	15.9	16.9	17.4	17.7	19.3	21.1	21.9
Change: peak to trough; trough to recovery	..	..	..	..	-3.6	..	..	..	4.5
Hypothetical accruals, high employment and prerecession tax rates	21.0	21.2	21.4	21.7	21.9	22.1	22.4	22.6	22.8
Shortfall: adjusted less hypothetical accruals	—	-1.2	-5.5	-4.8	-4.5	-4.4	-3.1	-1.5	-0.9

1957-59 recession and recovery

Item	1957			1958				1959	
	II	III-P	IV	I-T	II	III	IV	I	II-R
Actual accruals	..	20.2	18.1	15.5	16.1	18.0	21.1	21.6	24.1
Less estimated effect, small business tax act	..	..	..	-0.1	-0.1	-0.2	-0.2	-0.2	-0.2
Adjusted accruals, prerecession tax rates	..	20.2	18.1	15.6	16.2	18.2	21.3	21.8	24.3
Change: peak to trough; trough to recovery	..	..	..	-4.6	..	..	..	..	8.7
Hypothetical accruals, high employment and prerecession tax rates	..	20.2	20.5	20.8	21.1	21.4	21.7	22.0	22.3
Shortfall: adjusted less hypothetical accruals	..	—	-2.4	-5.2	-4.9	-3.2	-0.4	-0.2	2.0

1960-62 recession and recovery

Item	1960			1961				1962	
	II-P	III	IV	I-T	II	III	IV	I	II
Actual accruals	21.8	20.3	20.0	18.6	21.2	22.1	24.5[b]	23.9	..
Change: peak to trough	..	..	..	-3.2	..	..	..	..	..
Hypothetical accruals, high employment	21.8	22.1	22.4	22.7	23.0	23.3	23.6	24.2	..
Shortfall: actual less hypothetical accruals	—	-1.8	-2.4	-4.1	-1.8	-1.2	0.9	..	..

[a] GNP peaks, troughs, and terminal quarters of recovery are from Table 1. Seasonally adjusted quarterly totals at annual rates. Actuals are from national income accounts, U. S. Department of Commerce. Hypothetical accruals at high employment are computed by linear interpolation of GNP in current dollars from prerecession peak to the terminal quarter of recovery, assuming no change in prerecession ratio of profits to GNP.

[b] Figure is implicit in statistics published for the annual total and the first three quarters of 1961.

recovery. In all cases, adjustments have been made for changes in tax law that took effect during the relevant periods. No adjustment was required for 1960-62 since there was no significant change in the law prior to completion of this study. (Later in 1962, depreciation allowances were liberalized by Treasury regulation and an investment credit was enacted by Congress, with both changes retroactive to the beginning of the year.)

In the four recessions, the corporate profits tax (measured by accruals) generally showed coincident timing in the sense that it made its maximum contribution at the cyclical trough in GNP and reversed direction thereafter. In the 1953-54 recession, the actual accruals as recorded in the national income accounts, and the adjusted accruals at constant rates, reached their apparent trough even earlier, but this reflected some juggling of corporation accounts associated with the expiration of the excess profits tax on January 1, 1954. Because of collection lags, the cash flows associated with this tax show a distinctly slower response to both recession and recovery; this is the major reason why the entire cash (and administrative) budget surplus shows a similar lag behind the surplus or deficit on national income account.

Another way of judging the effects of corporate profits tax accruals as built-in stabilizers is to look at the changes in such accruals as a percentage of the change in gross national product. This is shown for the postwar recessions and recoveries[6] by the following figures:

Period	Recession	Recovery
1948-50	25.3%	21.1%
1953-55	36.4	13.2
1957-59	29.9	15.6
1960-61	57.1	14.3

The much larger offset in 1961 than in earlier recessions reflects a shallower rate of deline in GNP.[7]

[6] For the recession figures, the change is from peak to trough in GNP, and for the first three recoveries, from trough to terminal quarter, as in Table 1. For the latest period, the change is over the first three quarters of recovery only, or 1961-I to 1961-IV.

[7] To take the extreme case, a period of no change in the GNP would cause a drop in profits and in profits taxes, since many corporate costs, such as depreciation on investment undertaken earlier, would continue to rise.

Individual Income Tax

Several factors account for the fact that the federal individual income tax is one of the chief elements of built-in flexibility in the federal budget. One is its size; on the average, it accounts for about half of administrative budget receipts. Others are the prompt response of individual tax liabilities to changes in economic activity and the current-payment method of collection. Moreover, the progressive rate structure and personal exemptions theoretically should produce proportionately greater swings in tax yield than in income.

Measuring Built-in Flexibility

The factors affecting built-in flexibility of the individual income tax are numerous and rather complex. As with the corporation income tax, total built-in flexibility depends on the responsiveness of the tax base to changes in GNP and the structure of tax rates. While annual data provide imprecise means of measuring changes over recessions as brief and mild as the four studied here, many of the statistics required for examining changes in tax base are available only annually.[8] Accordingly, the tax base is examined using annual data, with estimates of yield flexibility on a quarterly basis following. As noted earlier, in measuring fiscal effects, the discussion in this chapter deals with accrued tax liabilities rather than tax payments. Although accruals are more directly related to before-tax income, this treatment does not necessarily imply that accruals more meaningfully measure the economic impact of the tax. However, since the question of lags in payment is logically separable, it will be dealt with in the next chapter. Finally, throughout the discussion, the effects attributable to the tax on realized capital gains are kept separate from the tax on ordinary individual income. This was not done on the presumption that capital gains income affects spending in some way other than ordinary income. Rather, it was done in order to derive better measures of the rate of change in tax relative to income.

The primary reason for separating the tax on capital gains from the remainder of the income tax is statistical. Capital gains exhibit

[8] From the U.S. Treasury, Internal Revenue Service, *Statistics of Income.*

a high degree of year-to-year volatility, and often move contrary to cyclical movements in personal income. The national income estimates exclude capital gains from personal income but do not exclude the tax on capital gains from personal taxes. Hence, either the national income statistics or a comparison of Treasury tax data which include capital gains tax with national income estimates will give a poor measure of the marginal rate of tax relative to the income on which the tax is based. This gives rise to somewhat anomalous results. For example, in the recession year 1954, receipts from total tax, including capital gains, increased (after adjusting for changes in tax rates). But in that year personal income decreased, as estimated by the U.S. Department of Commerce, because personal income did not include capital gains. These data would be appropriate if it could be assumed that disposable after-tax capital gains income has no effect on consumption or other private outlays, but that the tax on such gains does. But this assumption does not seem warranted. If the tax rates on capital gains are significantly different from those on ordinary income, the marginal rate of tax on ordinary income may not be a good approximation to the marginal rate of tax on total income. But it will be a better approximation than if capital gains taxes are included in the numerator while capital gains income is excluded from the denominator.

A second reason for treating separately the tax on capital gains is that the relation between realized capital gains and the general business cycle is unclear. This subject is briefly discussed later in this chapter.

Cyclical Changes in Personal Income

While corporate net profits decline relatively more than gross national product in recession, personal income declines relatively less. As shown in Table 8, while there has been no noticeable trend in the ratio of personal income to GNP over the postwar period, personal income has tended to rise as a percentage of GNP in each recession year except 1949. Largely, this increase reflects the absorption by corporate profits of much of the drop in earned income from reduced production. It also reflects the rise in recession-induced personal transfer payments, mainly unemployment compensation, and the tendency of corporations to maintain dividend pay-

TABLE 8. Relationship of Personal Income to Gross National Product, 1948-61[a]

(Amounts in billions of current dollars)

CALENDAR YEAR	PERSONAL INCOME		CHANGE FROM PRECEDING YEAR	
	Amount	Percent of GNP	Personal Income	GNP
1948	210.4	81.1	18.8	25.1
1949 (Trough)	208.3	80.7	—2.1	—1.4
1950	228.5	80.3	20.1	26.5
1951	256.7	78.0	28.2	44.4
1952	273.1	78.7	16.4	18.0
1953	288.3	78.9	15.2	18.4
1954 (Trough)	289.8	79.8	1.6	—2.3
1955	310.2	78.0	20.4	34.4
1956	332.9	79.4	22.7	21.7
1957	351.4	79.4	18.5	23.6
1958 (Trough)	360.3	81.0	8.8	1.8
1959	383.3	79.4	23.1	38.2
1960	402.2	79.7	18.9	21.7
1961 (Trough)	416.7	79.9	14.5	16.9

[a] Source, U.S. Department of Commerce, *Survey of Current Business*, July 1961 and February 1962.

ments even when profits are reduced. The distribution of a drop in earned income, as between profits and personal income, affects the size of the automatic stabilizing response of the federal budget, since marginal rates of tax differ for the two kinds of income.

Flexibility of the Tax Base

The differences between individual income for tax purposes and personal income as estimated by the Department of Commerce include taxable items that are not part of personal income (such as gains from sale of property) and nontaxable income (such as imputed income of various types and personal transfer payments).[9] In addition, a significant amount (about $30 billion) of income embraced conceptually by the tax code goes unreported—principally

[9] A tabulation for 1957, with amounts, of the major conceptual differences is presented by Joseph A. Pechman in "What Would a Comprehensive Individual Income Tax Yield?," *Tax Revision Compendium*, Vol. 1, House Ways and Means Committee, 86 Cong. 1 sess. (1959), p. 253.

because it is earned by individuals having small incomes and no tax liability. Of the major conceptual differences, transfer payments and capital gains affect the cyclical pattern of receipts while the other differences do not appear to do so to any significant extent. Finally, personal exemptions and deductions are subtracted from total reported income in arriving at income subject to tax. (Taxable income and personal income are compared in Appendix Table C-4.)

The overall ratio of taxable to personal income shows a strong upward trend. Over the period 1948-59 as a whole, taxable income increased by more than 50 percent of the increase in total personal income—a marginal rate of change well in excess of the average ratio of taxable to personal income for any of the years (Appendix Table C-4). This rise in the ratio of taxable to personal income reflects a decline in the proportion of income that goes unreported because it is received by families in low-income brackets with no tax liability. In a period in which average income rises faster than average personal exemptions, taxable income—income in excess of exemptions—becomes a larger share of total income.

However, there is reason to doubt that recession-year flexibility can appropriately be measured from data for years in which income was generally rising. In the first place, since population continues to grow, the potential value of tax exemptions and deductions rises, and this can reduce taxable income even if total income does not actually decline. Thus, as Cohen has pointed out, the combined increase in exemptions and deductions in the recession year 1958 operated to reduce taxable income (and tax) even though total income rose slightly. Other things being equal, this should produce a higher built-in flexibility during contractions than expansions.[10]

The rise in potential exemptions relative to total income in recession years is an explanation of the decline in those years in the ratio of adjusted gross to total income (Appendix Table C-4). This decline reflects an increase during recession in the proportion of families not filing returns because their income is too small to be taxable. However, the ratio of taxable to personal income in recession years also is affected by such other factors as changes in

[10] Leo Cohen, "A More Recent Measure of the Built-in Flexibility of the Individual Income Tax," *National Tax Journal*, Vol. 13 (June 1960), p. 126. Joseph A. Pechman had made this point in his comment in *American Economic Review*, Vol. 49 (May 1959), pp. 552-55.

capital gains (which in the recession years 1954 and 1958 operated to increase the ratio) and changes in transfer payments (which in recession years move to decrease the ratio).

Finally, the effect of not taxing income which falls below the level of personal exemptions and deductions has at least two aspects which, to a certain extent, work at cross-purposes so far as built-in flexibility is concerned. For individuals who experience a reduction from one level of taxable income to another, the whole drop in income is reflected in a reduction of taxable income. However, if the drop in income carries some individuals below taxable levels, a smaller proportion of the drop in total income is reflected in reduced taxable income, with the remainder reflected in a rise in unused exemptions.[11]

Exemptions claimed on taxable returns dropped in three recession years, 1949, 1954, and 1958; and, in 1949 and 1954, the drops were enough to increase the ratio of taxable income to adjusted gross income on taxable returns. The rise in unused exemptions plays a moderating role on the cycle sensitivity of the tax base analogous to the role played by loss corporations in the corporation income tax. This tendency is a function of the proportion of taxpayers with low taxable incomes going into the recession and, therefore, on the margin of being dropped from the tax rolls altogether, and will presumably decrease with secular growth in average income levels (provided personal exemptions are constant).

Secular change in the role of unused exemptions may be the

[11] An example will make this argument clearer. Suppose average total income for the population is $5,000, average exemptions and deductions $3,000, and income in excess of exemptions and deductions subject to a tax of 20 percent. Then the average ratio of taxable to total income is 40 percent (2,000 ÷ 5,000) and the average rate of tax 8 percent (.20 × .40). If in case 1, an individual having average exemptions and deductions and total income of $6,000 has a drop in income of $2,000, taxable income is reduced by 100 percent of the drop in total income (compared to the average ratio of 40 percent) and tax is reduced by 20 percent of the drop in income (compared to the average rate of 8 percent). If in case 2, on the other hand, an individual also having average exemptions and deductions, but having total income of only $3,500, experiences the same $2,000 drop in total income, taxable income is reduced by only 25 percent of the drop in total income (500 ÷ 2,000) compared to the average ratio of 40 percent, and tax is reduced by only 5 percent (.20 × 500 ÷ 2,000), compared to the average rate of tax of 8 percent.

explanation of the greater sensitivity of individual income taxes to changes in personal income during the 1958 recession than in the 1954 recession (of which more later) in spite of a lower starting tax rate.

Secular growth in the cycle sensitivity of the tax base is also implicit in estimates by Brown and Kruizenga.[12] For example, holding exemptions and income distribution constant, an increase in per capita income over two to three years—at the rate of, say, $100 per year—would be enough to offset the reduction of roughly 10 percent in built-in flexibility that took place when tax rates were reduced in 1954. This may account for Brown's finding, otherwise somewhat puzzling, that yield sensitivity was about 12 percent of personal income under 1953 rates and exemptions, and around 13 percent under the present structure.[13]

In short, the tax base has both a secular and a cyclical income elasticity significantly greater than unity, and there are a priori reasons for expecting the cycle sensitivity to increase with the secular growth of income if there is no change in exemptions.

Yield Flexibility, Annual Data

Flexibility of yield, as opposed to flexibility of the tax base, is remarkably small for a tax with rates nominally as progressive as those of the federal individual income tax. The comparison of annual tax liabilities to taxable income in Table 9 shows a decline in average rate of tax over the postwar period as a whole. Because of the possibility that adjustments for different tax rates prior to 1954 do not do full justice to the actual changes in law, this seeming decline perhaps should not be taken as conclusive. But there is certainly no evidence of the rise that one would expect as average income levels increase. The subperiod since 1954, which is uncomplicated by rate change, also shows no trend.

Yield flexibility depends on the bracket-by-bracket distribution of income changes. Perhaps two factors deserve mention in this

[12] E. Cary Brown and Richard J. Kruizenga, "Income Sensitivity of a Simple Income Tax," *Review of Economics and Statistics*, Vol. 41 (August 1959), pp. 260-69.

[13] E. Cary Brown, "The Personal Income Tax as an Automatic Stabilizer," *Tax Revision Compendium*, Vol. 3, op. cit., p. 2359.

TABLE 9. Income Tax Liability Compared to Taxable Income, 1948-59[a]

(Liabilities and income in billions of current dollars)

CALENDAR YEAR	INCOME TAX LIABILITY[b]		TAXABLE INCOME		TAX AS PERCENTAGE OF INCOME
	Amount	Increment	Amount	Increment	
Including capital gains					
1948	18.2	...	74.7	...	24.3
1949 (Trough)	17.1	—1.1	71.6	—3.0	23.8
1950	20.6	3.5	84.3	12.6	24.4
1951	23.2	2.6	99.3	15.0	23.4
1952	24.4	1.2	107.4	8.1	22.7
1953	25.9	1.4	115.6	8.1	22.4
1954 (Trough)	26.5	0.1	115.2	—0.3	23.0
1955	29.6	3.1	127.9	12.7	23.2
1956	32.7	3.1	141.4	13.5	23.2
1957	34.4	1.7	149.2	7.8	23.0
1958 (Trough)	34.3	—	149.2	—	23.0
1959	38.6	4.3	166.4	17.2	23.2
Excluding capital gains					
1948	17.3	...	72.7	...	23.8
1949 (Trough)	16.5	—0.8	70.2	—2.5	23.4
1950	19.5	3.0	81.8	11.6	23.8
1951	22.2	2.7	96.6	14.8	23.0
1952	23.7	1.5	105.2	8.6	22.5
1953	25.2	1.5	113.7	8.5	22.2
1954 (Trough)	25.4	0.1	112.1	—1.5	22.6
1955	27.9	2.5	123.5	11.3	22.6
1956	31.1	3.2	137.2	13.8	22.7
1957	33.2	2.0	146.0	8.8	22.7
1958 (Trough)	32.8	—0.3	145.2	—0.8	22.6
1959	36.4	3.6	160.6	15.4	22.7

[a] See Appendix Table C-4 for taxable income. Tax figures are from U. S. Treasury, Internal Revenue Service, *Statistics of Income* adjusted as explained in footnote b.

[b] Adjusted to constant (1959) tax rates. (See Appendix B, Table B-3). Tax liability figures on the basis of constant tax rates given by Leo Cohen in "A More Recent Measurement of the Built-in Flexibility of the Individual Income Tax," *National Tax Journal* (June 1960), were computed by a more thorough method since he considered other income brackets besides the first, but he gives no figure for 1948 which is the first year before a recession.

connection. First, the great bulk of taxable income is taxed at flat first-bracket rates. The first bracket, after all, is very wide for the majority of taxpayers enjoying income-splitting. (For joint returns, the minimum width of any bracket is $4,000.) As an example, for a married couple with three children, taking the standard 10 percent deduction, income up to just under $7,800 is taxed at first-bracket rates; and for most homeowners the limit is still higher since deductions are likely to exceed 10 percent. Given the preponderance of low incomes in the total, a substantial increase in average taxable income can take place without carrying many taxpayers into higher brackets.

Second, a relatively small reshuffling of income among the higher brackets may be enough to cause a drop in the average rate of tax. For example, an unexplained (but apparently temporary) decline in the proportion of property income reported on upper-bracket returns during the Korean War years caused a steady and decided decline in average tax in 1951-53.[14]

The cycle-sensitivity of yield also appears disappointing unless, as in the bottom half of Table 9, adjustment is made for capital gains. Unadjusted, the tax declined very little in 1958 and rose in 1954. Eliminating both capital gains and the tax thereon from the calculations, however, shows a decline in the average rate of tax in two of the three recession years tabulated. The decline in yield (at present tax rates) was from one-fourth to one-third of the decline in taxable income—a marginal rate somewhat in excess of the average rate, which is under one-fourth. Thus, the elasticity of tax for cyclical changes in taxable income is greater than unity even if the same cannot be said for secular changes.

Yield Flexibility, Quarterly Estimates

Treasury collection data, as published, make it difficult to trace the effect on individual income tax yields of a change in income, or to separate such effects from those due to changes in tax rates and other influences. About two-thirds of the individual income tax is collected through withholding by employers of a percentage of cur-

[14] See Leo Cohen, "An Empirical Measurement of the Built-in Flexibility of the Individual Income Tax," *American Economic Review*, Vol. 49 (May 1959), pp. 532-41, and Peckman's comments in the same issue, pp. 552-55.

rent wages and salaries in excess of exemptions. Individuals not sub-ject to withholding, or where withholding is insufficient, file and pay quarterly a declaration of estimated tax. By April 15 of the year after the tax year (March 15, prior to 1954), final payment is made, or a refund claimed for any underpayment or overpayment of withheld or estimated tax.

The time lag between accrued liability and cash transaction dif-fers for each of these components of the individual income tax, and the response of each to cyclical changes in individual income varies correspondingly. For the withheld portion of the tax, Treasury col-lections are reported on a "when received" basis, although the tax has been withheld by employers from one to four months earlier. Reported collections of taxes which are not withheld lump declara-tions and final payments together in one sum, although the liabilities are for different time periods. For example, such collections re-ported for the second calendar quarter of 1961 include, for most tax-payers, the first and second quarterly declarations on 1961 income (due in April and June respectively) and final payments on 1960 in-come (due in April). Both portions of the tax show seasonal, as well as cyclical and other, influences, the seasonal pattern for the tax that is not withheld being particularly pronounced.

The national income accounts make adjustments for both the payments lag and seasonality in the withheld tax, but record the portions which are not withheld and the refunds on a cash flow, rather than an accrual, basis. Furthermore, the method of seasonal adjustment used for these portions leaves something to be desired, at least from the standpoint of measuring the cyclical pattern of receipts on a part-yearly basis. Appendix B describes a method of estimating the individual income tax by quarters on the basis of "full accrual." The results are recorded there in some detail, as they would appear useful in applications other than the present study. The full accrual series described there has the following elements: Withheld tax is adjusted for seasonality and for the lag of collec-tions behind withholdings by employers. Quarterly declarations of estimated tax are adjusted for seasonality and for the payments lag by assuming that the first, second, third, and fourth declarations of a particular year's estimated tax represent liability accrued during the first, second, third, and fourth calendar-year quarters. Final payments for the year's liability are distributed on the same basis as the sum of seasonally adjusted withholdings and seasonally adjusted accrued declarations. Refunds are distributed on the same basis as withholdings for the year, on the assumption that refunds (or at least changes therein) arise from withholding too much, rather than declaring too much, of estimated tax. And, finally, capital gains taxes are eliminated from all portions of the tax, for reasons given earlier.

Table 10 summarizes the quarterly built-in stabilizer effects of the individual income tax during periods of recession and recovery in the postwar period. The changes in individual tax liabilities as a percentage of change in gross national product for these years are as follows:[15]

Period	Recession	Recovery
1948-50	2.3%	7.4%
1953-55	7.5	8.2
1957-59	11.1	8.9
1960-61	17.9	5.5

The small response recorded for the 1948-49 recession probably reflects an imperfect adjustment for the accrual of refunds associated with the retroactive 1948 tax cut. The large response in the 1960-61 recession probably reflects the shallowness of that recession, since the rise in personal exemptions associated with growing population tends to reduce the tax base even with no reduction in aggregate income.[16] For the 1957-59 and 1960-61 periods—for which the estimates are free of complications caused by adjustments

[15] The change in tax liabilities for the first three periods is on a full accrual basis (see Appendix B), excluding tax attributable to individual capital gains. For the 1960-61 change, national income account estimates were used. For the recession figures, the change is from peak to trough in GNP, and for the first three recoveries, from trough to terminal quarter, as in Table 1. For the last period, the change is over the first three quarters of recovery only.

[16] The fact that national income estimates, rather than the full accrual estimates, were used for the 1960-61 period probably is not the explanation, since both major differences between the two measures—the inclusion of capital gains tax in the national income estimates, and the absence of within-year movement of final payments and refunds in the national income measure—operate in the direction of a smaller rather than a larger change, peak to trough, in the national income measures.

TABLE 10. Individual Federal Income Tax Accruals, Postwar Recessions and Recoveries[a]

(In billions of current dollars)

Calendar-Year Quarters, Including Peaks (P), Troughs (T), and Terminal Quarters of Recovery (R)

1948-50 recession and recovery

Item	1948 II	1948 III	1948 IV-P	1949 I	1949 II-T	1949 III	1949 IV	1950 I	1950 II-R
Actual accruals			15.1	15.0	14.9	15.0	14.8	16.1	16.2
Change: peak to trough, trough to recovery					-0.2				1.3
Hypothetical accruals, high employment			15.1	15.3	15.6	15.8	16.1	16.3	16.5
Shortfall: actual less hypothetical accruals			—	-0.3	-0.7	-0.8	-1.3	-0.2	-0.3

1953-55 recession and recovery

Item	1953 II-P	1953 III	1953 IV	1954 I	1954 II-T	1954 III	1954 IV	1955 I	1955 II-R
Actual accruals	30.1	30.1	29.7	26.1	26.1	26.9	27.5	27.6	28.2
Less estimated effect, tax code changes:									
Decrease in rates, January 1, 1954				-2.9	-2.9	-2.9	-2.9	-3.0	-3.1
Revenue Code of 1954				-0.4	-0.4	-0.7	-0.8	-0.8	-0.8
Adjusted accruals, prerecession tax rates	30.1	30.1	29.7	29.3	29.4	30.5	31.2	31.4	32.1
Change: peak to trough, trough to recovery					-0.7				2.8
Hypothetical accruals, high employment	30.1	30.4	30.8	31.1	31.4	31.7	32.1	32.3	32.7
Shortfall: adjusted less hypothetical accruals	—	-0.3	-1.0	-1.7	-2.0	-1.2	-0.8	-1.0	-0.6

1957-59 recession and recovery

Item	1957 II	1957 III-P	1957 IV	1958 I-T	1958 II	1958 III	1958 IV	1959 I	1959 II-R
Actual accruals		34.4	33.6	32.7	32.7	33.8	34.7	36.4	37.7
Change: peak to trough, trough to recovery				-1.7					5.0
Hypothetical accruals, high employment		34.4	35.0	35.5	36.0	36.5	37.0	37.5	38.0
Shortfall: actual less hypothetical accruals		—	-1.3	-2.7	-3.3	-2.7	-2.3	-1.1	-0.3

1960-62 recession and recovery

Item	1960 II-P	1960 III	1960 IV	1961 I-T	1961 II	1961 III	1961 IV	1962 I	1962 II
Actual collections	41.5	41.6	41.3	40.5	41.5	42.2	42.8	...	...
Change: peak to trough, trough to recovery				-1.0					
Hypothetical collections, high employment	41.5	41.9	42.3	42.8	43.2	43.6	44.1	44.5	45.0
Shortfall: actual less hypothetical collections	—	-0.3	-1.0	-2.2	-1.7	-1.5	-1.3	...	...

[a] GNP peaks, troughs, and terminal quarters of recovery are from Table 1. Seasonally adjusted annual rates. Data for first three recessions and recoveries are based on individual income tax, excluding estimated capital gains tax (Appendix B). Data for 1960-62 are from the U. S. Department of Commerce national income account estimates, which include capital gains tax and include nonwithheld tax and refunds on the basis of collections. For hypothetical accruals and collections at high employment, see Appendix A, method 1.

for changes in tax rates—the figures are consistent with the expectation that the income tax should offset more of a decline than an increase in GNP. In general, they are also consistent with the expectation that the built-in flexibility of the tax in response to recession should become higher at constant tax rates and exemptions with growth in average levels of income. However, the evidence on these points cannot be described as conclusive.

Individual Capital Gains

The exclusion of capital gains tax from the foregoing measurement of built-in flexibility of the individual income tax has been on grounds that the tendency of the tax to increase in recession years makes for poor comparison with national income account measures of income. Since capital gains are associated with movements in security prices, a more or less systematic relationship between capital gains and the business cycle might be expected. The stock market, after all, is alleged to discount in advance the ups and downs in the economy, and stock market prices have long been used as a "lead indicator"—comprising, in fact, one of the eight series used by the National Bureau of Economic Research (NBER) in its original version of the lead indicator diffusion index. Of course, discounting of this nature can be right directionally without necessarily being precise quantitatively. Moreover, realized capital gains depend on when the individual sells, how long he has held, and other factors that weaken any direct link with overall economic activity.

The evidence on regularity of cyclical pattern in capital gains is slightly mixed. In the 1954 and 1958 recessions, realized capital gains underwent a sharp decline in the peak years prior to the recession (1953 and 1957) and a sharp rise during the recession years. The pattern in the 1949 recession differed in that capital gains changed little in the year prior to the recession, but fell sharply in the recession year. In all three of these, the year following the recession showed a sharp rise in capital gains. More recent experience may have been more like the 1958 and 1954 pattern. While the *Statistics of Income* figures on capital gains are not yet available, movements of stock prices suggest a drop in realized capital gains in 1960 and a substantial increase in the 1961 recession year. Prior to World War II, several minor recessions featured increases in realized capital gains, while sharper contractions featured decreases. It might be argued that the drop in capital gains in 1949, the first postwar recession, reflected unfamiliarity of the investment community with what is to be expected over the course of short recessions of the postwar variety. Continuing, it could be argued that more recent experience, in which capital gains fell in the year prior to recession and rose in recession years, reflects more accurately the probable cyclical response, now that expectations have been adjusted to short and temporary recessions. If this turns out to be the case, the capital gains tax might be viewed as an automatic destabilizer. But on this line of reasoning, capital gains income should be viewed as an automatic private stabilizer, with a contribution which is not negligible, although ignored in the usual national income framework. Table 11 gives realized capital gains and taxes thereon in two recessions. The amounts added to net income of individuals in the recession years 1954 and 1958 through this means must be regarded as a substantial source of stability, whether or not "automatic," and the stability would be reinforced by any liquidity effects of nonrealized capital gains, which presumably move in the same direction. To the extent that this is "automatic," it is a case of economic stability feeding on itself, and the results could easily be the reverse in a more serious depression.

TABLE 11. Realized Capital Gains and Capital Gains Tax in Two Postwar Recessions[a]

(In billions of current dollars)

CALENDAR YEAR	NET CAPITAL GAINS REALIZED	CAPITAL GAINS TAX Accrued[b]	CAPITAL GAINS TAX Paid	GAINS LESS TAX ACCRUED	GAINS LESS TAX PAID
1953	3.9	0.7	0.8	3.2	3.1
1954 (Trough)	6.7	1.2	0.7	5.5	6.0
Change	2.8	0.4	—0.1	2.4	2.9
1957	6.9	1.2	1.6	5.7	5.3
1958 (Trough)	8.6	1.5	1.2	7.1	7.4
Change	1.7	0.3	—0.4	1.4	2.1

a Net capital gains realized are net short-term gains plus 100 percent of net long-term gains (taxable and nontaxable returns), from U. S. Treasury, Internal Revenue Service, *Statistics of Income.* Data on capital gains tax, from Appendix B.
b Estimates of the accrued tax on realized gains.

Employment Taxes

An accurate direct computation of the cyclical sensitivity of employment taxes at constant tax rates is difficult because of the many changes in law. The appropriate adjustments for changes in payroll tax rates for old-age and survivors insurance (OASI) would not be particularly difficult. However, frequent legislation extending coverage of, or raising the limit on, taxable wages has also affected collections—with varying lags and with less certain effects. Moreover, receipts of the Federal Unemployment Trust Fund depend on merit rating[17] and other provisions of the laws of the several states which are subject to frequent change.

TABLE 12. Changes in Federal Employment Tax Accruals, Postwar Recessions and Recoveries[a]

(In billions of current dollars)

CALENDAR-YEAR QUARTERS	PRIVATE WAGES AND SALARIES	FEDERAL EMPLOYMENT TAX PAYMENTS		TOTAL[b]
		Employers[b]	Employees and Self-Employed	
Change, peak to trough				
1948-IV to 1949-II	—4.2	—0.08	—0.04	—0.12
1953-II to 1954-II	—3.6	—0.08	—0.05	—0.14
1957-III to 1958-I	—6.6	—0.20	—0.15	—0.35
1960-II to 1961-I	—4.9	—0.19	—0.15	—0.34
Change, trough to terminal quarter of recovery				
1949-II to 1950-II	6.4	0.13	0.06	0.19
1954-II to 1955-II	12.0	0.28	0.18	0.46
1958-I to 1959-II	21.4	0.64	0.48	1.12
1961-I to 1961-IV	15.0	0.60	0.45	1.04

[a] Peaks, troughs, and terminal quarters of recovery are as in Table 1, except for 1961 terminal quarters of recovery. Seasonally adjusted annual rates, with effects of tax rate and other legislative changes eliminated.

[b] Using prerecession ratios of total contributions to wages and salaries, and of employer to total, as computed in Appendix Table C-6.

[17] Under the laws of most states, employers are allowed reductions in the rate of unemployment insurance tax if they have had a low turnover of employees eligible for unemployment benefits. Under this practice, called merit rating or experience rating, an employer's tax rate is recomputed, usually annually, on the basis of his recent employment record.

TABLE 13. Relationship Between Wages and Salaries and Federal Employment Taxes, Postwar Recessions and Recoveries[a]

(In billions of current dollars)

CALENDAR-YEAR QUARTERS	PRIVATE WAGES AND SALARIES		SHORTFALLS IN EMPLOYMENT TAXES—ACTUAL LESS HIGH EMPLOYMENT[b]		
	Actual	Actual Less High Employment	Employer Contributions	Employee and Self-Employed Contributions	Total
1948-IV(P)	118.6	...	...	...	...
1949-I	116.0	—3.4	—.07	—.03	—.10
II(T)	114.4	—5.7	—.11	—.06	—.17
III	112.7	—8.2	—.16	—.08	—.24
IV	112.2	—9.5	—.19	—.09	—.28
1950-I	114.9	—7.5	—.15	—.07	—.22
II(R)	120.8	—2.4	—.05	—.02	—.07
1953-II(P)	164.8	...	...	...	...
III	165.7	—.5	—.01	—.01	—.02
IV	164.1	—3.6	—.08	—.05	—.14
1954-I	161.5	—7.6	—.18	—.11	—.29
II(T)	161.2	—9.4	—.22	—.14	—.36
III	160.8	—11.2	—.26	—.16	—.42
IV	163.9	—9.5	—.22	—.14	—.36
1955-I	167.5	—7.4	—.17	—.11	—.28
II(R)	173.2	—3.1	—.07	—.04	—.12
1957-III(P)	200.2	...	...	...	...
IV	198.0	—4.6	—.14	—.10	—.24
1958-I(T)	193.6	—11.3	—.34	—.26	—.59
II	193.5	—13.8	—.41	—.31	—.72
III	197.6	—12.1	—.36	—.27	—.64
IV	201.5	—10.5	—.31	—.24	—.55
1959-I	206.7	—7.7	—.23	—.18	—.40
II(R)	215.0	—1.8	—.05	—.04	—.09
1960-II(P)	224.6	...	...	...	...
III	224.2	—2.6	—.10	—.08	—.18
IV	221.6	—7.4	—.29	—.22	—.52
1961-I(T)	219.7	—11.6	—.46	—.35	—.81
II	226.0	—7.5	—.30	—.22	—.52
III	230.7	—5.0	—.20	—.15	—.35
IV	234.7	—3.2	—.13	—.10	—.22

[a] Peaks (P), troughs (T), and terminal quarters of recovery (R), are as given in Table 1. Seasonally adjusted annual rates.

[b] Using prerecession ratios of total contributions to wages and salaries, and of employer contributions to total, as computed in Appendix Table C-6. This eliminates the effect of changes in tax rates and other legislative changes.

An indirect method of measurement is used in this study, which seems indicative of the general orders of magnitude. Marginal changes have been computed on the assumption that employment taxes at constant rates would move proportionately to changes in private wages and salaries. This assumption may slightly overstate the cyclical sensitivity, since employment taxes have no lower limit on taxable earnings but do have an upper limit—a fact which could make the marginal changes in tax less than proportional to changes in total wages. (See Appendix C for explanation and details concerning employment tax rates.) Table 12 gives the results of applying the prerecession tax rates to changes in private wages and salaries during the recession. Table 13 shows the parallel estimates of the shortfalls in employment taxes below the high employment trend.

Since private wages and salaries tend to lag in recovery, the shortfall of employment taxes and, hence, their contribution as built-in stabilizers, reached a maximum after the cyclical trough in all but the 1960-61 recession. Not only in absolute terms, but also in relation to wages and salaries, the effect of these stabilizers has become larger in line with the secular growth in the rate of tax. This trend will continue in future years because of the increases in OASI tax rates already scheduled in present law. The employee contribution has become more important (reflecting the growth of OASI, to which both employee and employer contribute) relative to unemployment insurance, to which only employers contribute. The estimated distribution between employer and employee contributions is also given in Tables 12 and 13.

Because wages and salaries decline less than gross national product in recession, the GNP elasticity of this group of employment taxes is less than unity. The change in tax as an offset to GNP changes is persistently less in recovery than recession. But, as the figures[18] on page 55 also show, the change in employment taxes

---

[18] For the recession figures, the change is from peak to trough in GNP, and for the first three recoveries, from trough to terminal quarter, as shown in Table 1. For the last period, the change is only over the first three quarters of recovery.

TABLE 14. Cyclical Sensitivity of Federal Excise Taxes, Postwar Recessions and Recoveries[a]

(In billions of current dollars)

Calendar-Year Quarters	Actual[b]	Adjusted for Tax Rate Changes[c]	Change from Prerecession Peak	Assumed High Employment Estimates[d]	Shortfall from High Employment Estimates
1948-IV(P)	8.2	8.2	. . .	8.2	. . .
1949-I	7.9	7.9	—.3	8.3	—.4
II(T)	8.2	8.2	—	8.5	—.3
III	8.5	8.5	.3	8.6	—.1
IV	8.1	8.1	—.1	8.7	—.6
1950-I	8.0	8.0	—.2	8.9	—.9
II(R)	8.8	8.8	.6	9.0	—.2
1953-II(P)	11.3	11.3	. . .	11.3	. . .
III	11.3	11.3	—	11.4	—.2
IV	10.9	10.9	—.4	11.6	—.7
1954-I	10.3	10.3	—1.0	11.8	—1.4
II(T)	10.1	10.6	—.7	11.9	—1.3
III	9.7	10.7	—.6	12.0	—1.4
IV	10.1	11.1	—.2	12.2	—1.1
1955-I	10.5	11.5	.2	12.4	—.8
II(R)	11.3	12.3	1.0	12.5	—.2
1957-III(P)	12.3	12.3	. . .	12.3	. . .
IV	12.0	12.0	—.3	12.4	—.4
1958-I(T)	11.7	11.7	—.6	12.6	—.9
II	11.9	11.9	—.4	12.7	—.8
III	11.7	12.1	—.2	12.9	—.8
IV	12.2	12.7	.4	13.0	—.3
1959-I	12.6	13.1	.8	13.1	—
II(R)	12.7	13.2	.9	13.3	—.1
1960-II(P)	14.2	14.2	. . .	14.2	. . .
III	13.8	13.8	—.4	14.3	—.5
IV	13.8	13.8	—.4	14.4	—.6
1961-I(T)	13.3	13.3	—.9	14.5	—1.2
II	13.6	13.6	—.6	14.6	—1.0
III	14.0	13.8	—.4	14.7	—.9
IV	14.5	14.3	.1	14.8	—.5

[a] Peaks (P), troughs (T), and terminal quarters of recovery (R) are as given in Table 1. Seasonally adjusted annual rates.

[b] Indirect business tax accruals, national income account basis, U. S. Department of Commerce.

[c] Excise Tax Reduction Act cut rates effective April 1, 1954, on transportation and a number of consumer durables and other items with a combined annual effect estimated at $1 billion. Half this effect is assumed to take place on a national income basis in 1954-II, the full effect in 1954-III. The excise tax on freight transportation was removed effective August 1, 1958, with an estimated full year effect of $500 million. The Highway Act of 1961 raised excises on the trucking and rubber industries by an estimated $150 million annually effective July 1, 1961.

[d] See Appendix A (method 1).

as a percentage of the GNP change has increased significantly from one recession to the next.

Period	Recession	Recovery
1948-50	1.3%	1.0%
1953-55	1.4	1.3
1957-59	2.2	2.0
1960-61	6.1	2.5

Excise Taxes

Federal excise taxes, as measured by the Commerce Department's series on indirect business taxes, show a high degree of cyclical sensitivity. This series is on an approximate accrual basis, net of refunds, adjustments having been made for some of the collection lags and refunds. In this study, the Commerce series has been adjusted for changes in tax rates that took place during the 1954 and 1958 recessions and compared with a linear trend from peak to recovery. Such a comparison yields a shortfall, compared to presumed high employment yields, running as high as 8 percent to 12 percent of total collections at the trough, which is considerably higher than the percentage shortfall in GNP.

It is difficult from available data, most of which are annual, to pinpoint precisely the source of this sensitivity. Since the taxes are flat-rate levies, this behavior must reflect a sensitivity of the tax base rather than yield sensitivity. Of the major sources of excise revenue, sales of gasoline and tobacco show little tendency to decline in recession years. Alcoholic beverages show only mild cyclical sensitivity. By far the most important source of cyclical sensitivity of federal excises is the drop in sales of new cars in recession years. A rough estimate would be that this accounts for between half and two-thirds of the yield declines shown in Table 14.[19] Other consumer durables on which there is a federal excise

[19] Manufacturers' sales of motor vehicles and parts declined by $4.5 billion (seasonally adjusted annual rate) between the third quarter of 1957 and the first quarter of 1958, and $7.1 billion between the second quarter of 1960 and first of 1961 (U.S. Department of Commerce, *Business Statistics* (1961) and *Survey of Current Business,* February 1962). The assumption that 8 percent of these declines represents the decline in federal tax liability (the rate on automobiles, trucks, and buses) indicates a decline of $360 million in 1958 and $570 million in 1961 attributable to this source.

also tend to be sensitive to cycles. As far as timing is concerned, the shortfall in accrued tax followed the general course of the economy in 1953-55, 1957-59, and 1960-61. An erratic movement during the 1948-50 recession and recovery is of uncertain origin. But it may be traceable in part to the stronger demand for automobiles during the first of the postwar recessions, coupled with the effect of the steel strike in the fall of 1949.

Since the tax bases for excises are more specific, and much narrower, than those for income and employment taxes, a considerably less regular cyclical pattern can be expected depending on the particular product mix of changes in demand and production. The following figures[20] give the percentages of GNP decline and recovery which are offset by changes in federal excise taxes. The exceptionally large 1961 decline reflects the major role of declining automobile demand in this recession.

Period	Recession	Recovery
1948-50	–%	3.3%
1953-55	7.1	5.0
1957-59	3.9	2.7
1960-61	16.1	2.4

It is sometimes suggested that an ad valorem basis for levying excise taxes would enhance the cyclical sensitivity compared to the specific excises generally used by the federal government.[21] However, the federal excise with the greatest potential built-in flexibility, that on automobiles, is already on an ad valorem basis. Moreover, prices have shown little tendency to decline in recession for the items accounting for the great bulk of actual collections. It thus appears that the sensitivity to cycles is attributable mainly to the effect of demand on sales and output of taxable items, and that little additional flexibility in mild recessions would have been observed under the alternative method of taxation.

[20] For the recession figures, the change is from peak to trough in GNP, and for the first three recoveries, from trough to terminal quarter, as in Table 1. For the last period, the change is only over the first three quarters of recovery. The 1948-50 change in excises as a percentage of the change in GNP was less than the smallest unit recorded.

[21] See *Money and Credit*, The Report of the Commission on Money and Credit (Prentice-Hall, 1961), pp. 124, 126.

Unemployment Compensation Payments

Transfer payments in the form of insurance benefits to the unemployed constitute by far the most important built-in stabilizer on the expenditure side of the federal budget. The unemployment insurance system is administered by the states, but the underlying legislation is national, and the federal government gives grants to states for the administrative expense and also keeps custody of the trust fund balances. As in the case of employment taxes, this creates problems in measuring the fiscal effects of these transfer payments.

It is impossible to make a precise split between automatic and discretionary increases in unemployment benefits during recession because of the many changes in state laws which affect outlays. But from the point of view of federal fiscal action, changes in state laws (other than those prompted by federal action) may be regarded as exogenous. Such changes are frequent enough and numerous enough to give a more or less smooth trend to outlays (aside from cyclical ups and downs). In fact, as Lester's studies show,[22] there has been no noticeable trend in the percentage of wage loss offset by unemployment compensation in the postwar period. This is in spite of numerous increases in the coverage and expansion in benefit duration under state laws as well as the Federal Unemployment Tax Act which extended coverage in 1956 from employers of eight or more to employers of four or more workers. Such increases apparently have been offset by the lag in legislating increases in weekly benefit amounts to match rising wage levels. However, it is necessary, in measuring the system's built-in response to recession, to separate the effects of discretionary increases enacted by the federal government which took place during recessions. These were the temporary extensions of benefit duration, first enacted in 1958, and again in 1961.

[22] Richard A. Lester, "The Economic Significance of Unemployment Compensation, 1948-1959," *Review of Economics and Statistics*, Vol. 42 (November 1960), pp. 349-72, and the same author's *The Economics of Unemployment Compensation* (Industrial Relations Section, Princeton University, 1962). Also see Daniel Creamer, *Personal Income During Business Cycles* (Princeton University Press for NBER, 1956), for a study of wage loss offset by unemployment compensation in the 1948-50 recession and recovery.

TABLE 15. Unemployment and Unemployment Compensation in Postwar Recessions and Recoveries[a]

(Dollar amounts in billions)

	UNEMPLOYMENT				UNEMPLOYMENT COMPENSATION				
	Total Unemployment		Insured Unemployment		Actual Transfer Payments			Assumed High Employment Rate for Regular[c]	Actual Less High Employment
Calendar-Year Quarters	Number (thousands)	Percent Civilian Labor Force	Number (thousands)	Percent Total Unemployment	Total	TUC (Discretionary)[b]	Regular State Programs		
1948-IV (P)	2,291	3.7	1,138	49.7	.8	...	.8	.8	...
1949-I	2,866	4.7	1,540	53.7	1.5	...	1.5	.9	.6
II (T)	3,664	5.9	1,912	52.2	1.8	...	1.8	.9	.9
III	4,210	6.8	2,309	54.8	1.9	...	1.9	1.0	.9
IV	4,276	6.8	2,355	55.1	1.8	...	1.8	1.1	.7
1950-I	4,002	6.4	1,944	48.6	1.9	...	1.9	1.1	.8
II (R)	3,591	5.7	1,616	45.0	1.6	...	1.6	1.2	.4
1953-II (P)	1,687	2.6	862	51.1	.8	...	.8	.8	...
III	1,731	2.7	953	55.0	.9	...	.9	.8	.1
IV (T)	2,377	3.7	1,334	56.1	1.3	...	1.3	.8	.5
1954-I	3,381	5.2	1,712	50.6	1.7	...	1.7	.8	.9
II (T)	3,737	5.8	1,983	53.1	2.2	...	2.2	.9	1.4
III	3,846	6.0	2,004	52.1	2.3	...	2.3	.9	1.4
IV	3,495	5.4	1,841	52.7	2.2	...	2.2	.9	1.3
1955-I	3,067	4.7	1,452	47.3	1.5	...	1.5	.9	.6
II (R)	2,848	4.3	1,235	43.4	1.3	...	1.3	.9	.5
1957-III (P)	2,915	4.3	1,417	48.6	1.7	...	1.7	1.7	...
IV	3,378	5.0	1,891	56.0	2.4	...	2.4	1.7	.7
1958-I	4,321	6.3	2,412	55.8	3.1	...	3.1	1.8	1.3
II (T)	5,039	7.4	2,803	55.6	4.2	.2	4.0	1.8	2.2
III	5,069	7.4	2,599	51.3	4.8	.8	4.0	1.9	2.1
IV	4,389	6.4	2,229	50.8	4.2	.5	3.7	1.9	1.8
1959-I	4,032	5.8	1,809	44.9	2.9	.3	2.6	2.0	.6
II (R)	3,547	5.1	1,427	40.2	2.2	.2	2.0	2.0	—
1960-II (P)	3,707	5.2	1,689	45.6	2.4	...	2.4	2.4	...
III	3,990	5.6	2,011	50.4	2.9	...	2.9	2.4	.5
IV	4,499	6.3	2,462	54.7	3.8	...	3.8	2.5	1.3
1961-I	4,868	6.8	2,534	52.1	3.8	...	3.8	2.6	1.2
II (T)	4,968	6.9	2,290	46.1	4.5	.9	3.6	2.6	1.0
III	4,892	6.8	2,129	43.5	4.0	.8	3.2	2.7	.5
IV	4,469	6.3	2,025	45.3	3.8	.6	3.2	2.8	.4

a Peaks (P), troughs (T), and terminal quarters of recovery (R) are as given in Table 1. Seasonally adjusted. Data on total unemployed are from U. S. Department of Labor, Monthly Report of the Labor Force, January 1962. Insured unemployed, from U. S. Department of Labor, Bureau of Employment Security, shows average weekly volume, state unemployment insurance programs including Alaska and Hawaii. Actual transfer payments are from U. S. Department of Commerce, National Income and Output (1958) and Survey of Current Business, July 1961 and February 1962.

b TUC stands for temporary extended unemployment compensation enacted in 1958 and 1961.

c For first three periods, figures are based on linear interpolation, peak to recovery, after adjusting the latter for change in unemployment rate. The 1960-61 figures are based on an assumption of a little over 10 percent per year growth in line with the trend of recent years.

Although normally only about half of total unemployment is covered by the insurance system, a much larger portion of the recession-caused increase in unemployment is insured. Both insured and total unemployment tend to reach their peaks after the cyclical trough (as measured by output), and unemployment benefit payments likewise continue to rise after the trough. In part, this is the converse of what happens to corporate profits. Profits tend to rise more rapidly than output in recovery, reflecting among other things a lag in laying off employees during the downswing, so that the initial phases of the recovery feature a sharp rise in productivity. Moreover, hours of work of the existing work force tend to be expanded prior to the rehiring of additional employees. With respect to total unemployment, a further lag is caused by new entrants into the labor force; but this factor does not affect insurance benefits since new entrants typically are not covered in the insurance system.

The percentage of wage loss compensated by unemployment benefits varies from state to state, being twice as high in some states as in others. The compensation rate is considerably higher during the decline than during the recovery. This may be traced to the drop in insured unemployment relative to total unemployment due to exhaustion of benefit rights as the recession wears on. As is shown in Table 15, insured unemployment as a percentage of the total rises sharply during the decline, but then diminishes during the recovery to a point well below the prerecession peak. The net result of the rise, then decline, of compensation rates is that, as is shown in Lester's studies, recession-caused loss of wages appears to have been compensated at a rate no higher (about 15 percent, counting wage loss from partial unemployment) than the average rate for all types of unemployment.[23]

The amounts expended automatically under state programs in the three recessions are compared in Table 15 with a high employment trend, the difference being the amounts assumed attributable to the recession. As a built-in stabilizer, unemployment compensation has offset much larger fractions of the drop in gross national product in recession than of the subsequent rise during recovery. These figures on the changes in unemployment compensation (excluding special programs extending the duration of benefits enacted

[23] Lester, in *Review of Economic Statistics, op. cit.,* pp. 359-60.

in 1958 and 1961), as a percentage of the changes in GNP, are
as follows:[24]

Period	Recession	Recovery
1948-50	10.5%	1.1%
1953-55	14.1	2.6
1957-59	9.1	2.0
1960-61	25.0	1.4

In addition to the factors mentioned previously, this asymmetry
also reflects the fact that unemployment was, in the first three postwar recessions, substantially higher after the recovery than before
the recession, and that the 1961 figure is based on only the first three
quarters of recovery. The higher offset in the 1960-61 contraction
than in the three earlier ones probably reflects the shallower nature
of that recession. In the case of unemployment compensation, as
with corporation and individual income taxes, an actual decline in
GNP is not required for the federal budget to move toward a
deficit.[25]

Other Federal Stabilizers

For all practical purposes, the items already covered constitute
the federal built-in fiscal stabilizers that were operative in the
postwar recessions. In addition, there are certain programs which
might be expected to operate in the right direction more or less
automatically because they are set up on an open-end basis. These
include various categories of veterans benefits and federal matching
grants to states for public assistance. However, the cyclical sensitivity of such programs has been quantitatively insignificant.

Federal farm price supports are frequently listed as a major
built-in fiscal stabilizer. Because price elasticities of the supply of,

[24] For the recession figures, the change is from peak to trough in GNP, and
for the first three recoveries, from trough to terminal quarter, as in Table 1.
For the last period, the change is only over the first three quarters of recovery—
from 1961-I to 1961-IV.

[25] To take an extreme illustration, if GNP remained unchanged for several
quarters, the growth of the labor force would produce an increase in unemployment some of which would be insured.

and demand for, farm commodities are both low—at least in the short run—a relatively small recession-induced drop in demand could cause a large drop in farm prices and in farm incomes. To protect farm incomes, the Commodity Credit Corporation (CCC) undertakes to stabilize the prices of farm commodities either by direct purchase on the open market or by issuing nonrecourse loans to farmers secured by commodities which the farmer can subsequently sell or forfeit to the CCC, depending on market conditions. The effect of CCC operations on farm incomes is difficult to measure, since it depends on what prices would be in the absence of CCC operations—a debatable matter to say the least. However, a number of factors cast doubt on whether these operations should be considered a built-in fiscal stabilizer.

First, there has been little drop in demand for farm products traceable to the postwar recessions because disposable personal income has been insulated from the declines in activity and because the demand for food has little income elasticity in the short run. Small changes in supply due to weather and other growing conditions have had more influence on farm prices. Second, even when CCC operations raise farm prices, they do not necessarily increase total demand. The diversion of purchasing power of consumers away from nonfarm goods and services may be as great as the additional spending by farm families.[26] Third, it is questionable whether CCC operations should be considered an automatic response to recession and a built-in stabilizer in the sense that the term is here used. Farm price support payments increased in the recession years 1958 and 1961 owing mainly to exceptionally large production. These payments declined in 1954. Perhaps the nearest approach to the behavior expected of a built-in stabilizer was the increase in price support payments during the 1949 recession. As farm production increased abroad, U.S. sellers were left with heavy inventories and excess capacity, and the resulting drop in farm

[26] Karl A. Fox, "The Contribution of Farm Price Support Programs to General Economic Stability," *Policies to Combat Depression,* Conference of the Universities-National Bureau Committee for Economic Research (Princeton University Press, 1956), pp. 295-349; Comment by James T. Bonnen in the same volume, pp. 349-54; and Reply by Fox, pp. 354-56.

exports, prices, and incomes was one of the factors in that recession.

If fiscal stabilizers are examined in terms of the consolidated cash federal budget rather than the national income budget, a more or less automatic federal destabilizer is found in the secondary market operations of the Federal National Mortgage Association (FNMA). Charged, among other things, with the responsibility for improving the geographical distribution of funds available for home mortgages, FNMA, under its secondary market operations, has stepped up purchases of mortgages insured by the Federal Housing Administration (FHA) and those guaranteed by the Veterans Administration (VA) during periods of high employment and tight money; and it has reduced purchases (or increased sales) during the last three recessions.[27] Also working in an ostensibly perverse direction, more or less automatically, are the operations of the Federal Home Loan Banks System and the Federal Savings and Loan Insurance Corporation. The Home Loan banks act as reserve banks for the federally insured savings and loan associations. In periods of tight money and active demand for mortgage funds, the savings and loan associations reduce their reserve accumulations or borrow from the Home Loan banks. In recession periods, when the savings and loan associations tend to become more liquid, they resume reserve accumulation and reduce their indebtedness to the Home Loan banks.

These operations affect assets, but do not have direct income effects on the private economy, which is why they are excluded from the national income version of the budget. Also, they have less automaticity than the fiscal measures described earlier, since they depend partly on the administrative decisions of credit managers— which, while predictable to a certain extent, are not completely so. More important, while the direction of these operations apparently has been the reverse of that appropriate for economic stabilization, their effect on residential construction in the postwar cycles has been more than offset by fluctuations in the availability of mortgage credit, and by the way in which certain federal guarantee and insurance operations work.

[27] The FNMA secondary market operations worked in a stabilizing direction in the 1949 recession.

Some years ago, Hart[28] recommended criteria for judging automatic stabilizers that were not limited to federal receipts and expenditures. Hart would also label as "automatic stabilizer" any device which, without waiting for fresh policy decisions, expands the public's stock of cash in a slump and reduces it in prosperity, or which reduces the public's demand for cash in a slump and increases it in prosperity. He goes on to mention some monetary destabilizers, such as the tendency of banks to shift from bonds to instalment credit and stock market loans in an upswing, but his stabilizers are all of the fiscal variety. Clement[29] agrees with Hart's broader criteria for what constitutes a stabilizer, but asserts that "his tests concerning the supply of and demand for moneyness do not in practice admit a larger number of existing measures to membership." As a matter of fact, there are at least two federal programs of some importance that operate as built-in stabilizers through their effect on the liquidity of the economy rather than their effect on the federal surplus. These are the home loan insurance program of the Federal Housing Administration and the home loan guarantee program of the Veterans Administration, which will be discussed briefly in the following chapter.

[28] Albert Gailard Hart, *Money, Debt, and Economic Activity* (2nd ed., Prentice-Hall, 1953), pp. 462-66.

[29] M. O. Clement, "The Concept of Automatic Stabilizers," *Southern Economic Journal*, Vol. 25 (January 1959), pp. 303-14.

CHAPTER III

The Economic Significance
of Built-in Stabilizers

How IS THE LEVEL of economic activity affected by the built-in fiscal stabilizers? The economic effects of a rise or fall in tax liabilities or transfer payments induced by recession and recovery cannot be measured as precisely as the budgetary impact which was described in the preceding chapter. The economic significance depends on how consumers and business would have behaved in the absence of the budget changes—a conjectural matter, at best. But a systematic examination should permit judgments on general orders of magnitude.

In this study, as in most treatments of fiscal policy, attention is directed mainly to the influence of the built-in stabilizers on incomes in the private sector. A drop in the budget surplus, however, also affects the assets of the private sector. The asset effects are usually relegated to the sphere of monetary or credit policy,[1] but they cannot be completely isolated from the income effects. For example, the way in which the budget deficit is financed will influence liquidity and indirectly condition the income effects of the built-in stabilizers. Since the liquidity effects are independent of the source of the deficit, they will be examined briefly after the more specific effects of particular stabilizers have been considered. The

[1] A brief but informative discussion of the distinction between fiscal policy and monetary policy appears in the *Monthly Review* of the Federal Reserve Bank of Kansas City, August 1961.

initial part of the analysis of specific effects, like the measurement of fiscal impact, is on a liability basis, that is, any lag between the accrual of tax liabilities and tax payments is ignored. But, subsequently, the possible need to modify the conclusions to take account of lags is examined.

Nature of Fiscal Stabilizers

The major fiscal stabilizers come into operation when incomes decline or, as explained in Chapter II, when they fall below the hypothetical high employment trend. Thus the contribution of the stabilizers is in the nature of cushioning, rather than preventing or reversing, a decline or shortfall. Moreover, since taxes absorb less than 100 percent of income and unemployment benefits compensate for less than 100 percent of after-tax wage loss, the cushioning effect is only partial. This is evident when the stabilizers are measured against shortfalls from hypothetical high employment but is not always obvious when they are compared with actual declines in GNP. In 1960-61, for example, the fiscal stabilizers offset well over 100 percent of the actual decline in GNP, peak to trough, owing to the shallowness of the recession.

The built-in stabilizers do not stimulate the economy throughout the recession and recovery. When the trough of a recession is passed, the stabilizers automatically reverse direction and keep the expansion from proceeding as rapidly as it otherwise would, even though the economy is still below full employment. They not only cushion a decline; they also retard recovery.

The importance of built-in stabilizers stems primarily from their role in insulating private incomes from a decline in demand, thereby interfering with the cumulative magnification of a decline once started. This interference takes place with respect to both consumption and investment outlays in the private sector, and can be further classified as initial or primary effects and secondary or induced effects. It is useful to try to analyze these separately, in spite of the usual difficulties of segregating influences on aggregate demand in an economy in which there is interdependence of the major income flows.

The effects of stabilizers on consumption depend, in the first instance, on their effects on disposable personal income. Stabilizers that have their primary effects on disposable personal income may be called "direct stabilizers" to distinguish them from other—"indirect"—stabilizers. A drop in individual income tax liabilities, or a rise in unemployment compensation, is a direct stabilizer because it provides direct support for disposable personal income and thus keeps disposable personal income from falling as much as earned income in a recession. A decline in corporate profits tax accruals, on the other hand, is an indirect stabilizer because it affects disposable personal income only insofar as corporations are induced thereby to alter their employment policies or their dividend payments.[2]

Excise taxes probably resemble the corporation income tax in their built-in stabilizing effects. With respect to excise taxes, the temptation should be avoided to apply ordinary incidence theory— according to which excise taxes are for the most part paid by consumers—in assessing their effects as built-in stabilizers. Incidence theory applies to the result of changes in tax rates. But the effects of built-in stabilizers take place at rates assumed to be unchanged, and apparently represent mainly a drop in sales volume rather than a decline in the net proceeds from any given volume of sales.

Employee contributions for social insurance—payroll taxes paid by employees—resemble income taxes and unemployment benefits in having direct consequences for disposable personal income. The recession-induced drop in employer contributions for social insurance is ambiguous, and can be considered either direct or indirect in its effect on disposable personal income, depending in part on one's theory of corporate behavior.[3] In the present chapter, employer

---

[2] Changes in corporate rent or interest payments would also affect disposable personal income, as would changes in pricing policy, if one were analyzing real as well as money income effects. But these seem distinctly minor in importance compared to the possible effects on wages and dividends.

[3] For example, if corporations respond to a drop in sales by aiming at a calculated reduction in output and employment, the reduction in employer contributions for social insurance is in the nature of a windfall reduction in total costs of the corporation. However, if the response is aimed at a calculated reduction in total costs, the drop in payroll taxes cushions the decline in after-tax income of employees, and resembles the "direct" stabilizers in this respect.

TABLE 16. Change in Federal Surplus or Deficit Due to Direct and Indirect Built-in Stabilizers as Percentage of Change in Gross National Product[a]

Item	Percentage Change, Peak to Trough	Percentage Change, Trough to Terminal Quarter of Recovery
1948-50 recession and recovery		
Direct stabilizers	14	10
Indirect stabilizers	25	24
Total	39	34
1953-55 recession and recovery		
Direct stabilizers	23	12
Indirect stabilizers	43	18
Total	66	30
1957-59 recession and recovery		
Direct stabilizers	22	13
Indirect stabilizers	34	18
Total	56	31
1960-61 recession		
Direct stabilizers	49	. . .
Indirect stabilizers	73	. . .
Total	122	. . .

[a] Peaks, troughs, and terminal quarters of recovery are those given in Table 1. Seasonally adjusted annual rates. Figures from Table 5 and U. S. Department of Commerce. Direct stabilizers are individual income tax, unemployment compensation, and employment taxes; indirect stabilizers are corporate profits taxes and excise taxes.

contributions are classed with the direct rather than the indirect stabilizers; however, this item is shown separately in Chapter II, and readers who prefer to treat it as an indirect stabilizer can rearrange the figures.

Classified by direct and indirect, the fiscal effects of the built-in stabilizers relative to change in GNP are recapitulated in Table 16. The direct stabilizers comprise the individual income tax, employment taxes, and unemployment compensation; the indirect stabilizers, the corporate profits tax and the excise taxes. As noted earlier, the larger response relative to the contraction in GNP in 1953-54 and in 1960-61 probably reflects the smaller decline in those recessions, particularly in the latter case.

Direct Fiscal Stabilizers

The role of the direct fiscal stabilizers in cushioning disposable personal income from changes in aggregate demand (GNP) is illustrated in Table 17. As may be seen, the drop in disposable personal income is but a minor fraction of the drop in GNP in recession, and, in fact, disposable income actually increased slightly in two of the four recessions. However, the direct fiscal stabilizers are only a part of the explanation for this. Gross business saving (mainly retained corporate profits and depreciation allowances) and the indirect stabilizers have absorbed more substantial fractions of the declines. (Because the indirect stabilizers—excises and corporate profits taxes—are closely related in their economic effects to business gross saving, as is discussed later, the two have been lumped

TABLE 17. Built-in Stabilizers in Relation to Output and Income, Postwar Recessions and Recoveries[a]

(In billions of current dollars)

ITEM	CHANGE, PEAK TO TROUGH				CHANGE, TROUGH TO TERMINAL QUARTER OF RECOVERY			
	1948-1949	1953-1954	1957-1958	1960-1961	1949-1950	1954-1955	1958-1959	1961
Gross national product	—9.5	—9.9	—15.4	—5.6	18.0	34.1	55.6	41.4
Less:								
Indirect fiscal stabilizers and business gross saving[b]	—3.6	—6.3	—12.2	—5.6	7.4	11.1	19.8	11.5
Net increase in tax rates[c]	—	—1.9	—	—	.9	—.5	1.8	—
Direct fiscal stabilizers	—1.3	—2.2	—3.4	—2.7	1.7	4.2	7.2	3.9
Other adjustments	—.8	—1.5	1.5	1.1	—3.5	2.1	—.2	4.7
Disposable personal income	—3.8	2.0	—1.3	1.6	11.5	17.2	27.0	21.3

[a] Peaks, troughs, and terminal quarters of recovery are those given in Table 1, except for the change from trough in 1961 which covers only the first three quarters of recovery. Seasonally adjusted annual rates.
[b] Including capital consumption allowances and inventory valuation adjustment and changes in excise and corporate profits tax rates.
[c] Individual income and employment taxes only.

together in Table 17.) During recovery, the direct stabilizers have offset a smaller part of the rise in GNP and, partly for this reason, disposable personal income has shared a larger part of the increase —about a half in the last three recovery periods and more than that in 1949-50.

The importance of cushioning disposable income during recession stems from the fact that it is a major determinant of personal consumption expenditures. An initial change in autonomous demand and in GNP, by causing a change in disposable income, induces a further change in consumption. The relation between the initial change and the cumulative total change in income and demand is indicated by a multiplier. The size of the multiplier depends on the relation between (1) disposable income and GNP and (2) disposable income and consumption.[4] Because the direct fiscal stabilizers reduce the fraction of a change in GNP that is reflected in disposable income, they reduce the value of the multiplier and lessen the cumulative response of total income to any autonomous change in demand.

Annual data over a stretch of years, in most of which income was rising, indicate that personal consumption changed by about 0.9 of the change in disposable income.[5] This fraction is called the marginal propensity to consume with respect to disposable income. Assuming for the moment that the marginal propensity to consume is constant, the influence of the direct fiscal stabilizers on the multiplier can be roughly calculated on the basis of the relations shown in Table 17. In the 1953-54 recession, for example, business saving and the indirect fiscal stabilizers together offset about two-thirds of the decline in GNP, and the direct fiscal stabilizers offset roughly an additional fourth of the decline in GNP. With these relations and a marginal propensity to consume of 0.9, the multiplier would be only 1.08; in the absence of the direct fiscal stabilizers, but with the other relations assumed unchanged, the multiplier would be

[4] The multiplier is equal to $\dfrac{1}{1 - bc}$, where b is the fraction of a change in GNP that appears in disposable income and c is the marginal propensity to consume disposable income.

[5] Bert G. Hickman, *Growth and Stability of the Postwar Economy* (Brookings Institution, 1960), pp. 221 ff.

1.42.[6] In the absence of the direct fiscal stabilizers, the multiplier—
and the total change in income associated with an initial change in
demand—would be roughly one-third larger.

These illustrative calculations are based on certain simplifying
assumptions, and they abstract from several complications. No account is taken of the fact that the multiplier process is time-consuming and a process about which little is known empirically.
Attention is focused on the reaction of personal consumption to a
change in income without regard to the possibility that a change in
investment will also be induced. (Reference will be made to induced
investment in the later discussion of the indirect fiscal stabilizers.)
The role of business saving and the indirect fiscal stabilizers, moreover, is a changing one. In the 1948-49 recession, they offset only
about two-fifths of the decline in GNP, whereas in 1960-61 they
offset the whole decline in GNP from peak to trough (Table 17).

Another important qualification relates to the assumption that
the marginal propensity to consume as estimated from annual data
for a period of generally rising income is a reliable indicator of the
behavior of consumers during a recession. There are several reasons
why the marginal response may be less with respect to a drop in
disposable income during a recession. Individuals may make an
effort to maintain per capita consumption, particularly for food and
other "essentials," by saving less of current income and drawing
on liquid assets. Especially with a growing population, such tendencies may raise total consumption even when income falls.[7] Similarly, it seems plausible that individuals would regard a recession-
induced income change as transitory, in which case there probably

[6] With the direct fiscal stabilizers, the multiplier is equal to

$$\frac{1}{1 - .9(1 - .67 - .25)} = 1.08.$$

Without the direct fiscal stabilizers, the multiplier is equal to

$$\frac{1}{1 - .9(1 - .67)} = 1.42.$$

[7] See James Duesenberry, *Business Cycles and Economic Growth* (McGraw-Hill, 1958).

would be a smaller effect on consumption than if the income changes were viewed as permanent.[8]

On the other hand, there are factors that tend to make consumer expenditures sensitive to temporary declines in disposable income. Outlays for new automobiles and other consumer durables, which are treated as current consumption in the national income accounts, can be reduced without proportionately reducing current use of durables by consumers. The existence of large backlogs of consumer needs and large accumulations of liquid assets in the hands of consumers may have been more important in maintaining consumer expenditures in the face of a decline in disposable income in the early postwar years than in recent years. The statistics in Table 18 show an interesting, and perhaps significant, progression. In 1948-49, total consumption expenditures (in constant prices) rose in the face of a drop in disposable income; in 1953-54, they changed little; in 1957-58, they fell by about three-fourths of the decline in disposable income; and in 1960-61 they changed little despite a small rise in disposable income.[9]

The statistics suggest the possibility that consumption has become more sensitive to changes in disposable income in recessions than it was in the early postwar period. A marginal propensity to consume with respect to disposable income of the order of 0.9, or even higher, may not be an unrealistic assumption for recessions. A high marginal propensity to consume makes the economy more unstable and, at the same time, enhances the importance of the direct fiscal stabilizers, which cushion disposable income. Nevertheless, the significance of the direct fiscal stabilizers should not be exaggerated; business saving and the indirect fiscal stabilizers

[8] Milton Friedman, *A Theory of the Consumption Function* (Princeton University Press for National Bureau of Economic Research, 1957).

[9] Disposable income and consumption expenditures are in constant prices; the trough values are the averages of values for the trough quarter and for one quarter before and after, in order to avoid undue weighting of possible irregularities. If the trough values are measured by data for single quarters, the progression shown in Table 18 also appears; for 1960-61 disposable income declines by $1.9 billion from peak to trough while consumption expenditures decline by $2.5 billion.

72 Federal Fiscal Policy

TABLE 18. Consumption Expenditures in Four Postwar Recessions[a]

(Seasonally adjusted annual rates, in billions of 1954 dollars)

Item	Change, Peak to Trough
1948-49 recession	
Disposable personal income	—1.5
Consumption expenditures, total	2.2
(Consumer durables only)	(1.3)
1953-54 recession	
Disposable personal income	—.7
Consumption expenditures, total	.1
(Consumer durables only)	(—1.6)
1957-58 recession	
Disposable personal income	—3.7
Consumption expenditures, total	—2.8
(Consumer durables only)	(—3.2)
1960-61 recession	
Disposable personal income	.8
Consumption expenditures, total	—.1
(Consumer durables only)	(—2.8)

[a] Peaks and troughs are those designated in Table 1. The troughs are measured by average of value at trough and the quarter on each side, to avoid undue weighting of a single quarter's observation. Figures are from U. S. Department of Commerce, *U. S. Income and Output* (1958) and *Survey of Current Business*, July 1961 and February 1962.

combined are much more important as leakages in the flow between GNP and disposable income.[10]

The direct stabilizers must be assigned a role in reducing the magnitude of postwar contractions, although not as great as might be imagined if the other leakages that would operate—even in their absence—are ignored. In 1961, the direct stabilizers were more important than previously owing to the increased percentage of disposable income which was protected and possibly, also, to

[10] If the marginal propensity to consume disposable personal income were 1.0, the multiplier would be 1.49 without the direct fiscal stabilizers and 1.09 with the direct stabilizers. If the marginal propensity to consume were as low as 0.5, the corresponding values of the multiplier would be 1.20 and 1.04. These calculations are made in the same way as those in footnote 6, and are based on the assumption that business saving and the indirect stabilizers offset two-thirds of changes in GNP and the direct fiscal stabilizers offset another one-fourth of changes in GNP.

increased responsiveness of consumption to changes in disposable income. In addition to their influence on consumption, the direct stabilizers have important induced effects on investment, particularly inventory investment. These will be considered after looking at the first-round effects of the indirect stabilizers—the corporation income tax and excise taxes.

Indirect Fiscal Stabilizers

The primary, or initial, effects of the indirect fiscal stabilizers, mainly the corporation income tax, are intimately related to those of a major "private" stabilizer. Quite aside from any change in federal tax liability, the more than proportional drop in corporate profits in recession, coupled with the relative insensitivity of corporate spending to income changes in the short run, is itself a source of stability to the economy—as has been pointed out by several observers.[11] Corporations frequently appear to try to maintain dividends in accordance with some long-term pay-out policy at the expense, in recession years, of retained earnings.[12] Recessions typically feature substantial reductions in corporation investment outlays—mainly for inventory, but also for fixed capital—and also reductions in corporate wage payments (with a lag, however, because of slowness in reducing overhead labor). But it is reasonable to view such changes as a response to declining gross sales, irrespective of whether net profits are rising or falling at the moment. And in the case of corporate fixed investment, the decline to some extent may even be viewed as autonomous—that is, related to long-

[11] See, for example, a preliminary paper by Charles L. Schultze, "Short-Run Movements of Income Shares," National Bureau of Economic Research Conference on Research in Income and Wealth, April 28-29, 1961, mimeographed; Hickman, *op. cit.,* pp. 221-32; Leslie Fishman, "A Note on the Postwar Recessions," *Review of Economics and Statistics,* Vol. 43 (February 1961), p. 44.

[12] Regressions fitted by Lintner for annual data, and by Duesenberry, Eckstein, and Fromm for quarterly data, have a much higher coefficient on dividends of past periods than on income of the current period. See John Lintner, "Distribution of Income of Corporations Among Dividends, Retained Earnings, and Taxes," *American Economic Review,* Vol. 46 (May 1956), p. 97, and James S. Duesenberry, Otto Eckstein, and Gary Fromm, "A Simulation of the United States Economy in Recession," *Econometrica,* Vol. 28 (October 1960), p. 787.

run expectations, unexpected changes in the pattern of trade, or a correction of past overinvestment—rather than a response to cyclical reduction in either gross or net receipts.

In a national income accounting framework, a drop in retained corporate profits in response to a GNP decline implies that the decline in disposable personal income from the same drop in production is reduced by the same amount as the drop in retained profits. This is not strictly accurate, for if retained earnings were higher, and wages and salaries and other personal income such as dividends consequently lower, a good part of the change (perhaps 40 to 50 percent) would be offset by direct stabilizers—individual income and employment taxes, and unemployment compensation. In other words, a reduction in retained corporate profit is a net stabilizer if the marginal response of corporate spending to a change in retained earnings is less than 50 to 60 percent of the marginal propensity of individuals to spend from disposable personal income. The decision as to whether earnings should be retained or paid out in dividends is at least partly at the discretion of the corporation, and therefore presumably takes some account of investment plans. Thus it appears reasonable to regard investment as a major determinant of retained earnings in the short run, rather than the other way around. In short, the drop in corporate profits and retained earnings is an important built-in private stabilizer— it adds significantly more to personal spending than it deducts from corporate spending. The concern in this study is the extent to which this source of stability is enhanced by the fact that federal corporation income taxes decline by almost half of the decline in profits.

Effects of reduced tax liabilities on final demand could include direct alteration of corporation investment outlays, or indirect effects on consumption through changes in price, dividend, or employment policy. Taking consumption first, price cuts by corporations have not been a conspicuous feature of the postwar recessions, even with the drop in corporate tax liabilities. Moreover, price cuts are not unambiguously expansionary considering possible effects on expectations. Cyclical changes in corporate tax liabilities presumably have some effect on dividend distributions. However, the effect appears small and is subject to large leakages because marginal tax rates and marginal saving propensities of corporate stock-holders are probably higher than average.[13]

Employment by corporations, it may be presumed, would be geared in the short run primarily to gross sales and output expectations rather than net income, either before or after taxes. The fact that half of any increase in corporate costs is borne by the federal government through reduced taxes may cause somewhat less economizing with respect to management, research, and other overhead employment, and perhaps a somewhat easier attitude at the bargaining table if wage settlements fall due. Again, however, any such effects would be subject to leakages through income tax and personal saving and, in the case of employment increases, unemployment benefits would be smaller. In short, primary effects of the indirect stabilizers on consumption may be regarded as minor.

Of the two major determinants of corporate investment—availability of funds and rate of return—the latter would be essentially unaffected by the decline in tax liabilities, since these are approximately proportional to the decline in total profits. There remains then the possible effect on capital or inventory investment of the fact that corporate cash balances decline less than they would if there were no decline in tax accruals. Since capital markets have remained orderly in postwar recessions, and liquidity of financial institutions actually increased, it cannot be argued that reduced profits tax liabilities supply funds that corporations could not raise externally if needed. Against this must be set the fact that external funds are not substitutes for internal funds in the view of many corporations. However, as is shown in Table 19, rising depreciation allowances on past investment offset part of the drop in profits in recession years so far as funds on hand are concerned. Moreover, the need for corporate funds for inventory and capital investment declines in recession years by more than the decline in available

[13] For example, Lintner's equation (*op. cit.*) suggests a change in dividends equal to only 15 percent of the change in profits after tax. If the marginal tax rate typical for stockholders were, say, 35 percent, and their marginal propensity to save 20 percent, the effect on consumption would be only 8 percent (.15 × .65 × .80) of the change in federal corporate profits tax liability). The Duesenberry, Eckstein, Fromm equation (*op. cit.*) fitted to quarterly data would yield only 4 percent.

TABLE 19. Sources and Uses of Corporate Funds Over Three Postwar Recessions[a]

(In billions of current dollars)

Corporate Funds	1948	1949 (T)	1950	1953	1954 (T)	1955	1957	1958 (T)	1959
Sources									
Depreciation	6.2	7.1	7.8	11.8	13.5	15.7	19.1	20.3	21.5
Retained profits	12.6	7.8	13.0	7.9	6.3	10.9	8.9	5.7	9.1
External long-term financing	7.2	4.3	4.2	7.6	6.4	8.6	11.9	10.9	9.5
Payables and other short-term financing	2.2	−1.5	11.9	2.5	−.9	11.3	4.8	5.1	12.3
Federal income tax liabilities[b]	.9	−2.2	7.3	.6	−3.1	3.8	−2.2	−2.5	2.4
Uses									
Plant, equipment, and inventory investment	23.0	12.7	26.7	25.7	20.8	30.9	34.8	24.0	33.4
Increase in cash	.3	1.2	1.6	.2	2.3	1.2	.1	2.5	−.2
U. S. government security holdings	.7	2.0	2.9	1.6	−2.3	3.8	−.4	.2	3.8
Receivables and other	4.3	.6	14.1	1.1	3.0	14.7	5.8	8.6	14.9
(Discrepancy: uses less sources)	(−.8)	(1.0)	(1.1)	(−1.8)	(1.6)	(.3)	(−2.2)	(−4.2)	(−2.9)

[a] Troughs (T) are as given in Table 1. Figures are from U. S. Department of Commerce, *U. S. Income and Output* (1958) and *Survey of Current Business*, July 1961.
[b] Excess of accruals over disbursements.

funds. This is indicated by the fact that corporations in the aggregate added to their cash holdings in the 1949, 1954, and 1958 recession years more than they had in the preceding year of high income; and, in two of the three recessions they stepped up their purchases of United States government securities as well. They reduced their short-term indebtedness in two of the recessions.

That corporate funds are large relative to investment in recession years can be taken to indicate that the stability of the economy would not be greatly enhanced by further stepping up the cyclical sensitivity of the tax—say, by placing payments on a more nearly current basis.[14] This is not the same as saying that the nation could, with impunity, dispense altogether with the cyclical sensitivity of this tax. The drop in tax liabilities in recession years (compared to hypothetical collections at the same tax rates at high employment) has amounted to half or more of actual after-tax retained earnings. It seems unlikely that a decline this large would leave dividends, inventory investment, capital investment, and compensation of employees all unaffected. Moreover, some corporations would be much less liquid than the aggregate data in Table 19 suggest.

It is not possible to quantify these various tendencies with precision. Certainly some contribution to stability is obtained by having a cyclically sensitive corporation income tax rather than a completely insensitive tax. But it seems reasonable to argue that effects on investment as well as consumption of the indirect stabilizers—at least in short recessions where there is no great shock to long-term profit expectations—are small, and that their major impact is on retained corporate profits[15] All things considered, it would be surprising if the first-round addition to total demand were more than a small fraction of the amount by which federal tax collections decline. This is considerably lower than the effectiveness that can be attached to the individual income tax—perhaps enough so as to make these two major stabilizers roughly coordinate in value, in spite of the much greater decline in revenue associated with the corporation tax and excises. The probability that the decline in corporation and excise tax collections adds substantially less to private spending than is deducted from federal receipts may be a disadvantage if the resulting federal deficit inhibits government spending or tax cuts that would be appropriate as part of a high employment policy.

[14] E. Cary Brown reached a similar conclusion in considering the counter-inflationary effects of changing the corporate tax to a current-payment basis of collection. E. Cary Brown, "Pay-As-You-Go Corporate Taxes?", *American Economic Review,* Vol. 37 (September 1947), p. 641.

[15] This is essentially the conclusion reached by Richard Goode, "The Corporate Income Tax in a Depression," *Policies to Combat Depression* (Princeton University Press for National Bureau of Economic Research, 1956), p. 149.

Secondary Effects

Additions to aggregate demand from either direct or indirect stabilizers have secondary, or induced, effects on investment. Investment in plant and equipment may not be sensitive to changes in consumer demand over short recessions of the postwar type. But induced effects on inventory investment are far from negligible. Recession, after all, is characterized by efforts to liquidate inventories in line with reduced sales expectations. In fact, the decline in inventory investment has been the largest single category of decline in total demand in the postwar recessions. An attempt to liquidate inventories which caused a nearly equal decline in disposable income—and, therefore, consumption—would be largely self-defeating. In short, a reduction in the value of the multiplier, which the built-in stabilizers represent, means a still larger reduction in what has been called the "supermultiplier" (including inventory reaction).[16]

If the desired level of stock—inventory or fixed capital—bears a fixed relation to the level of total demand, then investment will change (although with a lag) as a result of changes in demand. The tendency toward accentuation of business fluctuations by the induced effects of demand changes on inventory or fixed investment is known as the "acceleration" principle, and the ratio of induced changes in investment to changes in demand is called the "accelerator." It can be shown that, if consumption depends (with a lag) on income and investment depends (with a lag) on the level of consumption, an initial change in aggregate income may, depending on the specific relations and the time required for the reactions to take place, generate a series of alternating swings in the economy. Some theories of the business cycle have leaned heavily on the interaction of the acceleration and multiplier principles.[17]

[16] Duesenberry, Eckstein, and Fromm, *op. cit.*, p. 763, compute a supermultiplier of 2.72 for 1957-58 conditions, compared to their 1.34 multiplier, which ignores inventory reaction.

[17] See John R. Hicks, *A Contribution to the Theory of the Trade Cycle* (Oxford University Press, 1950), and Paul A. Samuelson, "Interactions Between the Multiplier Analysis and the Principle of Acceleration," reprinted in *Readings in Business Cycle Theory*, selected by a committee of the American Economic Association (Blakiston Co., 1944).

A reduction in the duration, as well as amplitude, of contraction in the economy possibly can be attributed to the built-in fiscal stabilizers on either of two major explanations of business cycles. If cycles are explained by interaction of a multiplier and accelerator (inventory or otherwise), then a reduction in the value of the multiplier can reduce the period as well as amplitude of fluctuations. On the less mechanical explanation of cyclical turning points in terms of accidental developments or autonomous demand factors, then the slower the rate of decline (because of a smaller multiplier or supermultiplier) the sooner can the exogenous factors making for a rise exert themselves. The above argument assumes a reduction only in the value of the multiplier, and the tendency described would be reinforced by any influence of the fiscal stabilizers (most likely the indirect stabilizers) in also reducing the value of the accelerator.

On an accrual (mainly a national income budget) basis, the built-in stabilizers, with relatively minor exceptions, operate in the direction of curtailing both contraction and expansion in the economy. Measured from peak to trough and trough to recovery, the stabilizers offset a larger fraction of a decline than a recovery. This difference, however, is something of an optical illusion, which disappears if the performance of the stabilizers is measured by reference to shortfalls from hypothetical high employment values. Measured in terms of deviation from trend, the restraining influence of the stabilizers during expansion appears to be no smaller than their supporting influence during contraction. In fact, the tendency of profits to "over-recover" during the expansion, coupled with the high tax rates on this income, tends to give the stabilizers greater income sensitivity in recovery than in recession. These propositions can be clarified by an illustration. In the 1953-55 cycle, the actual decrease in corporate profits tax accruals from peak to trough was equal to 36.4 percent of the decline in GNP, and the increase in accruals of this tax from the trough to the terminal quarter of the recovery equaled 13.2 percent of the rise in GNP (Table 5). At the trough, however, the shortfall of corporate profits tax accruals below the hypothetical high employment level was only 17.6 percent of the shortfall of GNP; during the subsequent recovery, the decrease in the shortfall of corporate profits tax accruals equalled 19.5

percent of the decrease in the shortfall of GNP below hypothetical continued high employment.[18]

Liquidity Effects

In terms of liabilities, then, the fiscal stabilizers are at least as effective in offsetting recovery as in offsetting recession. Cash flows, on the other hand, are distinctly asymmetrical. It is well known that because of the lag between accrual of liability and payment of tax, the budget deficit on a cash basis reaches its peak a year or so after the recession trough. To what extent does this lag alter the automatic contribution of the built-in fiscal stabilizers?

Lags in Cash Flows

It is useful to keep in mind that part of the lag in the cash deficit is purely seasonal in origin, since it occurs in good years as well as recession years. Therefore, the lag which is of interest so far as recession is concerned should be measured by the lag between seasonally adjusted accruals and seasonally adjusted cash payments.

Ignoring seasonal factors, the lag in cash payments is negligible —something less than one quarter on the average—for payroll and excise taxes. There are lags in unemployment compensation owing to the waiting period under state laws and the failure of some individuals to file as soon as eligible; and, presumably, there is an additional lag while state employment offices process claims and make payment. Countering this, however, is the tendency of the states to draw down their balances in the Unemployment Trust Fund slightly in advance of anticipated need, so that the federal cash budget records unemployment outlays slightly in advance of unemployment transfer payments recorded in the national income accounts. While difficult to measure, these various lags appear relatively insignificant from the point of view of overall fiscal policy.

Perhaps slightly surprising, the lags also appear to be small for the individual income tax, although these lags are commonly thought to decrease the cyclical sensitivity of this tax. For the with-

[18] The estimates of the shortfall of corporate profits tax accruals, adjusted for changes in tax rates, are from Table 7; the estimates of GNP shortfalls, from Appendix Table A-1.

held portion of the tax, more than half of the amounts withheld by employers is deposited to the Treasury's accounts in the same quarter. The remainder is paid by the middle of the following quarter. There is a long collection lag on declarations of withheld tax caused by the heavy concentration of payments in the fourth fiscal quarter. But this is a seasonal phenomenon, and seasonally adjusted declarations respond promptly to business cycle turns. The lags are much greater—an average of nine months—for final payments and refunds. But, at least in ordinary years, these are opposite in sign and roughly offsetting in magnitude. For recession years, it is true, refunds tend to rise and final payments to decline. Precise measurement of the effect of this is difficult because of the lack of data on cash flows that are adjusted seasonally and for tax rate changes. However, if the 1958 experience is typical, the payment lags for individual income tax may be safely ignored.[19]

The major lag is that associated with the corporation income tax. Corporate profits tax liabilities decline promptly and recover promptly in response to movements in general economic activity. Payments, however, are lagged up to six months after the end of the year in which the liability is incurred, with the result of much poorer timing from a stabilization standpoint. It is often pointed out that corporations usually record taxes on their own books on an accrued liability basis, leading to the strong presumption that liabilities rather than cash payments represent the basic influence of taxes on investment, wage, price, and dividend policies. The failure of tax payments to decline in recession as much as liabilities, as shown in Table 19, constitutes an additional factor tending to dry up funds in the corporate sector, reinforcing the decline in profits and in other sources of funds. But since corporations are typically well stocked with cash at the trough of short recessions (relative to

[19] The change from peak to trough in accrued liabilities, seasonally adjusted, was $1.72 billion as shown in Appendix B. Replacement of accrued values of final payments and refunds (annual rates) at both peak and trough by the actual values for the entire preceding calendar year (as an approximation for seasonally adjusted cash flows) actually *increases* the decline (although by an insignificant amount) to $1.77 billion. Further, a comparison of seasonally adjusted cash collections from the individual income tax with seasonally adjusted accruals over the whole 1957-59 recession and recovery reveals that the former are somewhat more erratic, but not clearly slower in fiscal effects.

investment needs), more or less cash in the amounts at issue probably would not affect their expenditures significantly.

Since corporations frequently invest temporary cash balances in short-term liquid assets, the major effect during recession of a decline in cash balances relative to tax liabilities would appear to be on capital markets. With the payment lag, Treasury tax receipts are greater and corporate cash balances smaller during the recession than if there were no lag, whereas the reverse is true a year later during the recovery. If the Treasury neither hoards nor dishoards cash balances, its borrowing will be less during the recession and more a year later than would be the case with no lag. In effect, cash balances are thus transferred from the corporations during the recession and placed at the disposal of capital markets generally. Although the gross amounts reach several billion dollars at annual rates, the net amount is much less. This is because corporations would have returned much of the cash to the capital markets by investing in short-term securities or reducing their short-term indebtedness. Any net effect of the payment lag during recessions is slightly expansionary if, as seems likely, the expenditures of noncorporate borrowers are raised more than the expenditures of corporations are reduced. But the effect on the capital market could be largely offset by Federal Reserve operations, and probably is at least partly offset in this way.

During recovery, the lag causes the Treasury to borrow more, and corporations to borrow less, than they would if corporate tax accrual and payment were simultaneous. At that time, it is no longer possible to argue that liquidity effects on corporations are nil, since during recovery interest rates will ordinarily have started to rise and a variety of uses for funds will make themselves known. However, since noncorporate borrowers also demand cash during recovery, and the Treasury has to borrow more than with no payment lag, the net effect may be largely canceled—that is, corporate expenditures are raised, but other expenditures reduced, compared to the situation with no lag.[20]

[20] This differs from the conclusion reached by Michael E. Levy, "Federal Budget: Deficit or Surplus?", *Business Record of* the National Industrial Conference Board, February 1962. Levy argues that corporate profits tax accruals

In summary, collection lags are largely confined to the corpora-tion income tax and, insofar as they have an effect, it is mainly on capital markets generally rather than directly on taxpayer expendi-tures. On the assumption that the monetary authorities take partly offsetting steps, the economic effect of the lags will be small. It seems that estimates on the accrual basis (national income budget) adequately portray the timing of the contribution of the built-in stabilizers—even considering effects on assets or liquidity, and not just direct income effects. The lagged cash deficit, therefore, rep-resents primarily "accounting" effects and should not be misread by fiscal or monetary authorities as indicating economic effects. Even seasonally adjusted cash budget figures on occasion have been interpreted this way,[21] and the possibility is stronger if attention is focused on budget figures for the fiscal year, which are also affected by purely seasonal lags (as with the individual income tax). Atten-tion to cash flows, even seasonally adjusted, could lead to restrictive monetary and fiscal policies too early in recovery. As discussed later in this study, fiscal policy in late 1958 and in 1959 may have be-come overly restrictive partly because it was too much influenced by attention to cash flows.

Financing Aspects

As just implied, the effect of the built-in stabilizers partly de-pends on how the resulting Treasury deficit is financed.

At one extreme, the deficit caused by the stabilizers could be financed entirely by depletion of cash balances in Treasury tax and loan accounts at commercial banks. There then would be positive accretions to private assets and cash balances over and above the purely passive effects of cushioning part of the decline in private

---

in the national income budget exaggerate the anti-inflationary effect of the tax during recovery, because of the liquidity effect on corporations of the lag in tax payments. However, Levy fails to consider the liquidity effects of the Treasury's having to borrow more during recovery than it would if there were no such lag.

[21] The *Morgan Guaranty Survey* of the Morgan Guaranty Trust Company of New York, May 1961, for example, indicts counterrecession fiscal policy in the postwar period for poor timing on the basis of seasonally adjusted cash budget trends.

incomes. And depletion of Treasury balances at Federal Reserve banks would add equal amounts to commercial bank reserves and potentially multiple amounts to the money supply. Rolph is of the opinion that these additional effects probably would stimulate private expenditures, and not merely prevent a decline.[22] While this perhaps attributes too much to asset values and cash balances—particularly in recession—the direction of the effect is clear.

At the other extreme, the Treasury could keep its cash balances intact, the monetary authorities could keep the lid on commercial banks to prevent the emergence of idle balances, and the Treasury could sell long-term bonds to finance the deficit. Under such circumstances, the direct income effects of a budget deficit could be largely offset by a reduction of private liquidity.

Both of these extremes, of course, are unlikely. In practice, some middle course is ordinarily pursued—the Treasury keeps its cash balances largely intact and borrows the needed funds. But, for the most part, this borrowing takes place for the short term rather than the long term; and the monetary authorities take steps to increase the likelihood that idle balances, rather than privately needed loanable funds, are tapped by allowing bank reserves to increase by some fraction of the amount financed. The present study does not examine the adequacy of monetary and debt actions in the postwar recessions, or discuss the pros and cons of various proposals such as Friedman's to make the monetary effects as automatic as the fiscal.[23] Nevertheless, the so-called automatic stabilizers are not, under present arrangements, automatic with respect to the financing of the budget deficit, and any analysis requires some assumption about the behavior of the monetary and debt management authorities. Perhaps the best assumption—implicit in the foregoing analysis— is that debt managers will largely abstain from issuing long-term bonds and that monetary authorities will generally "lean against the wind"—that is, allow the money supply to decline in recessions by something less than the decline in demand for cash. The result

[22] Earl R. Rolph, "Built-in Flexibility and Monetary Management," *Tax Revision Compendium,* Vol. 3, House Ways and Means Committee, 86 Cong. 1 sess. (1959), p. 2349.

[23] Milton Friedman, "A Monetary and Fiscal Framework for Economic Stability," *American Economic Review,* Vol. 38 (June 1948), pp. 245-64.

of the latter policy will be generally lower interest rates, but nothing like the degree of liquidity that would be involved in allowing the money supply to increase by the full amount of the deficit. On these assumptions, a deficit produced by built-in stabilizers has some positive effect on private assets and cash balances in addition to income effects, although it is not clear how this can be quantified.

Other Factors Influencing the Behavior of Stabilizers

The apparently growing responsiveness of individual income and employment taxes to changes in GNP helps give the economy greater resiliency against decline. But it is not necessarily an unmixed blessing, because it can complicate the process of formulating fiscal policy to accord with stable growth.

Secular Trends

Since other taxes are at least proportional to their respective bases, other things being equal, a secular drift upward in employment and individual income taxes relative to gross national product would call for a reduction of tax rates or an increase in expenditures relative to GNP over time. However, the rise in revenue potential relative to high employment GNP may not exhibit itself adequately in an economy which is in either a recession or recovery stage during a third to a half of the time. Hence, if fiscal policies (tax rates and expenditure changes) are geared in part to realized budget surpluses, there may be a bias toward overly restrictive fiscal policies and a secular trend toward lower rates of factor utilization. Any such tendency would be aggravated if corporate profits are a residual income share. In that case, incomplete recovery from recessions might produce a declining share of corporate profits in total income. Given the high marginal tax rate on corporate profits, this could be enough to produce a regular bias towards understatement in actual budget totals of the underlying trend toward a bigger tax bite at high employment and constant income shares. Although this possibility is more relevant to discretionary policies—discussed later—it is mentioned here because the role of built-in stabilizers in this connection can easily be overlooked.

Long Depressions

A discussion of built-in fiscal stabilizers would be incomplete without consideration of how they might be expected to behave in a more serious depression than the four since World War II. For such an evaluation, the description "more serious" probably should be understood as a "more protracted" depression rather than a "steeper rate" of decline. As has been pointed out,[24] the order of magnitude of the first three postwar recessions is not different from that of the depression that started in 1929 with respect to rates of decline of exogenous demand factors; the difference, rather, is in the duration of the decline of the 1930's.

In a more protracted recession, the automatic contribution of unemployment compensation would be reduced as the exhaustion of benefit rights under state law mounted. The extent of this effect would depend on how much of the rising total unemployment represented "hard core," as opposed to a turnover of new unemployment. Moreover, the tax rate increases under state merit-rating provisions in the unemployment compensation system—which, because of the lags involved, are at least as likely to be in a stabilizing as a destabilizing direction in short recessions[25]—would become perverse. The exhaustion of benefits could be readily compensated by legislation. In fact, since legislation extending the length of federal benefits has been enacted in the two most recent recessions (1958 and 1961), re-enactment in the next recession appears so likely as almost to qualify as a built-in stabilizer—whether President Kennedy's proposal to make extended benefit periods automatic in recession has been enacted by then or not.

The relative efficacy of the individual income tax would also diminish in a longer recession, since the greater the drop in income, the larger the proportionate drop for individuals with no tax liability anyway because of exemptions and deductions. By a similar argument, but of much smaller importance, the fact that employment taxes have an upper, but not a lower, limit on income subject to

[24] Schultze, *op. cit.*
[25] See William H. Andrews and Taulman A. Miller, "Unemployment Benefits, Experience Rating, and Employment Stability," *National Tax Journal,* Vol. 7 (September 1954), pp. 193-209; Richard A. Lester, *The Economics of Unemployment Compensation* (Industrial Relations Section, Princeton University, 1962), Table 11, p. 70.

tax means that the more protracted the decline, the larger the change in taxable income relative to change in total income.[26]

For excise taxes as built-in fiscal stabilizers, there seems to be no a priori reason to expect a diminished relative contribution in a more protracted depression. However, for corporation income tax, and, more important, its "private stabilizer" counterpart—the shift of income from corporations to individuals, partly resulting from the lagged response in laying off employees—the support to the economy would diminish with the prolongation of depression. An accurate projection of corporate profits over a long depression is not feasible. However, a diminished rate of absorption of GNP shortfall by profits (and by profits taxes) seems clearly indicated.

Farm price supports would be more likely to operate in a stabilizing direction so far as fiscal effects and farm income are concerned. However, for reasons given previously, this would be no guarantee that the price supports would become a built-in stabilizer, even in severe depressions, for aggregate income—farm and nonfarm—in real terms. On the other hand, certain other federal programs which have shown little reaction to short recessions probably would take on the nature of built-in stabilizers. These include: old-age and survivors insurance, under which more people would find it advantageous to retire in depression than otherwise; certain of the veterans benefit programs, such as pensions and hospital and medical care; and open-end matching grants for public assistance.

On balance, automatic federal fiscal stabilizers could be expected to have a smaller relative effect as the duration of the depression increased. Working in the same direction would be the possibility that state and local finance, as in the 1930's, would turn fiscally perverse, rather than stabilizing, as it was during the brief postwar recessions.

Federal Housing Credit Programs

Federal government programs to guarantee or insure private home loan mortgages have been undertaken mainly to increase the availability of credit, particularly for veterans and low-income or middle-income individuals, for new residential construction. These

---

[26] The effectiveness would not be any higher than that indicated in Chapter II, since the method used there to measure fiscal effects did not take account of the limit on taxable wages.

programs have also been expected to help protect the economy, in the event of a serious decline, from a repetition of the disastrous liquidity scramble among financial institutions that aggravated the depression in the early 1930's. In the mild postwar recessions, there has been no great upsurge in mortgage defaults and no real pressure on financial institutions. However, the insurance of home loan mortgages by the Federal Housing Administration (FHA) and their guarantee by the Veterans Administration (VA) have played an important contracyclical role for another reason. Because of certain characteristics of mortgage markets and the way the federal programs operate, new residential construction has been stimulated by FHA insurance, or VA guarantees during periods when the economy was below high employment and held back when the economy was operating at relatively high levels.

Mainly because federally guaranteed or insured mortgages carry very low down-payment requirements compared to conventional mortgages, the total demand for housing has tended to increase when FHA or VA credit was available from private lenders, and to decrease when such credit was not available. In periods of high employment and tight money, when interest rates on other kinds of loans rise, the legal ceilings on interest rates on FHA and VA mortgages curtail the availability of credit for such mortgages. Discounts on FHA and VA mortgages rise, to make up for their low interest rate. This discourages some lenders—such as insurance companies, who do not like to lend at discount—and either adds to the costs of builders (if builders have to absorb the discounts) or adds to the initial settlement costs of prospective buyers. When recession comes, and money becomes easier, the limits on interest rates are no longer effective and a disproportionate increase occurs in the availability of mortgage money for federally guaranteed or insured mortgages. New housing construction increased significantly faster than total production in each of the postwar recoveries, after having declined significantly during the prerecession periods of high level activity, with the FHA and VA sectors of the market accounting for much of the volatility.

Other factors have tended to operate in the same direction. These include the stimulus to conventional mortgage loans from generally easy monetary policy during recessions and various discretionary changes in the insured and guaranteed programs affecting down-payment requirements, closing costs, maturity periods for loan repayment, and the maximum size of loan. The strength of residential construction during periods following mild contractions, in large measure, results from the maintenance of high consumer incomes and a high degree of bank and nonbank liquidity. For these reasons it is not indicative of what would happen in a severe depression in which consumer incomes and the liquidity of financial institutions might be impaired.

Conclusions

There is little doubt that the combined effect of the various fiscal stabilizers has been a substantial source of stability in the postwar period. The direct stabilizers—individual income tax, employment taxes, and unemployment compensation—have been more important in this than the indirect stabilizers—corporation income and excise taxes—certainly per dollar of deficit, and probably in total contribution in spite of the larger budgetary effects of the latter.

Measured on an accrual basis—the significant basis for fiscal policy purposes—the stabilizers are well timed to counteract contraction, reverse direction promptly after the trough, and also retard recovery. Cash payment lags are of relatively minor importance to the economic impact of the stabilizers, and their effect in delaying the appearance of the maximum deficit on a cash basis should not be allowed to call forth overly restrictive fiscal and monetary policy during recovery. There is some evidence that the income-sensitivity of personal consumption expenditures during recession has increased, which heightens the importance of the direct fiscal stabilizers. The fact that the yield of the individual income tax increases faster than income over a period of years and the increase of employment tax rates together give the fiscal stabilizers a growing effectiveness in counteracting recession—although the difficulty of formulating fiscal policy to accord with the requirements of stable growth in an economy subject to periodic recessions is perhaps increased. Including secondary effects on inventories, it appears that the fiscal stabilizers have significantly limited the duration, as well as the magnitude, of decline in the postwar recessions. However, fiscal and related stabilizers would provide relatively less support in a prolonged depression than in the short postwar recessions.

But fiscal stabilizers are not the only stabilizing forces set in motion in mild recessions. Among private and nonfiscal stabilizers, the absorption by corporate saving of much of the decline, which cushions the fall in personal income, is particularly important. Also, residential construction has tended to give (with different timing to be sure) a strong and semiautomatic stimulus to the economy in the postwar recoveries. State and local capital outlays have tended to show a stabilizing response to easy credit conditions in recession years, although they are less volatile in this respect than residential construction. And an increase in exports relative to imports—normally expected in response to recession, either because of price or income effects, or both—has occurred three out of four times.

Finally, fiscal and other automatic stabilizers, while important factors, are not the whole explanation of postwar stability. Monetary policy, fortuitous developments in exogenous private demand, and discretionary government fiscal actions have all played a role. The last influence, discretionary government fiscal policy during the postwar recessions, is the subject of the chapters which follow.

CHAPTER IV

Recession and Recovery,
1948-1950

THE RECESSION which began near the end of the calendar year
1948 was the first real test of the federal government's ability and
willingness to use its powers—as promised in the Employment Act
of 1946—to counteract a decline in economic activity. A depression, with massive unemployment, had been expected as one of the
consequences of the end of World War II, and was still feared. Instead, the main problem with which fiscal policy had to cope in the
first three postwar years was one of excess demand and inflation.
Consumers, businessmen, and state and local governments, following the long depression of the 1930's and four years of wartime
shortages, had huge backlogs of needs and much of the purchasing
power required to fill them. The economy had inherited, as a result
of the wartime federal deficits, a large volume of liquid assets in the
form of U.S. government securities, and the policy followed by the
Federal Reserve authorities of maintaining orderly government
bond markets at low and stable rates of interest permitted these
securities to be turned into cash rapidly and without capital loss.[1]

[1] For a brief analytical description of the U.S. economy during this period,
see Bert G. Hickman, *Growth and Stability of the Postwar Economy* (Brookings
Institution, 1960), pp. 51-71.

When the recession finally came, it turned out to be considerably milder than the long-expected postwar readjustment. It was partially obscured by some signs of further inflation and by a lag of statistics behind events; and it came at a time when the government had been taking a particularly strong anti-inflationary stance. Significantly, during that recession, the precepts of compensatory fiscal policy were less widely accepted than they were to become later. For these and other reasons, recognition of the recession was slow and the switch in government policy from countering inflation to countering recession was extremely cautious.

Inflation and Tax Reduction

Some signs that the postwar inflation might be coming to an end could have been detected as early as the first quarter of 1948. Investment demand weakened in the business and housing sectors, and a decline in net exports which had begun earlier accelerated.[2] In February, a sharp break in farm and food prices and relatively stable industrial prices represented marked departures from earlier trends. Also, the Senate Finance Committee, in hearings on pending legislation to reduce taxes, received some testimony forecasting recession, and used this point as an argument for tax reduction in its report on the bill.[3]

But these were only straws in the wind. When the Revenue Act of 1948 became law on April 2, over President Truman's veto, there was little disagreement with the belief that inflation was a greater current threat to the economy than deflation. Some of the proponents of the Revenue Act even supported it on grounds that a tax reduction, by encouraging production, would reduce the inflationary gap.[4] Holmans makes the point that other aims—striking

---

[2] *Ibid.*, pp. 65-67.

[3] A. E. Holmans, *United States Fiscal Policy 1945-1959* (Oxford University Press, 1961), pp. 91-92. This book contains an especially interesting review of the early postwar years from an outside point of view.

[4] E. Cary Brown, "Fiscal Policy in the Postwar Period," in Ralph E. Freeman (ed.), *Postwar Economic Trends in the United States* (Harper and Bros., 1960), p. 154.

a symbolic blow at the New Deal and forestalling further increases in government spending, improving tax equity and incentives, and winning the fall elections—weighed more heavily than economic stabilization with the legislators who were pushing tax reduction.[5]

The 1948 Revenue Act increased personal exemptions from federal income tax from $500 to $600, reduced rates in all brackets, allowed income-splitting for married couples, increased the standard deduction, and extended additional exemptions to the blind and aged. These provisions reduced liabilities on a full-year basis by an estimated $4.7 billion, with withholding rates reduced effective May 1. In addition, estate and gift tax liabilities were reduced by an estimated $250 million. Since the bill was retroactive, liabilities for the calendar year 1948 were reduced by the full amount but collections did not fall until after enactment. As a result, refunds were exceptionally large in early 1949—fortunate, if largely accidental, timing from the standpoint of the recession.

The administration's opposition was vigorous, based largely, but by no means exclusively, on the argument that a budgetary surplus was needed to combat inflation. Secretary of the Treasury John W. Snyder, testifying before the House Ways and Means Committee in January, had opposed tax reduction on the grounds that "present economic conditions, budgetary considerations, inflationary pressures, and debt management problems require the maintenance of government revenues at the present level."[6] By March, in testimony before the Senate Finance Committee on the same bill, only a slight change in Mr. Snyder's emphasis can be discerned. The March testimony, however, dropped explicit reference to inflation and was couched instead in terms of "financial integrity" and "sound financial structure." These, he explained, meant adequate revenues, a balanced budget, and debt retirement—aims which, on some occasions at least, have been regarded as ends in themselves, more or less independent of their short-run economic impact.[7]

In at least one passage, the President's veto message was ex-

---

[5] Holmans, *op. cit.,* pp. 56-96.

[6] *Annual Report of the Secretary of the Treasury, 1948,* p. 301. (Cited hereinafter as *Treasury Report,* with the year to which it refers included in the title.)

[7] *Ibid.,* pp. 305-10.

Chart 2

Gross National Product, Unemployment, and Federal Receipts and Expenditures, Quarterly, 1948-50

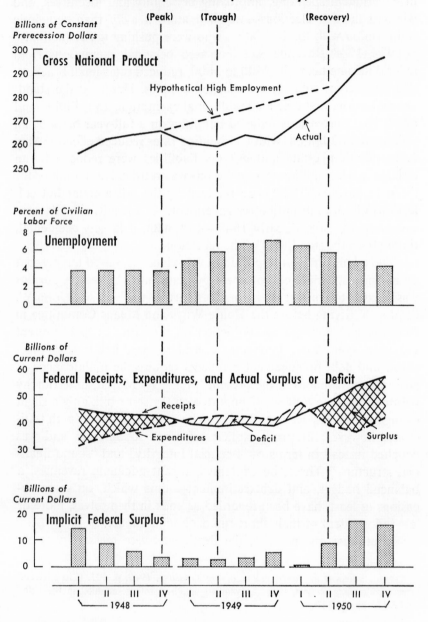

Source: Appendix D.

94

plicit on the inflation point: "The national income is at a record level. Employment is at a record level. Production is at a record peacetime level. The resources and labor force of this country are fully employed. Under these circumstances, tax reduction could only result in higher prices—not in higher production." But in spite of this strong language, there is evidence elsewhere in the message that President Truman was aware that inflationary forces had abated at least temporarily. For example, "Preliminary estimates indicate that corporate profits during the first quarter of 1948 have substantially maintained the very high level of 1947." Again, "Inflation is still here and the cost of living *has not descended* to reasonable levels."[8]

It is also clear that the President objected strongly on equity grounds to the distribution of benefits under the Republican-sponsored bill. While not pursuing its recommendations vigorously, and standing little chance in competition with the pending tax reduction, the administration had put forward its own ideas on tax revision that could hardly be described as anti-inflationary. The President had recommended a "cost-of-living" tax credit of $40 per capita to compensate low-income individuals for losses suffered from inflation, with the revenue loss to be offset by an excess profits tax on corporations. This exchange, as Brown points out, while preserving the government's financial position, at best would have been neutral in short-run economic impact, and more likely expansionary—particularly if the administration's argument is accepted that an excess profits tax would not significantly crimp investment.[9]

Finally, the discussion of budget uncertainties in the President's veto message raised the issue of balanced budgets and fiscal responsibility—not identical with the issue of inflation. Although he had proposed in January 1948 a budget surplus of $4.8 billion for fiscal year 1949, later legislation and appropriations enacted by Congress had raised the expenditure estimate, and it seemed likely that a tax cut of $5 billion would unbalance the budget. More important, there had been growing international tensions, including

[8] *Ibid.*, pp. 326-27. (Italics added.)
[9] Brown, *op. cit.*, pp. 153, 158.

the first Russian moves to seal off Berlin. These had prompted the President—the day before his veto of tax reduction—to recommend substantial additional appropriations for the armed forces. He pointed out that the precise expenditure results of such needs were not certain—and further increases might well be likely. Describing a tax cut under such circumstances as an "erratic and vacillating tax policy," he said he could not endorse action involving revenue reduction that "in all likelihood" would have to be corrected by a tax increase the next year.[10]

That the President in his charge of fiscal irresponsibility had hit on a potent political issue is indicated by the efforts of the Republican Congress to hide the prospective 1949 deficit by a bookkeeping device. Although tax liabilities for calendar year 1948 were reduced by the full amount, collections in fiscal year 1948 were affected to a relatively minor degree, and a surplus of over $7 billion was expected. A rider was tacked to the Economic Cooperation Act, approved April 3, 1948, that would in effect have charged $3 billion of fiscal 1949 expenditures against fiscal 1948 revenues, leaving budget surpluses in both years.[11]

A New Round of Inflation

The drop in farm prices in February proved temporary, and a new round of price and wage increases took place in the summer and early fall. Had these developments been evidence of surging demand, the Revenue Act of 1948 would have been fiscally perverse, as was generally thought to be the case at the time. Actually, however, demand was already beginning to flag; the Revenue Act was a well-timed blow at recession; and tax reduction played little part in the following price inflation, other than a possible effect on expectations. In fact, the additions to disposable personal income resulting from the tax cut were largely hoarded for the remainder of 1948.[12]

[10] *Treasury Report, 1948*, p. 327.

[11] The President subsequently chose to ignore this provision except to indicate by a footnote in later budget documents and Treasury Department reports that figures for fiscal years 1948 and 1949 did not give effect to the provisions of Section 114(f) of the Economic Cooperation Act of 1948.

[12] See Hickman, *op. cit.*, Chart 5, p. 54, and pp. 69-70. Holmans (*op. cit.*, pp. 97-99), argues that since the jump in the rate of personal saving which started

The President's Council of Economic Advisers (CEA) at the time was still a relatively new experiment in policy formulation and had not been steeled in the fires of recession. Moreover, there were arguments among its members and others about the proper relationship between the Council and the President (whether CEA was advisory to, or spokesman for, the President; and whether or not CEA was entitled to its own public views if such views were not necessarily in accord with the President's).[13] While the differences were certainly more theoretical than operational, it may be prudent to avoid completely identifying the views of the CEA with those of the administration.

Some passages in the July CEA report to the President show an awareness of both inflationary and deflationary forces at work, and some uncertainty as to which was going to predominate.[14] However, the general tone of the CEA report seemed more concerned with counteracting inflation than deflation.

The President called a special session of Congress, which began on July 27, 1948, and in his message opening the session laid down an eight-point anti-inflationary program. As Fredland puts it, Truman's recommendations "went well beyond the normal limits of fiscal and monetary policy into powers reminiscent of the war economy."[15]

---

in the second quarter of 1948 was larger than could be accounted for by the reduction in tax, the increase in saving was autonomous rather than the result of lower taxes. On this basis, he is willing to assign to the tax cut enough of an effect on consumption to have postponed the start of the recession for two or three quarters. The issue has an important bearing on the efficacy of tax cuts as antirecession devices, and is discussed in more detail at a later point in this study.

[13] Edwin G. Nourse, who was at that time Chairman of the Council of Economic Advisers, later advised analysts to distinguish between (a) the Council's reviews, (b) the President's program, and (c) the positions taken by those members of the Council who appeared before the Joint Committee on the Economic Report in Congress. See Nourse, discussant, "Stabilizing the Economy: The Employment Act of 1946 in Operation," panel at the December 1949 meeting of the American Economic Association, *American Economic Review,* Vol. 40 (May 1950), p. 183.

[14] Council of Economic Advisers, *The Economic Situation at Midyear 1948,* printed with the *Midyear Economic Report of the President, July 1948,* pp. 44 and 47, for example.

[15] John R. Fredland, "Keynesian Ideas as Reflected in the Domestic Fiscal and Monetary Policies of the United States, 1945-53" (unpublished Ph.D. dissertation, The American University, 1956), p. 165.

It is clear that the President's recommendations were shaped by political considerations as well as the state of the economy. In his July 15 acceptance address at the Democratic National Convention, the President had indicated a number of recommendations, including proposals to deal with inflation, he planned to lay before the special session. Commenting later on this address, Mr. Truman stated frankly that he had known "the special session would produce no results in the way of legislation." Rather, he called Congress back "to prove to the people whether the Republican platform really meant anything or not."[16] Furthermore, the inflation and the fiscal responsibility themes were both used repeatedly by Mr. Truman in his successful campaign for re-election in the fall of 1948.

Another theme which emerged at that time reappeared in the period which followed. It is of some interest because of a possible role in shaping the administration's fiscal policies and recommendations. In August, before the Senate Committee on Banking and Currency, Leon Keyserling, a member of the CEA, argued that it was even more urgent to bring inflation under control in a period such as the current one, when only some prices were rising, than in a period of generally rising prices. This, he said, was because economic imbalance—particularly the threat to consumer buying power from rising consumer prices—increased the danger that inflation would breed contraction.[17]

The special session did temporarily authorize the Federal Reserve Board to reimpose consumer credit controls and to increase reserve requirements which, after increases of February and June of 1948, had reached their legal limits. The Board soon lifted reserve requirements two percentage points on all demand deposits, and Regulation W, restricting the use of consumer credit, was reinstated in September 1948. In this connection, the CEA in its January 1949 *Annual Economic Review* said, "Regulation W probably has tended to restrict additional installment credit for certain purposes, including the purchase of automobiles and some other durable goods."[18]

"Thus," as Caplan writes, "just when the boom in the economy

[16] *Memoirs of Harry S. Truman, Years of Trial and Hope*, Vol. 2 (Doubleday, 1956), pp. 207-08. (Cited hereinafter as *Truman Memoirs*.)

[17] *Control of Inflation*, Hearings before the Senate Committee on Banking and Currency, 80 Cong. 2 sess. (1948).

[18] Printed with the *Economic Report of the President, January 1949*, p. 17.

was tapering off and the trend changing, new anti-inflationary controls were imposed."[19]

The Contraction—Conflicting Evidence and Goals

Wholesale prices, which had spurted 5 percent since February, reached a peak in August 1948; consumer prices, in September; and industrial production, in October. The National Bureau of Economic Research (NBER) places the cyclical turning point in October.

From the peak in the fourth quarter of 1948 to the trough in the second quarter of 1949, the gross national product (GNP) declined 3.6 percent—from an annual rate of $265.9 billion to $256.4 billion. Over the period, a change in business inventories, which switched from net investment of $4.3 billion to net disinvestment of $5.3 billion, accounted for virtually the whole GNP change. Aside from business inventories, the major decline in demand was for business fixed investment, which continued down throughout calendar 1949. Federal, state, and local government purchases all rose during the contraction period. Federal defense orders, which had been rising earlier in 1948, apparently declined,[20] although the precise adjustment which should be made for seasonality is not entirely clear.

Disposable personal income was bolstered by the automatic declines in federal tax liabilities and increases in transfer payments, as well as by the 1948 reduction in tax rates. Although a tapering-off of consumption after the first quarter of 1948 undoubtedly had been one of the initiating factors in the contraction,[21] the decline in consumption, once the recession began, was extremely modest and was soon reversed. The backlogs of demand for automobiles and housing were still large, and both of these played an important role in the mildness of the 1949 recession.

There is some evidence of awareness in administration circles that inflation was ceasing to be the major problem toward the end

[19] Benjamin Caplan, "A Case Study: The 1948-1949 Recession," *Policies to Combat Depression*, report of the Conference of the Universities—National Bureau Committee for Economic Research (Princeton University Press, 1956), pp. 27-53.

[20] Norman B. Ture, "Fiscal Policy," Chapter 8, *Staff Report on Employment, Growth, and Price Levels*, Joint Economic Committee, 86 Cong. 1 sess. (1959), p. 230.

[21] Hickman, *op. cit.*, pp. 69-70.

of 1948, but there was no clear-cut change of direction. For example, Caplan cites a CEA staff memorandum of September 21,[22] which forecast declining, rather than advancing, overall wholesale prices over the coming six to nine months. Caplan points out, however, that this forecast was qualified, and some conflicting evidence was noted. As another example, the White House asked CEA Chairman Nourse, on November 15, to take over the task of coordinating the administration's anti-inflation program; and shortly afterwards expressed gratification with the newspaper and radio reception of this move.[23] And, again, a staff memorandum to the Director of the Bureau of the Budget,[24] in early December, noted a mixed outlook for the coming year, although it reported, on balance, more likelihood of inflation than deflation. Expressing the view that an anti-inflationary stance was probably good strategy, it nevertheless suggested that, because of the uncertainties, the President's forthcoming annual messages make recommendations that could be reversed if the outlook changed.

In mid-December, Secretary of the Treasury Snyder described the situation this way to the American Bankers Association: ". . . our economy is at present in a basically sound condition, and shows encouraging signs of stability in the vicinity of the present high levels. There is today no strong evidence of overbuying by consumers, nor of overexpansion by industry." While the Secretary acknowledged that there was some feeling of apprehension about the economic outlook in business circles, he placed no more credence in these than in fears of unemployment in previous years that had failed to materialize.[25]

Apropos the rather slow official recognition of the recession, it is fair to point out that indexes continued mixed for some time after the turning point. Furthermore, the lag of statistics behind events was somewhat greater at that time than in later years. It is also pertinent that, both in the second quarter of 1947 and in the

[22] Op. cit., pp. 39-40.

[23] Edwin G. Nourse, Economics in the Public Service (Harcourt, Brace, 1953), pp. 228-29.

[24] From the Bureau's fiscal division; information obtained from the Bureau of the Budget archives.

[25] Treasury Report, 1949, p. 317.

first of 1948, fears of recession had been aroused by temporary hesitations in the economy, only to be quickly dissipated by new rounds of inflation.

In January 1949, Congress received from the administration a distinctly mixed picture of current and recent economic trends. The Council of Economic Advisers noted in its *Annual Economic Review*[26] that while total employment had increased, there had been layoffs in some lines and reduced hours of work (p. 1), and that "the pattern of price changes during 1948 was far more uneven than at any time since the end of price control," with farm, food, and some industrial prices declining significantly, others rising significantly (p. 4). While mainly concerned with inflation, the *Review* also referred to the disappearance of war-created backlog demand and major improvement in supply in many fields, a drop in inventory buying, and increasing competition for the consumer's dollar. It recommended caution in interpreting the divergent trends and said "we are moving into a period where much more highly selective efforts will be needed to achieve workable price relationships for the maintenance of economic stability." (Pp. 6 and 8.)

The CEA *Review* also reflected an emphasis—not unique to the Council at that time, and interesting in the light of certain bills that later came up in Congress—on the need for "balance" in the industrial composition of output and the distribution of income. Thus CEA expressed concern over "bottlenecks," particularly inadequate capacity in the steel industry, and also about maldistribution of income as between business and consumers. These matters were dealt with not only as questions of equity and of long-term growth, but also there was the strong implication that bottlenecks, on the one hand, or an inadequate consumer share of income, on the other, could lead to a contraction in economic activity. Trends in corporate profits and depreciation allowances were surveyed in relation to investment and working capital needs, with the conclusion that profits on the whole were still above the level necessary to furnish

---

[26] Printed with *Economic Report of the President, January 1949*. (Page references given in the following paragraphs refer to this CEA review and the President's 1949 *Report*.)

incentives and funds for investment "and to promote the sustained health of the economy." Considering the impact of World War II and progressive income taxes on relative shares, modified by the income-splitting provisions of the 1948 act, CEA concluded that "we are still far from obtaining the amount and distribution of consumer income in relation to the other component parts of the economy which seem essential for balanced economic growth." (Pp. 10 and 17.)

Along with this diagnosis of a very mixed situation, the administration in January presented specific policy proposals in both the *Budget* and the *Economic Report* which were distinctly anti-inflationary.[27] In the *Economic Report,* the President requested extension of the June 30 expiration date of (1) the Federal Reserve's temporary authority, granted the preceding August, to increase reserve requirements as a means of avoiding the release of a substantial volume of bank reserves; and (2) authority to regulate consumer installment credit. In addition, he asked for legislation enabling him to study and correct specific deficiencies of capacity that would be bottlenecks in production in a maximum employment economy, and for authorization for mandatory allocation powers, selective price and wage controls, and extension of existing controls on rents and exports.

Less consistent with the anti-inflation program, the President in his *Economic Report* expressed an intention to continue the policy of maintaining stability in the government bond market which, he said, engendered business confidence and made it easier for business and industry to obtain capital for expansion. There was also a request for increased coverage of the Fair Labor Standards Act and an increase in the minimum wage from 40 cents to 70 cents an hour.

Finally, and perhaps most controversially, the President asked for an increase of $4 billion in taxes, offering corporate profits and estate and gift taxes as the most logical sources of increased revenue. And he defended an increase in social security contributions

[27] The President's *Economic Report, 1949, op. cit.,* and *The Budget of the United States Government for the Fiscal Year Ending July 30, 1950* (January 1949). (Cited hereinafter by text page references or *Economic Report, 1949* and *Budget, Fiscal 1950.*)

for its additional anti-inflationary effect. This proposal of a tax increase in a period of recession often has been singled out as a particularly inept application of federal fiscal policy in the postwar period.[28] The factors leading to the proposal warrant examination in some detail.

The first factor was the inclusion in the *Budget* of a number of proposals for new or increased expenditure programs which, like the tax increase, were not enacted by Congress. The President's program called for a $5.7 billion increase in cash payments to the public in fiscal 1950. In the regular administrative budget, there were major increases for defense and several other activities. Proposals were made for new or expanded federal programs of aid to education, slum clearance and urban renewal, low-rent public housing, a comprehensive medical care insurance system, public assistance, foreign economic aid, and also an increase in employee pay. With allowance for expected reductions in veterans readjustment benefits, occupation and relief costs in Germany and Japan, and a few other items, total expenditures in the administrative budget were expected to rise by $1.7 billion.

Outside the administrative budget, the President recommended a sweeping liberalization of social security benefits. Under his plan, the increase in outlays would be met not only by the addition of taxes on newly covered employees, but also by advancing the next scheduled increase in the payroll tax rate from January 1, 1950, to July 1, 1949, and raising the ceiling on taxable earnings. The President said that the result would be initially a larger increase in taxes than benefits but that this would be desirable from an anti-inflationary point of view.[29] He also proposed extension of coverage under the unemployment system to employees in small establishments and to federal employees—the former would have resulted in a larger increase in trust fund receipts than expenditures; the latter would not. Outside the administrative budget, too, was a plan to have the National Service Life Insurance Trust Fund—administered by the Veterans Administration (VA)—pay a special one-time dividend of

---

[28] See Brown, *op. cit.;* Henry H. Villard, "The Council of Economic Advisers and Depression Policy," *American Economic Review,* Vol. 40 (December 1950), pp. 600-04; and Ture, *op. cit.*

[29] *Economic Report, 1949,* p. 10.

something over $2 billion in the latter half of calendar-year 1949. This dividend was certainly not originated as an antirecession action, since the basic decision had been made, and the program was "well under way," by June 30, 1948.[30] Moreover, if there were any attempts to accelerate payments because of the recession, these were not very successful, since the payments were not made until 1950.

A second factor which undoubtedly shaped fiscal attitudes was international tension. The Berlin airlift of supplies had been building up for more than six months, and there was no sign the Russians might soon relax their blockade.[31] Negotiations with the North Atlantic allies for a mutual defense pact had been under way for almost a year, and showed promise of coming to fruition in the near future, although no estimate of expenditures was included in the budget.

The President's Budget Message assumed a "continuance of full employment and approximately the current levels of economic activity," but under existing law, he said, revenues would fall far short of budget expenditures for both fiscal 1949 and fiscal 1950. Under these circumstances and in view of the international uncertainty, he felt the increase in taxes was needed:

> In a period of high prosperity it is not sound public policy for the Government to operate at a deficit. A Government surplus at this time is vitally important to provide a margin for contingencies, to permit reduction of the public debt, to provide an adequate base for the future financing of our present commitments, and to reduce inflationary pressures. I am, therefore, recommending new tax legislation to raise revenues by four billion dollars. Because of the normal lag in the collection of taxes, however, tax receipts in the fiscal year 1950 would be considerably less.[32]

The principles that should govern tax legislation were laid out in CEA's *Annual Review:* Additional measures should (1) provide a budget surplus; (2) absorb some of the current high profits, while avoiding measures which would lead business firms to charge

---

[30] *Annual Report of the Veterans Administration, 1949.*

[31] *Truman Memoirs,* Vol. 2, Chapter 9. The first Russian moves toward a change in the blockade policy were not noticed until late January 1949, and restrictions did not end until May 12.

[32] *Budget, Fiscal 1950,* p. M5.

higher prices or impair their ability to maintain desirable rates of expansion; (3) guard against aggravating any recessionary tendencies and provide sufficient fiscal flexibility to enable quick readjustments if such tendencies should become strong; and (4) reduce the inequities of previous legislation and strengthen the enforcement of the tax-collection system (pp. 38-39). It may be noted in passing that, if taxes were to be increased at a time of threatened recession, it would be hard to choose increases less damaging to aggregate demand than those selected by the administration.

One of the arguments advanced by CEA for a tax on profits was that such a tax is sensitive to changes in business conditions, and therefore will rapidly reduce its demands on taxpayers in the event of a recession. The Council also argued on grounds of equity that increases in personal income taxes under existing conditions "should be limited to the middle and upper brackets." However, it warned that "a further substantial increase in defense and military aid budgets would call for an increase in personal income taxes in all brackets." (Pp. 39-40.)

Thus, the Council cannot be accused of ignoring the possibility of recession altogether. Rather, CEA viewed its problem as one of navigating a cautious passage between the Scylla of recession and the Charybdis of inflation. This was not merely a conflict between a short-run need for antirecession action and a long-run need for redistribution of income for equity purposes. Both redistribution of income and restraint on consumer prices were required to avoid secular stagnation and perhaps contraction itself. The President, also, in listing his "guides to economic policy," had this reminder: "A prosperity that is too uneven in the distribution of its fruits cannot last." In short, in an economy with both inflationary and deflationary trends, a blow aimed at those factors which were inflationary was not inconsistent with remaining alert to the dangers of recession. "In fact, curbing inflation is the first step toward preventing depression." (P. 9.)

Still other influences probably affected the tax increase proposal. Orthodox canons of fiscal prudence (the respect for balanced budgets) undoubtedly exerted a constraining influence, as they did in later recessions. Moreover, the competing tenets of Keynesian compensatory fiscal policy were less widely held in 1949 than later. Then, too, there was the lag of statistics behind events and of policy behind statistics. Caution on the part of responsible public officials in reversing policies prior to a rather unambiguous indication of need is clearly prudent. And the extraordinary political attention given the inflation problem just prior to the 1949 recession made reversal even more difficult than it might otherwise have been.

Finally, there is some evidence that the administration was less than completely sincere in its proposal for tax increases. For example, neither the *Budget* nor the President's *Economic Report* was very specific as to which taxes should be increased by how much, or when. Although there was a statement that the corporate profits tax should provide the major increase, there was no estimate of the revenue effect by fiscal years. While spokesmen for the administration defended the general proposition of a tax increase in testimony before the Joint Committee on the Economic Report, they were no more specific than the President, and it does not appear that the administration made the kind of push required for enactment. It may be, then, that the President's tax proposal was made primarily "for the record," with little hope for, or danger of, enactment.

None of the foregoing considerations could convert the proposed tax increase into sound fiscal policy. But this provides a good illustration of a number of the recurring constraints on Presidential policy that are sometimes overlooked.

The "Gentle Art of Disinflation"

Shortly after the President's January messages to Congress, concern shifted, almost imperceptibly, from inflation to "disinflation." Apparently the first hint passed on to the President from the Council of Economic Advisers came in the form of a cautious warning inserted by Mr. Nourse in the Council's regular monthly memorandum of February 4, 1949, the basic tone of which continued to be inflationary:

Mr. Nourse believes that there are other facts than those cited above, additional developments not yet reducible to a statistical basis, and questions of business attitudes which lead him to an interpretation materially different from that contained in the remaining paragraphs of this memorandum. In a word, he does not believe there are clear indications that inflationary pressures are increasing or unabated, although developments are conceivable which might renew the process of inflation.[33]

At about this same time, the Joint Committee on the Economic Report was receiving testimony from other administration officials on the need to reduce inflationary pressures.[34] On February 10, Secretary of the Treasury Snyder told the Joint Committee "economic stability at the present high levels of employment and production depends to a great degree on continued confidence in the government's credit." Calling additional revenues "imperative," Snyder mentioned contingencies that might make the deficit even larger than forecast. One of these was the development of unemployment and a drop in business; but he apparently viewed this possibility as no more likely than that business levels and revenues would exceed the budget estimates (pp. 145-75). The two CEA members, with whom Nourse had indicated some disagreement on the outlook, also testified. Keyserling pointed to both inflationary and deflationary trends, and repeated his earlier argument that the deflationary danger caused by imbalances and divergent price trends made it that much more urgent to eradicate remaining inflationary pressures (pp. 7-54). John D. Clark concentrated on inflationary tendencies, including the expected forthcoming rise in federal expenditures (pp. 130-44 and 425-42).

Shortly afterwards, CEA Chairman Nourse, who had declined to testify before the Joint Committee, delivered an address to the Executives' Club of Chicago, under the title "The Gentle Art of Disinflation," in which he expressed the belief that the economy would be able to "take off some fat" without being hurt.[35] This was his way of expressing an idea, rather widespread at the time, that some deflation following the severe postwar inflation was not only inevitable but desirable, the trick being to achieve "disinflation" of prices without causing a serious contraction in output.

The Joint Committee issued its own findings on the *Economic*

[33] Nourse, *Economics in the Public Service, op. cit.*, pp. 234-35.

[34] *Hearings on the Economic Report of the President,* Joint Committee on the Economic Report, 81 Cong. 1 sess. (1949). Page references that follow in the paragraph refer to this report.

[35] Nourse, *Economics in the Public Service, op. cit.*, pp. 235-36.

Report of the President on March 1, 1949.[36] Although the Democratic majority agreed that current economic trends were "mixed," and its policy conclusions were essentially the same as the administration's, the Committee leaned less heavily on the inflation argument in defending them. The Joint Committee recognized that "it may be that deficit spending cannot be avoided in times of depression," but it argued that the current period was really rather prosperous by historical standards. Furthermore, expenditures, because of heavy defense needs, could not be reduced enough to balance the budget; a balanced budget was important for the maintenance of business confidence; taxes on profits would not impinge significantly on investment funds, given the current levels of corporate liquidity; and taxes on profits and individuals in upper income brackets would help redress the adverse distributional effects of inflation. It also approved the administration's policy of supporting the price of long-term government bonds at a yield level of 2½ percent. The Republican minority members filed separate views, stating "we see no justification for the claim that there now exists any serious danger of inflation."[37] While "subscribing completely to the idea that we should balance the budget and have something left to apply to reducing the national debt in 1950," the Republicans opposed tax increases and asked for expenditure reduction instead. They also argued that the administration's real motives in asking for selective controls and a study of inadequate steel capacity was a passion for economic planning rather than a fear of inflation.

On March 8, CEA members Keyserling and Clark sent the President a memorandum stating that the pulse of the economy was still strong, and that the only possibly adverse development would be loss of confidence by business investors. They pointed out that the President's program should, and did, contain weapons to combat both inflation and a substantial downturn in business.[38]

The optimism of the Council of Economic Advisers during this period has come in for considerable criticism. Villard, who called

[36] *Joint Economic Report,* Joint Committee on the Economic Report, 81 Cong. 1 sess. (March 1, 1949), pp. 4-14.

[37] *Ibid.,* p. 2.

[38] Nourse, *Economics in the Public Service, op. cit.,* pp. 236-37.

CEA's public position "fantastic optimism," hypothesized: "I suspect that an important factor retarding recognition by the Council of the change in economic circumstances in the first half of the year was the need to wait until the President found it politically possible to withdraw his request for tax increases."[39] Certainly, the caution with which CEA undertook to disenchant the President is consistent with this hypothesis. The Council's quarterly report, on April 1, 1949, undertook to tell the President "frankly" that the first quarter was one of mixed trends, and the immediate outlook uncertain. It listed three possibilities: first, and least likely, further inflation; second, the long-feared substantial downturn in business; third, and most to be hoped for, healthy price adjustments with only moderate temporary departure from maximum levels of employment and production. Although CEA said the government should extend every feasible encouragement to the third of these alternatives, it apparently made no specific suggestions in this connection.[40]

In the meantime, the Budget Bureau staff was discussing informally with the staff of CEA—also the Federal Reserve and the Federal Security Agency (FSA)—possible government actions in the event of a recession;[41] mainly focusing on unemployment compensation and various federal loan programs. Then, on April 8, the Director of the Bureau of the Budget asked for "plans—and possible programs that should be given consideration in the event of a downturn in economic activity." The bureau staff undertook a comprehensive survey, classifying possible program changes under the headings "automatic," "administrative," and "requiring legislation," and cross-classifying these by "moderate recession" and "deeper recession." Almost ninety separate items were listed. Of the listed changes in automatic expenditures, there were more decreases (because of expected price declines) than increases. On the revenue side, there was discussion of a proposal not to move up the scheduled old-age and survivors insurance tax rate increase to July 1, 1949, as previously recommended.

[39] *Op. cit.*
[40] Nourse, *Economics in the Public Service, op. cit.*, pp. 237-38.
[41] The information here and in the following paragraph was obtained from a review of the archives of the Bureau of the Budget.

Concern over a possible contraction in output still had not altogether replaced the appealing notion of "disinflation." For example, in addition to studying possible anti-recession actions, the Budget Director was also having a survey made of possible budgetary savings to be achieved by recapturing any price declines experienced in federal agency procurement programs, which could be done by placing budgetary reserves on appropriated funds. In this connection, the experience of the Bureau of Reclamation during fiscal 1950 is interesting.

It was estimated in April that, because of declining construction costs, the Bureau of Reclamation might accomplish its fiscal 1950 construction program with 15 percent lower dollar obligations than had previously been estimated. The possibility of placing reserves on these estimated savings was considered so that they would not be spent on items outside the original program. But apparently this was not undertaken in light of a subsequent speed-up in the Bureau's program. The Bureau of Reclamation had an unexpected leveling-off of construction costs and an increased rate of accomplishment by contractors on many projects, which required revisions in payment schedules and additional funds.[42] In reporting this development, however, no mention of the recession was made, although the speed-up was largely a result of slack in the construction industry which led contractors to step up performance and claim earlier reimbursement on government contracts. And the Bureau drew no conclusions in reporting an increase in the number of bidders on new work and a smaller spread between high and low bids, and also that contractors were accepting contracts "without including in their bids large contingency items to cover every possible expenditure." Except for the fact that a decision on budget apportionment policy would ordinarily be required, this phenomenon might be classified as a built-in stabilizer. However, the amounts involved were relatively small and comparable developments in later recessions have not come to the writer's attention.

By the start of 1949's second quarter, economic assumptions were being determined for use in the preview of the 1951 budget—to be transmitted to Congress the coming January. Among these

[42] See *Annual Report, Secretary of the Interior, 1949*, pp. 2-7.

were the assumptions that farm prices would continue to drop, and that unemployment would remain at a seasonally adjusted figure of 2.5 million from July 1, 1949, to December 1950. However, on the advice of CEA, higher unemployment estimates of up to 5 million were considered for agencies whose outlays would be affected by the level of unemployment. According to Nourse,[43] CEA members were invited that spring by the Budget Director to participate in discussions on the size and timing of a stockpiling program in connection with the forthcoming budget, but the extent to which economic stabilization goals shaped the eventual budget recommendations for stockpiling is not known.

During the first half of 1949, the policy of maintaining stable prices for government bonds—which earlier had led to expansionary monetary policy in the midst of inflation—had become the occasion for restrictive monetary action in the face of deflation. When the decline in business brought higher bond prices and lower interest rates, the Federal Reserve began to sell bonds, substantially reducing its holdings of governments and the reserves of member banks. It was not until June 1949, that the Open Market Committee of the Federal Reserve announced publicly it would stop trying to maintain a fixed pattern of interest rates, and that its policy would be to direct purchases, sales, and exchanges of government securities by the Federal Reserve banks with primary regard to the general business and credit situation and the supply of funds available to commerce, business, and agriculture.[44]

On the congressional front, Chairman Joseph C. O'Mahoney of the Joint Committee on the Economic Report announced, in late June and early July, the appointment of four special sub-committees to study and report on the problems of (1) investment needs and sources of funds, (2) the coordination of monetary, credit, and fiscal policies, (3) low-income families, and (4) unemployment. When initially discussed by the Joint Committee in March, these subjects were considered topical in relation to the recession.[45] But hearings were not held until the following fall and winter, and then

[43] *Economics in the Public Service, op. cit.,* p. 249.
[44] *Federal Reserve Bulletin,* Vol. 35 (July 1949), p. 776.
[45] Joint Committee on the Economic Report, *Report on the Economic Report of the President, 1949, op. cit.,* pp. 108-10.

the subcommittees treated their respective subjects in terms that were more general than topical. In the meantime, during the spring months, the approach suggested by the minority members of the Joint Committee—to balance the budget by cutting expenditures in the face of deflation—had gained considerable bipartisan support. For example, on April 1, 1949, Democratic Senator Walter F. George and Republican Senator Robert A. Taft had separately announced their opposition to Truman's proposed tax increases, and said they would work for lower expenditures instead.

The Economic Situation, Mid-1949

In retrospect, it is not hard to recognize that deflationary forces were about spent by the middle of 1949, but this was by no means clear at the time. In fact, as statistical evidence piled up, it confirmed that a decline had been under way for some time and showed few signs of reversal.[46] During June, the economic projections which were being used for preliminary plans in connection with the 1951 budget were based on rising unemployment through the second half of 1950.

On July 8, 1949, the Budget Director submitted a memorandum to the President covering the possibilities of expanding public works to alleviate unemployment.[47] It examined the volume of unfinished work on projects already under way; the volume of authorized, but unstarted (and for the most part unfunded), construction; agency estimates for unauthorized projects; and the status of various pending bills that could have some effect on public works. The conclusion was that perhaps $500 million could be added during fiscal 1950 to combined federal, state, and local government expenditures for public works construction. This could be accomplished, according to the memorandum, without additional leg-

[46] Present national income estimates place the trough in the second quarter of 1949 for gross national product, but for several years the trough was indicated as 1949-IV which is still the reference cycle trough used by the National Bureau of Economic Research. See Caplan, *op. cit.,* p. 29, for a brief history of successive upward revisions of GNP data for this recession.

[47] Information in this paragraph was obtained in a review of Bureau of the Budget archives.

islation or increase of the federal share of grant-aided projects—through the release of reserves,[48] supplemental appropriations early in the next session, and a coordinated effort to persuade states and localities to expand their public works. An additional $500 million might be added if Congress increased the federal share for grant-aided highways. However, these were outside estimates and it was also pointed out that, under a concerted effort of this type, the major impact would come in future years when the employment-generating projects might no longer be needed. Various bills already being supported by the administration would have the effect of stepping up advance planning and site acquisition, but would have no effect on construction in 1950 unless supplemental appropriations were enacted. For the time being, the administration was confining its acceleration efforts to the planning stage.

The recession was given official public recognition by the administration in July. The President's midyear report[49] said "a moderate downward trend characterized most phases of economic activity in the first half of 1949." He gave up hope for a balanced budget for the time being; indicated that government actions would be helpful, but that a large share of responsibility for keeping the correction within tolerable limits rested with businessmen and labor; and was cautiously optimistic about the outlook. Government fiscal transactions, which had switched from a large surplus to a small deficit over the year, were called "a source of support against other factors making for decline in the economy." (P. 4.) Crash programs were explicitly eschewed, since ". . . our economy is still operating at high levels of employment and production. The kind of Government action that would be called for in a serious economic emergency would not be appropriate now." (P. 5.) The January request for an increase of $4 billion in taxes was

[48] The technique of holding a portion of appropriated agency construction funds in reserve, through the Bureau of the Budget's apportionment process, had been employed in previous years as an anti-inflationary device. This was implied in President Truman's instructions for "budgetary controls" as described in his statement of August 3, 1946, on *The Review of the 1947 Budget.*

[49] *Midyear Economic Report of the President, July 1949.* (In the following summary of the President's recommendations, page references to this report are given in the text.)

specifically withdrawn. Instead, the President recommended an increase in estate and gift tax rates, offset by elimination of the excise tax on freight transportation and a liberalization of the loss carry-over provisions of the corporation income tax laws. "The net effect," he said (p. 8), "of these three changes in our tax structure, taken together, will be favorable to the expansion of business activity, without causing a significant net loss in total receipts."

The Council of Economic Advisers, in its review of *The Economic Situation at Midyear 1949* which accompanied the President's report, said ". . . the appearance of a government deficit will have to be accepted." Under the circumstances, the role of government, CEA said, should be to: (1) maintain business confidence; (2) "support the maintenance and exercise of consumer purchasing power"; (3) provide "such protection as our rich economy can reasonably provide" to the unemployed; and (4), "finally, without a premature commitment of resources . . . prepare and make ready those programs of government action which should be available to support economic expansion if the forces of the market alone should fail to provide the needed uplift." (P. 12.)

The President, in a section called "Policies for Economic Stability and Expansion" (pp. 5-13), listed eleven measures which he said were of "vital importance" in the current economic situation. The immediate expansionary impact of these measures, even had all been put into effect, would not have been large. In brief, the measures and some indication of their possible effects, are as follows:

1.   The President requested legislation to extend the maximum maturity periods for loans by the Reconstruction Finance Corporation (RFC), and stated that the RFC was already, under existing authority, basing its policy upon reasonable assurance of repayment, not under depressed conditions, but under generally prosperous long-run conditions. "The Corporation is also very properly focusing its loan activities towards areas where unemployment has become serious." If the maturities had been extended, the cost would have been an estimated $5 million at most. With respect to the alleged administrative liberalization of RFC loan policies, a Bureau of the Budget staff memorandum

shortly afterwards stated that there was considerable evidence, including a recent field investigation, that this policy of the President was not in fact being implemented throughout the RFC loan organizations.[50]

2.   Federal standards for the joint federal-state unemployment insurance program were recommended, along with an extension of coverage, and establishment of a federal reinsurance system to allow states to immediately meet the federal standards. Compared to the administration's January proposals of extended coverage, the July proposals, which would require higher benefits in many states, would have a more expansionary short-run fiscal impact. But as the President pointed out, increased benefits would require action by state legislatures, and obviously it would take time for new standards to take effect. Little if any additional short-run impact was implicit in the reinsurance recommendation, since the balances in most state accounts were adequate at the time.

3.   A one-year extension of the expiration date for unemployment benefits for veterans was requested. This would have cost an estimated $200 million to $300 million in fiscal 1950, but was not enacted.

4.   The President's January 1949 recommendation of increased old-age and survivors insurance benefits, on which Congress had taken no action, was repeated, with some modifications which made the July suggestions less contractionary. Whereas the January recommendations would have advanced, to July 1, 1949, an increase in the combined payroll tax rates on employees and employers to 3 percent, with a further increase by January 1, 1950, together with an increase in taxable wages, the July recommendations accepted the 3 percent combined rate already scheduled for January 1 and said nothing about enlarging the taxable wage base.

5.   With respect to public works, the President noted that the already budgeted federal program, in conjunction with expected private, state, and local programs, was substantial. "The economic situation does not now call for an immediate and sweep-

[50] Memorandum to the Director of the Bureau of the Budget, August 2, 1949 (from the archives of the Bureau).

ing expansion of public works." However, since planning activities needed rounding out to provide a larger backlog of planned projects in case the business downturn should worsen and stronger measures be required, he asked for legislation to: (a) provide for loans to assist in state and local advance planning (b) provide funds for the Public Buildings Administration for advance planning and site acquisition, (c) enable the Bureau of Public Roads to make advances to states for acquiring and clearing rights-of-way, and (d) provide for surveys and planning for school construction previously recommended.[51] The funds requested for public works planning and site acquisition were estimated to involve outlays of $7 million in fiscal 1950.

6.   Legislation was recommended to increase technical assistance to, and encourage investment in, the underdeveloped countries for reasons of both foreign policy and domestic economic policy. "The expansion of foreign investment . . . will improve the rest of the world's ability to buy from us." The President noted that the decline in business activity was reducing United States imports, and that this, if long continued, could have very serious adverse effects on the rest of the world. The international technical assistance program (proposed in the Point IV program sent to Congress earlier) was estimated to cost about $30 million.

The remaining proposals (numbers 7 through 11 following) were described at the time as activities involving negligible, or no, federal outlays. These were:

7.   A request for authority for a broad study of investment and development needs and market opportunities in an expanding economy.

[51] Interestingly, the view was expressed several months later in a publication of the Council of Economic Advisers (*Business and Government,* December 27, 1949, p. 19) that public works and other expenditures should be geared to long-range program goals, rather than economic stabilization needs. "The intrinsic purpose of public works is not to take up slack in employment, but rather to build up our national wealth by procuring certain end products which the country needs but which cannot be produced in any other way. Similarly, a decision to expand our educational facilities should be related closely to the priority value which we place upon education, rather than to the usefulness of school construction in taking up a business slack." The logic of this view would rather suggest tax cuts, although this particular publication expressed doubts whether even tax cuts and public works combined could correct a truly severe depression (p. 13).

8.   A recommendation for direct production payments for agriculture (the Brannan Plan) as an alternative to the pegging of market prices.

9.   Renewal of the January recommendation of an increase in the minimum wage to 75 cents an hour, and an extension of coverage.

10.   A renewed recommendation that federal public assistance grants be extended to the field of general assistance.

11.   And, concluding the list, the President said his Executive Office was being directed to review and coordinate the channeling of regular government activity, especially construction and procurement, into areas of serious unemployment.

Thus, while recession was recognized as the problem of the day, the measures outlined by the President for dealing with it were rather modest and cautious. Of this report, Holmans said: "The Midyear Economic Report of 1949 was just as confident as either the 1954 or 1955 Economic Report; if the charge of complacency could be fairly made against the Eisenhower administration in 1954, it could be made with equal justice against the Truman administration in 1949."[52] But this view slights the important break with tradition that was involved in the simple act of deliberately tolerating a budget deficit. A radio address by the President about the time of his *Midyear Economic Report* defended the budget deficit as both necessary and helpful under the circumstances. Notwithstanding the far more trying conditions in the 1930's, there had not been in that period a clear official endorsement of deficit spending as a support of purchasing power. While the Employment Act of 1946 was generally thought to imply the desirability of deficits in recessions, specific language to this effect was dropped from the final bill; and, of course, there is a wide gulf between abstract endorsement and specific proposal.

That the President's recommendation of a budget deficit ran directly counter to his own strong instincts is indicated by views he expressed later about the desirability of balanced budgets.[53] In this, he was obviously aligned with the predominant view of all

[52] A. E. Holmans, "The Eisenhower Administration and the Recession, 1953-55," *Oxford Economic Papers,* Vol. 10 (February 1958), pp. 34-54.

[53] Holmans, *United States Fiscal Policy, op. cit.,* p. 130.

but a handful of officials in both the executive and legislative branches. Even CEA Chairman Nourse subsequently revealed that he was "by no means free of apprehension . . . about going into deficit financing" at the time of the midyear review.[54] It is also necessary to avoid taking public expressions of optimism during such times entirely at face value.[55] Moreover, fiscal policy deliberations, during July 1949, were concerned with more than recession. As described by Nourse,[56] the Council of Economic Advisers became heavily involved with budget planning for defense.

The Department of Defense was seeking $23 billion for the 1951 budget, to be presented in January 1950, and some preliminary estimates had run as high as $30 billion. The President, on July 1, gave the Joint Chiefs of Staff a ceiling of $13 billion out of a tentative total budget of $41.8 billion. Although these were close to the January 1949 estimates for fiscal 1950, a deficit was in prospect under existing tax rates,[57] and the President enlisted CEA help in his campaign to hold down the military. The President asked CEA to advise him on the economic effects of his preliminary budget plans, as contrasted with lower expenditures or higher taxes. He also wanted to know the economic consequences of moderately higher or lower military and foreign aid outlays than contemplated in the ceiling determinations. In subsequent efforts to answer these questions, CEA Chairman Nourse maintained stoutly that the President's tentative budget figures, though no higher than already planned for 1950, conveyed a serious inflationary threat; the other members of the Council, Keyserling and Clark, calculated that these estimates, given normal economic growth, would be consistent with budget surpluses in 1952 and thereafter under existing tax rates. Separate CEA representations conveying these two points

[54] Nourse, *Economics in the Public Service, op. cit.,* p. 282.

[55] A CEA staff member at that time told the author that this midyear report was regarded by many of the staff as "whistling in the dark," and that, considering the often expressed fears of a truly serious postwar depression, maintaining the confidence of the business and investor community was an important aim of the Council.

[56] *Economics in the Public Service, op. cit.,* pp. 249-52 and 279-83.

[57] The calculations being used at the time must have been based on considerably less than full-employment revenues in fiscal 1951 (which is to say calendar 1950 private incomes) since the expenditure figures cited by Nourse (*ibid.*) would otherwise have allowed a surplus.

of view were presented to the President and the Budget Director in August.

On July 25, President Truman had placed his signature on the North Atlantic Treaty, ratified a few days earlier by the Senate and, on August 24, he requested congressional authorization for military assistance under the Treaty in the amount of $1.4 billion. Since this Treaty had been under consideration by the Senate since April, it must have been a factor in fiscal and budgetary planning for some time.

Finally, if the administration's proposals were modest by the standards of an economist, they were radical from the viewpoint of Congress—which at that time was busily engaged in efforts to balance the budget.

The widespread economy drive in Congress in 1949 reflected, on the part of many of its supporters, the belief that expenditures should be cut back to match the recession-reduced level of receipts. A resolution requiring the President to make across-the-board cuts of from 5 to 10 percent in his January budget barely missed enactment. Describing such activities, Holmans states: "The significant point is not that these extreme and obscurantist views were to be heard, but that they were to be heard so often and the contrary argument so rarely."[58]

When the 81st Congress, first session, adjourned in October 1949, Congress had reacted as follows to the President's proposals: It had cut defense appropriations by over a billion dollars from the President's requests; and had reduced appropriations for highways, aviation, and water resource public works. It had not given the President his aid to education bill; had not acted on the administration's social security or unemployment recommendations or extended veterans unemployment compensation; had not eliminated the transportation excise tax or taken any other tax actions recommended either in January or July; and had not raised postal rates. It had enacted a housing bill; and had given the President $500 million of his supplemental request for mutual defense assistance.

The Housing Act of 1949, signed on July 15, initiated new

---

[58] Holmans, *United States Fiscal Policy, op. cit.*, p. 117.

programs of federal aid for slum clearance and for farm housing. It authorized 810,000 additional units of low-rent public housing over a six-year period, and gave the President discretionary authority, on advice of the CEA, to accelerate or retard this program for economic stabilization purposes. However, the Housing Act should not be considered an antirecession move. Its provisions had been under consideration in Congress since 1945, and had been proposed several times by the President. Moreover, expenditures under the Act were negligible so far as the recovery was concerned.

Recovery Before the Korean Invasion

By mid-1949, inventory liquidation had gone far enough in relation to current sales to allow an early rise in production, although the switch to net accumulation of inventories did not occur until the first quarter of 1950. Although the National Bureau of Economic Research places the cyclical trough as late as October 1949, recovery, led by outlays for consumption and for residential construction, really started about the middle of 1949. The expansion was interrupted in the fall by coal and steel strikes, but resumed and increased rapidly after the turn of the year. Employment and industrial production began rising toward the end of 1949, and the quarterly peak in rate of unemployment came in October-December 1949. Business fixed investment continued down through the first quarter of 1950, but the fact that recovery of this important category of demand started prior to the outbreak of hostilities in Korea probably means that expansion would have been sustained for some period, even in the absence of wartime demand conditions.[59]

By September, economic assumptions and policy guidelines to be followed in preparation of the 1951 budget were based on "a high level of employment, production, and business activity," with unemployment assumed to average 3 million for the fiscal year. However, agencies for which unemployment was an important factor in the budget program were told an additional amount should be included in the contingency reserve to provide for a possible

[59] Hickman, op. cit., pp. 76-78.

increase in unemployment to 5 million. It was assumed that construction costs would be 5 percent below the July 1949 level, and farm prices even with it. Estimates for 1951 were to be based on operations at, or below, the 1950 level where possible, and expansion of existing activities or initiation of new activities should not be included "unless required by law or to meet urgent public needs." Nevertheless, "favorable consideration will be given to estimates for catching up on deferred maintenance on physical assets such as buildings and roads to prevent excessive deterioration of Government plants." Civil public works construction should allow only for the minimum rate of progress, with due regard to logical order and timing of the work; and new projects should be started only where the public need was so urgent that it was not in the national interest to postpone them. Sufficient allowance was to be provided for advance planning, but pending a more specific policy directive, there should be no particular emphasis on projects in "distressed areas."[60]

The Secretary of the Treasury was generally unwilling to admit that a recession had in fact occurred, or a deficit was needed. For example, on October 31, 1949, Snyder said in reply to a congressional questionnaire concerning fiscal policy that there were no hard and fast rules applicable to overall taxing and spending policy which would be good for all times; that receipts and expenditures had to be examined item by item in each fiscal period; that it was not possible to give an immutable rule in terms of national income on when the budget should and should not be balanced; and that taxing-spending policy should be determined only after careful consideration of the situation at any given time. However, he added, "Both President Truman and I have stated on a number of occasions that it is essential to reduce the public debt in years of prosperity, *such as we have enjoyed since the end of the war.*" And, in testimony on December 2, 1949, Snyder went still further in disagreeing with the deficit, the necessity—if not the propriety—of which the President had reluctantly accepted.[61]

In January 1950, the Council of Economic Advisers announced

---

[60] Information obtained from Bureau of the Budget archives.
[61] *Treasury Report, 1950*, pp. 159 and 179. (Italics added.)

in its annual review that the time for a more restrictive fiscal policy had come. It pointed out that the upturn since July—when "the Council did not favor general tax reductions"—made reductions "even less desirable in the present budgetary situation." Noting the belief also that taxes should not have been reduced in 1948, the Council emphasized the importance currently of reducing the deficit and moving "as rapidly as the need to maintain business progress will permit toward attaining a surplus to apply upon the Government debt. For this purpose, some increases in taxes may be made, without threatening the recovery of business now under-way."[62]

Although the economic assumptions in the President's budget for fiscal 1951 were for less than full employment,[63] the President proposed both reduced expenditures and increased revenues. Rec-ommended expenditure reductions took the form of scattered econ-mies through "improved management efficiency." The increase in revenues would be the net effect of (1) proposals for reduced excise tax rates; (2) tightened provisions with respect to depletion allow-ances, tax-exempt charitable and educational organizations, and life insurance companies; (3) increased rates and lower exemptions for estate and gift duties; (4) increased rates on corporation in-come; and (5) a variety of other reforms involving relatively small amounts of revenue. As pointed out by Holmans, the fact that these revenue proposals could hardly have encouraged investment at a time when the Council of Economic Advisers saw a need for such encouragement clearly indicates that they were shaped by consider-ations of equity rather than stabilization objectives[64]—that is, long-run rather than short-run considerations.

While a more expansionary budget might have been appropri-ate under the circumstances, it is significant that the reduced ex-penditures and increased revenues as proposed by the President would still leave a budget deficit. Moreover, the deficit was de-

[62] Printed with the *Economic Report of the President, January 1950*, pp. 105-06. (Cited hereinafter as *Economic Report, 1950*.)

[63] "The estimates of receipts assume economic activity at approximately the same level as the present time." (*Budget of the United States Government for the Fiscal Year Ending July 30, 1951*, p. M16.)

[64] Holmans, *United States Fiscal Policy, op. cit.,* p. 130.

fended as correct policy—certainly a milestone in Presidential budgets.

The President amplified his tax proposals in a special message to the Congress on January 23, 1950. In it, he expressed as his budget philosophy the proposition that "our general objective should be a tax system which will yield sufficient revenue in times of high employment, production, and national income to meet the necessary expenditures of the Government and leave some surplus for debt reduction." He went on to explain that the maintenance of a sound fiscal position on the part of the government is a long-range matter, that "nothing could be more foolhardy than to attempt to bring about a balanced budget in 1951 by measures that would make it impossible to maintain a balanced budget in the following years," and that "drastic increases in tax rates, just as in the case of drastic cuts in essential expenditures, might prove to be self-defeating."[65] The Secretary of the Treasury apparently was not entirely satisfied with the President's explanation for the deficit. A week or so later before the Ways and Means Committee he took pains to explain why the current period was, as the year 1949 had been, a period of "high employment, production, and national income" within the specific meaning of the President's terms. However, he mustered a defense of the deficit in terms of the extraordinary nature of military, foreign aid, and other vital postwar federal expenditures.[66]

The generally mild public and congressional concern with the 1948-49 recession was indicated by the *Report of the Subcommittee on Monetary, Credit, and Fiscal Policies* of the Joint Committee on the Economic Report, which was published in January 1950. Although the Subcommittee, under the chairmanship of Senator Paul H. Douglas, had heard testimony during 1949, the report was primarily concerned with the general question of inflation. Dealing mainly with debt policies during and after World War II—particularly the inflationary implications of the action of the Federal Reserve in pegging government bond prices—it had little to say about the current economic situation. The subcommittee did take the stand that fiscal policy should contribute to economic stability and

[65] *Treasury Report, 1950,* p. 181.
[66] *Ibid.,* pp. 186 and 201.

not be dominated by faith in annually balanced budgets. However, it said the effectiveness of fiscal policy was limited because of the imperfections of economic forecasting and the inflexibility of tax and expenditure policies under existing procedures.

Some concern about the vigor and duration of the recovery lingered until mid-1950. Although the unemployment rate did not decline to its prerecession level until 1951, the invasion of South Korea, in June 1950, shifted private and official attention to mobilization and the renewed dangers of inflation.

Conclusions—1948-1950

With the advantage of hindsight, and judged from the viewpoint of economic stabilization without regard to various political and institutional obstacles, one must conclude that the record of federal government policy, as reflected in official pronouncements and recommendations during the 1948-49 recession, was fairly poor. The credit tightening in the fall of 1948 and proposals for tax increases in January 1949 were badly timed. Administration counterrecession proposals were slow in coming. When expansionary proposals were finally made in July 1949, they were modest, although data then available did not indicate that the trough had been passed. Even so, the administration proposals were not accepted by the Congress, which showed much less concern over recession than the administration, and, in fact, tried hard to cut back expenditures. As a result, deliberate counterrecession actions played an insignificant role in the recovery.

Inability to forecast economic trends reliably was an obstacle, but not so great an obstacle as might be supposed on the basis of official utterances. There was concern backstage, and preliminary staff work was done at relatively early dates on various counterrecession proposals. A far more important restraint was the inflexibility which tends to be built into a position publicly taken by government. Policy reversal is always difficult, even when the need for action is no longer in doubt, but reversal was particularly difficult in 1949. Having harped on inflation so long and so loudly, officials found it difficult to change keys.

Other constraints tended to discourage the government from taking earlier and more strenuous expansionary actions. These were:

1. The reluctance of many officials—including the President —to compromise what had long been regarded as an intrinsically meritorious goal—"fiscal responsibility," which is to say balanced budgets.

2. The view held by many observers—including the chairman of the President's Council of Economic Advisers—that a little "disinflation" after the sharp postwar price rises would do no harm.

3. Uncertainty over the international situation and the possible need for increased defense and foreign aid outlays above and beyond the amounts planned for these purposes.

4. The apparent conflict between (a) measures appropriate for short-run stabilization purposes and (b) those required for long-range goals of equity and the avoidance of unsound "structure" in the composition of private output.

With respect to the first of these constraints—fiscal orthodoxy —notable progress, from the economist's point of view, was made during the recession and recovery. Starting from a proposal in January to balance the budget by raising taxes, by mid-49, the administration was defending a "passive" budget deficit as the proper policy for the fiscal year then under way. By January 1950, it was defending this policy for a fiscal year which had not even started. This break with tradition, however, did not extend so far as embracing deliberate additions to the more or less inevitable deficit produced by falling federal revenues.

If expansionary federal government fiscal policy can be justified only when needed to keep recession from turning into a cumulative downward spiral, then the administration's handling of the 1949 recession was largely vindicated by subsequent developments. The administration's diagnosis that this was not the long-feared postwar depression—but only a temporary adjustment that would be brief, mild, and self-correcting without drastic federal action— proved to be essentially accurate.

Judged by the stricter view that government action should reduce the time spent below full employment, even in the face of an imminent upturn, then more aggressive action was warranted. But this view, which calls for very fine tuning of fiscal policy, places a high premium on accurate forecasts. It is in this connection that defense "contingencies" become important. The possibility that defense outlays might be higher than planned was strong at the time of the President's veto of the 1948 tax cut, and again at the time of the annual presidential messages in January 1949. Hindsight is not an altogether fair judge of whether the exchange rate established by the administration between defense uncertainties and economic uncertainties was appropriate for the time.

Whether the government would have been able to act more aggressively if its contingent forecasts had proved to be wrong and a more serious depression had occurred is doubtful. Apparently the administration's secondary line of defense was public works, in connection with which it did some cataloging and took some steps to accelerate advance planning. There is little evidence that tax cuts were considered as a possible line of defense. Some preparation of stand-by proposals for tax reduction would have been prudent, since the lead times involved in public works programs are too long for them to be of much value as countercyclical devices. Also, the strong congressional opposition to expenditure proposals made by the administration in 1949 casts doubt on whether a request for additional appropriations for public works would have met with much success.

While counterrecession fiscal policies during 1949 left something to be desired, a number of federal fiscal actions undertaken for other reasons were helpful in limiting the extent of decline and initiating a recovery. The tax cuts embodied in the Revenue Act of 1948 (enacted six months or so before the cyclical peak and at a time when inflation was generally thought to be the problem of the day) turned out to be a fortuitous counterrecession action.

Incidentally, the apparent effect of this tax reduction does not lend a great deal of encouragement to the view that timely and sizable tax cuts make good counterrecession tools. The timing was far more prompt than can reasonably be expected for discretionary antirecession actions in the normal functioning of the political system. Indeed, it was even more prompt than would be the case under most of the proposed formulas for automatic reduction of tax rates based on the performance of various statistical indicators. The amount (about 14 percent of total federal receipts on a national income account basis) was sizable as tax cuts go; and the cut, being permanent (at least that was the expectation), should have had considerably more impact than a temporary one of comparable size. Nevertheless, consumer outlays did not respond quickly, and the inventory liquidation and general contraction which ensued were comparable in magnitude to other postwar contractions. On the other hand, the effect of the tax cut on personal savings and consumer assets was undoubtedly a factor in the extremely shallow decline in consumption expenditures once the recession started. If this is a correct view, then the 1948-49 recession might have been the most severe of the first four postwar recessions had it not been for the timely 1948 tax cut.

Once the recession began, the federal surplus on a national income account basis—because of built-in stabilizers and further increases in defense and foreign aid outlays—swung sharply from a surplus of $3.8 billion (annual rate) in the final quarter of 1948 to a deficit of $3.9 billion in the second quarter of 1949. This net change of $7.7 billion compares to a decline in the gross national product from peak to trough of $9.5 billion.

The factors affecting the federal surplus or deficit over the period of recession and recovery are summarized in Table 20. A distinction is made in this table between what were described in Chapter I as "active" and "passive" changes in the federal surpluses or deficit. It was argued there that federal fiscal activity may be considered passive if the total change from the prerecession peak value of the federal budget surplus is accounted for by the built-in stabilizers (measured from high employment). With only passive changes, complete recovery of the economy will take place only with the removal of the original depressants to private spending, or their offset by increases in other sources of private demand. Table 20 shows that the change from surplus to deficit over the contraction period was too large to be accounted for by the built-in

TABLE 20. Factors Affecting the Federal Surplus, 1948-50 Recession and Recovery[a]

(In billions of current dollars at seasonally adjusted annual rates)

Item	1948 IV-P	1949 I	1949 II-T	Change Peak to Trough	1949 III	1949 IV	1950 I	1950 II-R	Change Trough to Terminal (R)
Surplus at prerecession peak	3.8	3.8	3.8	...	3.8	3.8	3.8	3.8	...
Factors not due to recession									
Increase in receipts, high employment, constant prerecession tax rates	...	0.6	1.2	1.2	1.8	2.4	3.0	3.6	2.4
Plus: OASI payroll tax rate increase	...	...	...	...	...	...	0.9	0.9	0.9
Less: expenditure increase—									
Purchases, goods and services:									
National defense	...	1.4	1.6	1.6	2.0	0.9	0.5	-0.1	-1.7
Other	...	-1.4	-1.8	-1.8	-1.9	-1.8	-3.5	-4.8	-3.0
Transfer payments to persons:									
Dividend, National Service Life Insurance	...	...	...	...	...	...	8.4	2.0	2.0
Other	...	0.5	0.6	0.6	0.7	0.6	0.6	0.5	-0.1
Transfer payments abroad	...	0.8	1.8	1.8	0.9	0.7	0.7	1.2	-0.6
Grants to state and local governments	...	—	...	—	0.3	0.2	0.3	0.4	0.4
Net interest paid	...	0.1	0.1	0.1	0.1	0.1	0.2	0.2	0.1
Subsidies less current surplus of government enterprises	...	-0.1	...	—	0.1	0.1	0.2	0.4	0.4
Subtotal = Implicit high employment surplus	3.8	3.1	2.7	-1.1	3.4	5.3	0.2	8.5	5.8
Less: effect, built-in stabilizers									
Corporate profits tax accruals	...	-1.3	-2.8	-2.8	-2.5	-2.9	-2.2	0.1	2.7
Excise taxes	...	-0.4	-0.3	-0.3	-0.1	-0.6	-0.9	-0.2	0.1
Employment taxes	...	-0.1	-0.2	-0.2	-0.2	-0.3	-0.2	-0.1	0.1
Individual income tax accruals	...	-0.3	-0.7	-0.7	-0.8	-1.3	-0.2	-0.3	0.4
Unemployment compensation	...	-0.6	-0.9	-0.9	-0.9	-0.7	-0.8	-0.4	0.5
Other adjustments[b]	...	-1.8	-1.7	-1.7	-1.7	-1.6	0.3	0.7	2.6
Total = actual surplus (national income account basis)	3.8	-1.4	-3.9	-7.7	-2.8	-2.1	-3.8	8.3	12.2

[a] See Appendix D for sources and methods. Both receipts and expenditures in this tabulation exclude estimated amounts included in the national income tabulation of receipts and expenditures for the extraordinary (intragovernmental) payments in 1949 from the budget to the National Service Life Insurance trust fund. The net federal surplus is the same either way.

[b] In addition to adjustments explained in Appendix D, there is an adjustment here for the approximately $2.5 billion (annual rate) increase in corporate profits tax and excess profits tax accruals included in the national income account tabulation starting in the first quarter of 1950, but excluded in the above tabulation of implicit surplus at high employment. The tax increase was not enacted until late in 1950, and probably did not affect private expenditure decisions before mid-1950 at the earliest.

128

stabilizers. The implicit federal surplus, in which actual expenditures are compared with receipts as they would appear at high employment, declined by a little over $1 billion from the fourth quarter of 1948 to the second of 1949. Thus, the federal budget exerted an active as well as a passive offset to the decline in private spending.

As said before, this was not the result of deliberate counterrecession actions. However, the increase for other reasons in defense and foreign aid outlays, which should be considered in calculating the need for counterrecession action, was not unexpected at the time.

After the cyclical trough in the second quarter of 1949, the built-in stabilizers reversed direction, thereby exerting a restraining influence on the recovery. Moreover, federal expenditures leveled off in the second half of 1949 and the implicit surplus began increasing again. Then, the implicit surplus fell sharply in the first quarter of 1950, with the payment of large National Service Life Insurance dividends to veterans, but rose sharply in the second quarter of 1950. The decline in federal purchases of nondefense goods and services over the period of recession and recovery was caused mainly by price support operations of the Commodity Credit Corporation. These, while higher in 1949 than in 1948, declined steadily over the period on a seasonally adjusted quarterly basis.

Thus, by the second quarter of 1950, the actual federal surplus on a national income account basis reached a rate of $8.3 billion, $4.5 billion higher than the rate at the prerecession peak, although the unemployment rate was still considerably above the level prevailing prior to the recession. Approximately $2.5 billion of this increase, representing the accrual of increased corporate tax rates increases not enacted until later in the year, was hardly a factor in private spending decisions in the second quarter of 1950, and can be set aside. Even so, there was a net tightening of the federal fiscal system over a period of increased unemployment. Had there been no Korean war to make this a somewhat academic question, such fiscal tightening would have been appropriate only if the private spending expected to be set in motion during the recovery was somewhat greater relative to potential gross national product than was the case prior to the recession.

Two other government actions, not reflected in Table 20, played a role in supporting the economy during this period. First, on a cash basis, refunds of individual income tax were large in the spring of 1949 because of the retroactive features of the 1948 tax cut. It is probable that these exerted an expansionary effect which is not reflected in the tax accruals recorded in Table 20. Second, credit actions are excluded from the national income budget, and several government housing credit actions—particularly the issuance of advanced purchase commitments by the Federal National Mortgage Association—were factors in the spectacular housing boom of 1949 and 1950 that was an important part of the recovery. Aside from the fact that these were credit actions, rather than fiscal actions in the ordinary sense, they were aimed at housing instead of the general state of the economy. The goal of housing stability is not necessarily compatible with the goal of general economic stability—in fact frequently is incompatible—so that these actions in 1949 were fortuitous from the point of view of countering recession.

CHAPTER V

Recession and Recovery,

1953-1955

FISCAL ACTIONS started by the federal government before the recession in 1953—as in 1948—subsequently had a major impact on the course of the recession. In 1953, such actions were part of the attempts of the newly elected Eisenhower administration, with the cooperation of the first Republican Congress since 1947-48, to reduce federal expenditures and eliminate the budget deficits which had characterized the Korean War years.

When President Eisenhower took office in January 1953, he inherited a budget prepared by the outgoing Truman administration. That budget, for the 1954 fiscal year to start six months later, included increased expenditures of $4 billion and a sizable deficit. Moreover, a number of major tax reductions were provided by existing law. The excess profits tax was scheduled to expire on June 30, 1953. Individual income tax rates were to drop by 10 percent on January 1, 1954. On April 1, 1954, not only was the corporation income tax rate to drop from 52 percent to 47 percent, but also various temporary increases in excise taxes were to expire. Direct controls were to end for prices and wages on April 30, 1953, and for material and product allocations on June 30, 1953.

The final report of the outgoing Council of Economic Advisers (CEA) had forecast a reasonably stable general price structure which

131

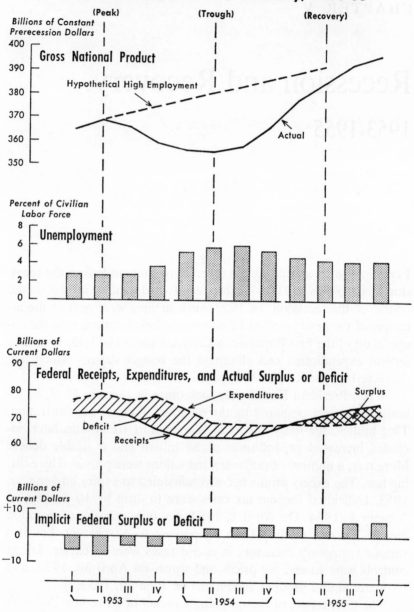

Chart 3

Gross National Product, Unemployment, and Federal Receipts and Expenditures, Quarterly, 1953-55

(Peak)   (Trough)   (Recovery)

Billions of Constant
Prerecession Dollars

Gross National Product

Hypothetical High Employment

Actual

Percent of Civilian
Labor Force

Unemployment

Billions of
Current Dollars

Federal Receipts, Expenditures, and Actual Surplus or Deficit

Expenditures   Surplus

Deficit

Receipts

Billions of
Current Dollars

Implicit Federal Surplus or Deficit

I   II   III   IV   I   II   III   IV   I   II   III   IV
└── 1953 ──┘   └── 1954 ──┘   └── 1955 ──┘

Source: Appendix D.

did not warrant any "sharp changes in public policy." The report was more concerned with whether an adequate volume of consumer expenditures would replace the defense outlays, scheduled to level off during 1953. It was cautiously optimistic on this score, also, stating that "for the major portion of the year 1953, the weight of evidence is clear that . . . a deflationary movement is not in prospect."[1]

Controlling Federal Expenditures

The incoming administration was noticeably more worried than its predecessor about the prospects of inflation. Indeed, the Democratic presidential candidate during the campaign also had expressed considerable concern about the possibility of inflation. Although consumer prices had drifted up only slightly during 1952, and wholesale prices had declined steadily since the spring of 1951, the extent to which direct controls were responsible was not altogether clear. In his State of the Union Message on February 2, 1953, President Eisenhower promised to reduce the planned deficits, balance the budget, lengthen the public debt, and check the menace of inflation.[2] The President emphasized that these tasks were made more difficult by the large outstanding balances of appropriations and commitments for future spending inherited from the Democratic administration.

In deference to the economy as "a highly complex mechanism," the President insisted that action must be gradual, and he promised to watch trends closely and recommend legislation if needed. However, Robert J. Donovan, who had access to records of behind-the-scenes activities during this period, makes it rather clear that the President was bothered more by the possibility that removal of direct controls would be inflationary than that reducing government expenditures might be deflationary.[3]

[1] Council of Economic Advisers, *The Annual Economic Review,* printed with the *Economic Report of the President, January 1953,* pp. 74-75. (Cited hereinafter as *Economic Report, 1953,* or with indications of subsequent dates.)

[2] National Archives and Record Service, *Public Papers of the Presidents of the United States, 1953* (1960), p. 12. (Cited hereinafter as *Public Papers, 1953,* or with indications of subsequent dates.)

[3] Robert J. Donovan, *Eisenhower, The Inside Story* (Harper and Bros., 1956), p. 30.

On February 3, 1953, a White House directive instructed all agencies of the government to review their budgets in an effort to progressively reduce the number of government personnel. In addition, they were to proceed only with clearly essential construction projects meeting the strictest tests of economy and to operate all programs at minimum levels of costs and expenditures. Obligations were to be held at the January rate, except when specifically authorized otherwise or where increases would be necessary to meet requirements fixed by law. Agencies were to aim at a downward adjustment of program levels, to review new legislative proposals in the same light, and to transmit budget revisions for fiscal 1954 to the Bureau of the Budget for review by the President as early as possible in March.[4]

The first bill introduced in the House when the 83rd Congress convened in January—sponsored by Representative Daniel Reed of New York, new Republican chairman of the Ways and Means Committee—proposed reduction of individual income tax rates on July 1, 1953—six months sooner than scheduled. And although the President told his legislative leaders he was opposed to a tax cut until a balanced budget was in sight, and indicated a possible extension of the excess profits tax was being studied,[5] the bill was reported out of Committee on February 16.

By March, price and wage controls had passed away without major incident. There is evidence of some uncertainty, as early as February and March, about the economic outlook, at least at the staff level. In working up preliminary receipt estimates for the 1955 budget, the staff of the Bureau of the Budget weighed the possibility of a decline starting sometime in fiscal 1954. Calculations of the depressing effect on revenues of reductions in government expenditures were made, and, in subsequent discussions of revenue projections with the staff of the Treasury Department, alternative economic assumptions were used incorporating various degrees of decline in gross national product (GNP).[6]

On April 11, 1953, Senator Ralph Flanders, Chairman of the Joint Committee on the Economic Report, released a staff paper

[4] *Public Papers, 1953*, pp. 53-54.
[5] Donovan, *op. cit.*, p. 60; and *Public Papers, 1953*, pp. 47-49.
[6] Information supplied by Bureau of the Budget officials.

that had been prepared on the possible economic consequences of a Korean truce. The Committee staff foresaw no break in spending for plant and equipment, and said "the present outlook for private business activity and continued high levels of production and employment remains good." However, it noted that "the usual rolling adjustments in certain segments of the economy or more general inventory-price fluctuations of the 1949 type might be expected."[7]

Also in April, the Secretary of the Treasury announced the sale for cash of $4.25 billion of 3¼ percent bonds with a 25-year to 30-year maturity—the first cash issue of marketable debt other than bills or tax anticipation certificates since the autumn of 1945, and the longest-term Treasury issue since 1941.[8] Secretary George Humphrey, in a statement at the time, placed debt-lengthening in an anti-inflation context, saying "The concentration of short-term debt in the banks by the previous administration was one of the causes of inflation in the cost of living which was costing the American people billions of dollars. A gradual placing of more securities in the hands of nonbank investors is a necessary step for economic stability."[9] Shortly after the issue was distributed on May 1, the Federal Reserve Open Market Committee authorized operations to ease credit, with the intention, in the later words of its chairman, of providing "assurance to financial markets and to business that legitimate needs for funds for stability and growth would be met. . . ."[10]

Concurrently with the President's April 30 press conference, the White House released a statement in which the President said he had been struggling for three months to balance military needs with the nation's ability to pay for them, and had been able to reduce requests for new spending authority by more than $8 billion below the Truman budget for fiscal 1954 without reducing military strength. On the contrary, "Deliveries actually will be speeded up

[7] Printed in *Joint Economic Report,* Joint Committee on the Economic Report, 83 Cong. 2 sess. (February 26, 1954), pp. 94 ff. (Cited hereinafter as *Joint Economic Report, 1954,* or with later dates where appropriate.)

[8] *Annual Report of the Secretary of the Treasury, 1953,* pp. 30–32. (Cited hereinafter as *Treasury Report, 1953,* or with later dates where appropriate.)

[9] *Ibid.,* p. 255.

[10] *Hearings on the Economic Report of the President, 1954,* Joint Committee on the Economic Report, 83 Cong. 2 sess. (1954), p. 110. (Cited hereinafter as *Hearings of the Joint Committee, 1954,* or with later dates where appropriate.)

through the reduction of lead times and concentration on producing those items which make the most military sense for the immediate future."[11] Speeding up deliveries might have sounded like higher, rather than lower, expenditures—and higher expenditures would have been possible even with reduced appropriations because of the large carry-over balances of prior year authorizations. However, this is not what the President meant, as became apparent twenty days later.

In a radio address on May 19, 1953,[12] and in a special message to Congress the next day, the President objected to the hump in defense spending planned by the previous administration around the concept of a specific date of maximum danger, and proposed instead a defense program that could be maintained over an extended period. He announced that, despite his having trimmed roughly eight and a half billion dollars in new obligational authority and four and a half billion in expenditures from his inherited budget, a substantial 1954 deficit was still in prospect. How earlier deliveries were to be reconciled with lower expenditures was not explained.

In the light of this situation, Congress was asked to make the following changes in scheduled tax reductions: a six-month extension of the excess profits tax; postponement of the cut in corporation income tax rates; and temporary postponement of the various excise tax reductions, pending review of the whole excise tax system. However, the President also asked for postponement of increases in payroll tax rates for old-age and survivors insurance (OASI) from 1.5 percent to 2 percent on both employers and employees, which were scheduled for January 1, 1954. The reasons given were not only that current receipts of the fund were adequate to cover expenditures, but also that the delay would be a "worthwhile saving to wage earners" and "simple justice." At the same time, the President said that the reduction in personal income taxes scheduled for January 1, 1954, could and should go into effect. Thus, as E. Cary Brown has pointed out, it appears that the administration was pledged to tax reduction prior to the downturn

[11] *Public Papers, 1953*, p. 228.
[12] *Ibid.*, p. 306.

primarily because of budgetary considerations rather than for economic-stabilization purposes.[13]

Hedging Against Decline

Perhaps some awareness of the need to support private purchasing power while expenditures were being cut can be imputed to this fiscal program. While in his radio address the President had expressed confidence that with continued effort "a balanced budget will come within sight," a balanced budget had not been achieved.[14] Nevertheless, the administration acquiesced in some reductions of tax rates. The President tied his suggested reduction in individual income tax rates to the cutbacks in expenditures, and said the tax cut would have been inflationary under President Truman's budget. Thus, by implication, tax reductions, even when the budget was unbalanced, were not inflationary when expenditures were being reduced.

Among possible alternatives, extension of corporation and excess profits tax rates would be among the less depressing to private spending in the short run, and a reduction (or cancellation of an increase) in individual income and OASI payroll tax rates among the more stimulating. This mix would have been consistent with a policy of supporting private purchasing power while reducing government expenditures with the smallest possible deficit in the administrative budget. However, there is no evidence that this was the administration's intention. For example, Secretary Humphrey at one point described the wish to have the excess profits tax expire no sooner than individual income tax rates could be reduced as a matter of equity,[15] and others have pointed out the political implications.[16]

[13] Brown, "Federal Fiscal Policy in the Postwar Period," in Ralph E. Freeman (ed.), *Postwar Economic Trends in the United States* (Harper and Bros., 1960), pp. 164-68.

[14] However, Secretary Humphrey argued that because expenditures were declining, and the budget deficit in prospect for fiscal 1955 was smaller than that in prospect for 1954, a balanced budget was "in sight."

[15] *Treasury Report, 1953,* p. 214.

[16] ". . . the more astute Republicans were reluctant to allow a tax on business to drop before taxes came down for individuals. Politically it was wiser to have both reductions occur simultaneously." Donovan, *op. cit.,* p. 60.

Also, the recommendation to cancel the scheduled increase in OASI payroll tax rates was interpreted by some as an attempt to stem future growth of the program.[17]

The staff of the Budget Bureau, in May and June, were using economic projections for preliminary calculations on the fiscal 1955 budget based on the following expectations: gradual declines in federal outlays and in spending for plant and equipment, with a leveling of GNP in the second half of 1953 or first half of 1954; and a GNP decline starting in the second half of 1954 or first half of 1955. However, revenue estimates prepared by Treasury staff were based on projections that had virtually no change in GNP from calendar 1953 to calendar 1954.[18] And, on June 1, Secretary of the Treasury Humphrey defended the administration's recommendations for extension of the excess profits tax and no acceleration of the scheduled reduction of individual income taxes on the grounds that "further inflation must be stopped and the dollar must be kept sound to provide a solid base for a healthy economy."[19]

Meanwhile, there is evidence that at least one federal agency viewed recession as more than a remote contingency. On June 5, 1953, the Bureau of Employment Security of the U.S. Department of Labor sent a letter to state employment security agencies furnishing economic assumptions to be used as a common background in preparing estimates of work loads for the 1955 budget. The coming decline in defense outlays plus the effects of a temporary catching-up of private investment were expected to turn the economy down by the middle of calendar 1954. However, factors of strength for the longer term were noted which would produce an upturn by the middle of 1955.

Policy letters to govern the preparation of the fiscal 1955 budget were sent to federal agencies by the Budget Director on July 10,

[17] See the CIO Convention Resolution on Social Security, adopted November 1953: "We oppose any postponement. . . . We reaffirm our previous stand that labor is willing to bear its fair share of the cost of an adequate program, and that lower payments now can only mean higher payments or lower benefits later. The American people are entitled to confidence that benefit provisions enacted into law will be met." *Social Security Act Amendments of 1954,* Hearings before the House Ways and Means Committee, 83 Cong. 2 sess. (1954), p. 656.

[18] Information obtained from Bureau of the Budget archives.

[19] *Treasury Report, 1953,* pp. 214 ff.

1953. The agencies were told that the expenditure reductions achieved so far for 1954 were only the first steps; that further reductions as large or larger would be required in 1955; and that progressive reductions in levels of obligations and expenditures during the 1954 fiscal year were needed to reach the lower expenditure level. Budget policies listed for fiscal 1955 included:

1.   A continued withdrawal of the federal government from activities more appropriately carried on in some other way.

2.   Continued limitations on new or resumed construction starts, holding construction to "minimum economic rates" and maintenance and repair of government facilities to the minimum required for safe operation and the avoidance of costly deterioration.

3.   Substituting guaranteed or insured loans for direct government loan and mortgage purchase programs wherever possible.

4.   Pursuing aggressive interest rate policies with respect to existing loan and mortgage portfolios.

5.   Using existing inventories rather than new purchases to the fullest extent possible, and stepping up the sale of excess inventories, property, or other assets.[20]

The otherwise restrictive guidelines contained a passage recommending that plans be drawn to meet a situation in which an expansionary policy would be appropriate: "Increased emphasis will be given to the development of plans for authorized high priority projects to a stage where these projects could qualify for construction at a time when new construction starts would be consistent with a less restrictive budgetary policy."[21]

In July, at the request of the Chairman of the Council of Economic Advisers, the staff of the Bureau of the Budget began a study of potential budget flexibility.[22] Although the staff regarded inflation as less likely than recession, the study embraced actions to counter both inflation and recession. On the counterrecession side, Bureau

[20] Information obtained from Bureau of the Budget archives.
[21] *Hearings of the Joint Committee, 1954*, p. 28.
[22] U.S. Bureau of the Budget, Budget Procedures Memorandum 29, July 13, 1953.

staff made estimates, for each federal program, of potential expenditure increases in 1954 and 1955 in four categories:

  1. Automatic increases in response to recession requiring neither administrative nor congressional discretion.

  2. Automatic increases requiring no discretionary action except supplemental appropriations.

  3. Expenditures based on authorizations to expend from debt receipts, requiring less, if any, congressional action than appropriations.

  4. Increases based on administrative discretion only.

Thus, the administration was apparently studying a hedge against possible recession in July 1953 at the same time it was issuing restrictive budget policies.[23]

The Korean armistice was signed July 26, 1953. However, since actual fighting had stopped earlier, the armistice already had been partly discounted in the administration's defense plans. In fact, the substantial decline in defense orders that started even before the new administration took office soon would have resulted in decreased defense spending. Nevertheless, the armistice made possible a more rapid decline in defense spending than had been previously anticipated.

On July 30, the administration requested an increase of $15 billion in the public debt limit, from $275 billion to $290 billion, but did not pursue the matter vigorously. And on August 1, the President sent a special message to Congress recommending extension of coverage under the OASI trust fund to some 10.5 million additional persons.[24] Properly, no suggestion was made that the extension of OASI coverage was a counterrecession proposal, since—unless the persons included were already past retirement age—increased revenues would have been at least as much as benefits in the early years.

Congress, by the time of adjournment on August 3, had gone farther than the President in cutting back 1954 appropriations, and

_____

[23] The results of this exercise are discussed in more detail later in this chapter in the section on "Expenditure Flexibility Compared to Tax Cuts."

[24] *Social Security Bulletin,* August 1953.

TABLE 21. Estimates of Federal Budget Receipts, Expenditures, and New Obligational Authority, Fiscal Year 1954

(In billions of dollars)

Source of Estimate	Budget Receipts	Budget Expenditures	Surplus	New Obligational Authority
Truman Budget, Jan. 1953[a]	68.7	78.6	—9.9	72.9
Eisenhower Message to Congress, May 20, 1953[b]	68.5[c]	74.1	—5.6	64.4[d]
Midyear Review, Aug. 27, 1953[e]	68.3[c]	72.1	—3.8	63.2[f]

[a] *Budget of the United States Government for the Fiscal Year Ending June 30, 1954* (January 1953).

[b] National Archives and Records Service, *Public Papers of the Presidents of the United States, 1953* (1960), p. 318.

[c] Change in revenue estimate from January includes upward revision for extension of excess profits tax, offset by downward revisions of January yield calculations.

[d] Based on statements that new obligational authority had been reduced by $8.5 billion from the January estimate.

[e] U. S. Bureau of the Budget, *Review of the 1954 Budget* (August 27, 1953).

[f] Including $400 million in anticipated supplemental authorizations from the coming session of Congress.

left without increasing the public debt limit. It had taken no action on extended coverage of OASI or the earlier request to postpone the scheduled increase in payroll tax rates; and none on scheduled reductions of corporation and excise taxes. But, after considerable pressure, Congress had gone along with the administration's other tax proposals. Thus, on January 1, 1954, the administration could expect a drop in individual tax rates by approximately 10 percent; expiration of the excess profits tax; and an increase of OASI payroll tax rates to 2 percent for both employers and employees.

The score, as Congress adjourned, on the budget for the fiscal year which had started July 1, 1953, is shown in Table 21. The military programs of the Department of Defense and the Atomic Energy Commission (AEC), together with foreign aid, accounted for $5.6 billion of the reduction of $6.5 billion below the Truman estimates of budget expenditures. The short-run inflexibility in the federal budget is indicated by the fact that, in spite of the administration's intensive efforts to trim expenditures, reductions outside the national defense and foreign aid categories were modest. Natural resource estimates were reduced $200 million by stretching out construction of water resource projects. Most other nondefense reductions resulted from re-estimates of work loads or, as in the case of certain lending operations, had little economic significance. Estimates for social security, welfare, health, education, and highways were little changed, and agriculture and interest were higher than in January.

The Contraction: Mid-1953

The cyclical peak as measured by the National Bureau of Economic Research (NBER) came in July 1953. Before then, however, production in a number of lines had tapered off and the peak on a quarterly basis—measured both by GNP and the more comprehensive NBER method—came in April-June 1953. In current dollars, GNP declined by 2.7 percent from an annual rate of $368.8 billion in the second quarter of 1953 to $358.9 billion in the second quarter of 1954. Although this was a little less in percentage terms than the 1949 contraction, prices did not decline significantly this time, and the contraction in real terms was somewhat larger in 1954 than in 1949.[25] Unemployment in 1953 stayed within a narrow range, averaging about 2.6 percent of the labor force through August—a lower rate than had prevailed even in 1951 and 1952 during the Korean war. The unemployment rate rose during the contraction and continued to rise until September 1954, when it reached a peak of a little over 6 percent.

The large cutback in federal government expenditures for defense was perhaps the major cause of the recession. The decline of defense purchases during the second half of 1953—$2.9 billion, at seasonally adjusted annual rates, between the second and fourth quarters—understates the economic impact of the cutback, since defense orders had started to drop earlier and fell by much more in this period. With disposable personal income supported by private and fiscal stabilizers and, after January 1, 1954, by the reduction of personal income tax rates, consumer purchases dipped only slightly in the fourth quarter of 1953, and then began rising again.

[25] See Bert G. Hickman, *Growth and Stability of the Postwar Economy* (Brookings Institution, 1960), pp. 99-120, for an analysis of the 1953-54 contraction.

However, a diminished rate of growth in consumption—which showed up even before the cyclical peak—was no doubt a factor, along with the cutback in defense orders, leading to business efforts to adjust inventory positions.

Inventory investment swung from accumulation at a rate of $3.1 billion in the second quarter of 1953 to liquidation at a rate of $4.6 billion in the fourth quarter. This change was equal to the whole GNP decline during this phase, with the relatively small changes in final demand approximately offsetting one another. After the turn of the year, inventory liquidation lessened as the gap between production and final sales narrowed, but defense purchases then began to decline precipitously—at an annual rate of over $6 billion (national income account basis) in the first half of 1954, and an additional $3 billion in the second half.

Residential construction, which has been a strong element in all the postwar recoveries, held steady during the first three quarters of contraction and began a sharp rise, even before the GNP trough in the second quarter of 1954. This rise lasted well into 1955. The reduction in business fixed investment was a considerably smaller factor than in the other postwar contractions, declining altogether by about $2 billion at annual rates from the third quarter of 1953 to the fourth of 1954.

On August 6, 1953, the President sent a letter to the heads of executive departments and major agencies—which re-emphasized the July letters of the Budget Director—requesting renewed vigor in the matter of efficiency and economy and substantial reductions in new obligational authority and in expenditures for both the remainder of fiscal 1954 and budget planning for fiscal 1955.[26] The same day, the staff of the Bureau of the Budget was instructed to base quarterly apportionments over fiscal 1954 on the policy of a progressive reduction in 1954 obligations and expenditures looking toward the reduced 1955 target levels.[27]

At the end of August, the staff of the Joint Committee on the Economic Report forecast continued high levels of production

[26] *Public Papers, 1953,* pp. 563-64.
[27] U.S. Bureau of the Budget, Budget Procedures Memorandum 32, August 6, 1953.

and employment "for the remainder of 1953 if not, indeed, well into 1954." It was optimistic about the long run, and saw for the more immediate years a mixture of forces, but at worst a rather mild and selective decline on the order of the 1949 contraction.[28]

In an address of September 22, 1953, before the American Bankers Association, Secretary of the Treasury Humphrey recognized a connection between declining government spending and the current uncertainty in the economic outlook, but counseled confidence: "It is the definite policy of this administration, through tax reductions, to return to the people for them to spend for themselves all the real savings on Government spending which can be reasonably anticipated." He went on to promise that the administration would do nothing to prevent expiration of the excess profits tax and reduction of the individual income tax scheduled for January 1.[29] Since, with Congress not in session, there was not much the administration could have done, even if it wanted to forestall the reductions, this may seem a gratuitous promise. It is possible, however, that Humphrey's statement dispelled uncertainty about the tax reduction.

This Humphrey address has been used several times as evidence of the administration's willingness to use tax cuts as antirecession measures.[30] E. Cary Brown is sharply critical of this view, arguing that the administration had committed itself to these tax reductions before the recession started and for different reasons.[31] Also, as Flash points out,[32] the excess profits tax reduction would have taken place six months earlier without the administration's vigorous efforts to extend them. Moreover, the administration could hardly have won an argument for further extension even had Congress been in session. The importance of this point is not whether the administration had foresight, but whether the incident demonstrates

[28] *Joint Economic Report, 1954,* pp. 78 ff.

[29] *Treasury Report, 1953,* pp. 246 ff.

[30] See, for example, the *Economic Report of the President* for both 1954 (p. 54) and 1955 (p. 20), and Arthur F. Burns, *Prosperity Without Inflation* (Fordham University Press, 1957), p. 30.

[31] Brown, *op. cit.,* pp. 167-68.

[32] Edward S. Flash, Jr., "The Council of Economic Advisers, A Situational Study of the Functioning of Advice" (Ph.D. thesis, Cornell University, 1961), p. 322.

that the federal government is able and willing to cut taxes to counteract recession. From this standpoint, the 1954 evidence is on the side of the skeptics. There have been several occasions when the executive and legislative branches were willing to adjust taxes to major changes in government expenditure, but few indications of willingness to change tax rates for purely stabilization purposes.

Hints of Concern

From September to the end of 1953, there were increasing signs —admittedly, more apparent with hindsight—that the administration was becoming concerned over the economic outlook. In September, interagency task forces at the staff level were established under the auspices of the Council of Economic Advisers to examine the economic aspects of a number of government programs.[33] These included home modernization and repair, federal credit aids to construction, public works, unemployment compensation, tax revision, community and business programs to expand employment, and programs to strengthen the financial system. While the task forces were also concerned with long-range structural matters— perhaps primarily so—the list suggests some concern with short-range stabilization.

Also in September, at the President's cabinet meeting, CEA Chairman Arthur F. Burns cited a number of unfavorable indicators and warned that a "readjustment" might be on the way. The President's reaction was that the Republican party must be ready to use the full power of the government, if necessary, to prevent "another 1929." Burns also cited some favorable factors and stated the situation was not critical, but said that planning was called for as a precaution against further decline.[34] The thinking of the CEA at that time was "less in terms of increased government spending and more in terms of monetary policy, the activities of private business, tax reduction and government programs emphasizing loans rather than construction undertaken by the government itself."[35]

[33] This move was announced later in the *Economic Report, 1954,* p. 123.
[34] Donovan, *op. cit.,* pp. 209-10.
[35] *Public Papers, 1953,* p. 615.

There was a hint, too, at the President's September 30 news conference that the debt ceiling was somewhat uncomfortable, but the President said the latest revenue estimates suggested that government could squeeze by without a special session of Congress. He declined to say whether the tax code revisions being worked up by Treasury would aim at higher or lower levels of receipts. At his news conference, a week later, the President refused to forecast when the budget would be balanced, stating a balanced budget was still a goal, but not necessarily one overriding all others.

The *Survey of Current Business* confirmed in October that gross national product had declined between the second and third quarters of 1953, with a drop in inventory investment accounting for more than the total decline.

Operations of a Cabinet Committee on Minerals Policy, appointed by the President in late October, offer an interesting example of the way in which short-term stabilization goals intrude into long-term policy decisions. In appointing the Committee to study overall production and use of metals and minerals, President Eisenhower indicated that depressed conditions in numerous mining districts, largely the result of post-Korean adjustment, were of grave national concern. He asked that every effort be made to find an equitable solution to this problem because strong and prosperous mineral industries form a primary component of a sound mobilization base. The Committee subsequently indicated that purchases for the long-term stockpile were to be made, whenever possible, from domestic producers, and ordinarily at times when the government decided that purchases would help to reactivate productive capacity and alleviate distressed conditions in industries producing strategic minerals and metals.[36] An interim report, in March 1954, called for acquisitions of 35 to 40 metals and minerals with the objective of virtually eliminating risk of shortage in time of emergency.

In November 1953, the Office of Defense Mobilization (ODM) issued revisions of its Manpower Policy No. 4 (originally issued in March 1952) directing government procurement agencies to promote the placing of contracts and facilities in areas of labor sur-

[36] *Annual Report of the Secretary of the Interior, 1954,* p. xxi.

plus.[37] Under this directive, however, since price differentials were prohibited,[38] aggregate purchasing power and employment could not be significantly increased except on rather artificial assumptions. Thus, as a countercyclical fiscal policy there is little substance to such actions, although similar actions have been pointedly announced in other postwar recessions. In this connection, it is interesting that the President, at his press conference on January 13, 1954, cautioned against exaggerating the effects to be achieved by channeling defense contracts to areas of high unemployment. The proportion set aside for this purpose, he pointed out, is generally small and then requires that the low bid be equaled or bettered in the depressed area. "But I believe that there has been an exaggerated idea that an entire contract would be shoved somewhere just because they had unemployment. There is no such intent."[39]

The President assured reporters at his November 18, 1953 press conference—apparently the first time the question of recession arose at these meetings—that the economic situation was under constant study. He pointed out that he met weekly with CEA Chairman Burns; that there had been discussion of what the government could do, should do, how and when; that the current indices were mixed; and that if and when government action was necessary he would not hesitate to take it. In answer to a different question, the President revealed that a balanced budget for 1955 no longer looked possible, given the inflexibility of so many expenditures. A decision on whether to seek an increase in the public debt limit, the President said, would not be made until late December when the budget figures become firmer.

Under questioning, the President revealed at his December 2 press conference that, although the budget could not be balanced for fiscal 1955, the tax proposals would not be aimed at increasing the level of revenues. Rather, the emphasis would be on establishing a downward trend in expenditures.

[37] On December 29, a White House press release referred to the "recently issued" ODM directive and stated the President's "complete agreement" with these policies.

[38] U.S. Department of Commerce, Business and Defense Services Administration, *Federal Programs of Assistance to Labor Surplus Areas* (1960).

[39] *Public Papers, 1954*, p. 50.

Reduced Expenditures or Stabilization Objectives?

Recognition that the economy was in recession was widespread by January 1954 when the President's program for the coming year was revealed in the usual trio of presidential messages to Congress[40] and an unusually large number of special messages covering such programs as housing, agriculture, and social security. Officially however, the situation was referred to as a rolling adjustment, a readjustment from wartime to peacetime conditions, a minor contraction, or some similar term. For example, in his *Economic Report,* the President said "there was a slight contraction in business leading to unemployment in some localities . . . due mainly to a decline in spending by business for additions to inventory" (p. iv); and "an inventory readjustment in the second half of 1953" was described as a reaction to "sluggishness of retail sales" and "excessively sanguine production schedules" in the early months of the year (pp. 19-20). Congressional critics chided the administration for its aversion to the term "recession" and earned in response the epithet "prophets of gloom and doom."

The President's program suggests a conflict between stabilization and budget goals. In a section of the State of the Union Message devoted to maintenance of a "strong economy," the President expressed confidence that the transition from a wartime to a peacetime economy could be completed without serious interruption in economic growth. He said he would not leave this vital matter to "chance," promised a number of specific recommendations and plans later that would demonstrate the administration's "economic preparedness," and stated that the federal budget should be a stabilizing factor in the economy. However, in the same message, he gave far more attention to his administration's achievements in reducing budget expenditures, and promised further reductions in

[40] Annual Message to the Congress on the State of the Union, *Public Papers, 1954;* Budget Message of the President, *Budget of the United States Government for the Fiscal Year Ending June 30, 1955* (hereinafter cited as *Budget, Fiscal 1955*); and the *Economic Report, 1954.* (Because of the frequent references to these sources in the following summary of developments, parenthetical page references, where the meaning is clear, are given in the text.)

both spending and new appropriations. Proposed tax code revisions were justified in terms of equity and incentives for enterprise and growth, with no mention of stabilization goals.

The Budget Message, too, was addressed to the reductions in expenditures already achieved, the additional reductions proposed for the coming year, and the proposals for tax structure reform. Under the administration's proposals, the deflationary impact of the federal budget would be further increased, though slightly, in 1955. Proposed budget expenditures would be cut by over $5 billion in fiscal 1955, and the requests for new obligational authority were down $4.4 billion. Proposed reductions affected a number of programs, but defense accounted for most of the amounts involved. On the revenue side, the long-heralded package of tax reform proposals would reduce revenues by about $1.3 billion. There would be a further revenue loss from the full-year effect in fiscal 1955 of the tax cuts that took place on January 1. But even with these combined revenue losses, the net effect would be a smaller deficit in fiscal 1955 and the cash budget would move to a small surplus.

The administration's recommendation of a reduction in revenues when the prospective budget was still in deficit—given its known strong attitude towards such matters—represented a partial victory for the proponents of increased purchasing power, or perhaps for political arguments.[41] In this connection, the Budget Message said: "The reductions in expenditures already accomplished, together with those now proposed, justify the tax reductions which took effect January 1 and the further tax revisions I am recommending. These lower taxes will encourage continued high capital investment and consumer purchases." (P. M6.)

The *Economic Report* gave only a mild hint of possible conflict between the administration's budget objectives and the econ-

---

[41] Revenue estimates were based on the assumption that personal income would average for the calendar year 1954 slightly less than the rates reached in 1953 and profits about a billion dollars down from year to year. The former assumption turned out to be slightly too pessimistic; the latter, too optimistic. But, in any event, the estimates clearly implied a recession and recovery. (*Hearings of the Joint Committee, 1954*, p. 56). Full employment throughout calendar 1954 would have balanced the fiscal 1955 budget given the expenditures and tax rates proposed by the administration.

omy's stabilization needs. After referring to the "disconcerting magnitude" of the budget deficit, the *Report* promised continuation in the "months and years ahead" of efforts to reduce both expenditures and tax receipts. It noted, however, that

. . . the precise rate of both the one and the other may need to be varied according to general economic conditions and the state of our international relations. In a rapidly changing world, such as we live in, there is no simple fiscal formula that will be suitable under all conditions (p. 56).

Thus, the impact of the recession on the administration's overall fiscal policy in January 1954 was ambiguous. So, too, were the specific program recommendations. The *Economic Report* singled out a number of elements of the administration's program for their special relevance to the stability of the economy, but gave fair warning of the difficulty of labeling particular policy actions as anti-recessionary:

The new concept that is emerging in the practical art of government . . . is to subject every act of proposed legislation or administration decision, as far as that is humanly possible, to review from the standpoint of the contribution it is likely to make, whether in the immediate or a more distant future, to the attainment of an expanding economy with maximum employment and without price inflation (pp. 111-12).

1953 Policy Actions

In the *Economic Report*, the administration expressed pride in six policy actions already taken during 1953 (pp. 49 ff.):

First was the speedy reaction of the Federal Reserve authorities to the credit squeeze that developed in May. This action—which actually started before the turning point—certainly was fortunate, and lends support to the usual view that monetary policy can be used with more flexibility than fiscal policy. Early action on the monetary front probably was a more important factor in the earlier recovery and spurt in residential construction in the 1953-54 recession than in other postwar recessions.[42] The initial Federal Reserve easing of

[42] See Hickman, *op. cit.*, pp. 117-19, and p. 340; and Leo Grebler, *Housing Issues in Economic Stabilization Policy*, National Bureau of Economic Research, Occasional Paper 72 (1960), pp. 16-36.

credit seems to have been a response to an unexpectedly great reaction to the restrictive monetary policy of early 1953 and to the Treasury's issuance of a new 30-year bond in April. In part, then, the Federal Reserve action merely corrected earlier miscalculations which created, in the words of the *Economic Report* (p. 50), an "incipient, and possibly dangerous scramble for liquidity."

Second was the fact that the Treasury, while continuing to lengthen the debt, in the latter half of the year "brought out issues that competed to a minimum with the demands for long-term credit by business firms and State and local governments." (P. 51.) While the Treasury debt actions were hardly expansionary, they were an indication of coordination of debt management with the easier credit policy of the Federal Reserve.

Next on the list was the "unequivocal promise of tax relief" made in late September by the Secretary of the Treasury. At best, this provided a psychological lift, since—as noted earlier—the change had already been scheduled. Although most businessmen probably were already aware of the pending reductions, the firm statement by the Secretary may have reassured some who feared that reductions would be canceled or postponed when Congress reconvened.

The administration noted that it had requested, and Congress granted, permissive flexibility in insurance terms of the Federal Housing Administration (FHA). Despite success on this front, the resulting presidential authority to reduce down payments and extend the maturity on loans was not used in the 1953-54 recession. Moreover, the stabilizing effectiveness of such flexibility is questionable. Private mortgage funds usually become more readily available in recession years, owing to changes in general credit conditions.

The fifth item was price supports and other aid extended to farmers. But the stepped-up outlays for farm price supports had offsetting effects in reducing the real income of consumers. The outlays were in response to changes in supply, rather than demand, and were largely automatic under the law. The administration's attitude toward such outlays is reflected in the fact that its proposals at that time—which were pushed vigorously through a reluctant Congress in subsequent months—featured "flexible price supports," a euphemism for hoped-for reductions in government outlays.

Finally, steps to improve and coordinate public works planning were among the actions cited. This policy—accelerated in various ways during following months—should be classified as a long-range reform, or a hedge against a more serious depression, since 1953-54 came and went without an effort by the administration to use such plans for economic stabilization. The distinction between construction and advance planning stands out sharply in the Budget Message discussion of natural resource development (p. M79). Noting that for fiscal reasons "some improvements and programs which might be desirable have not been included in this budget," it emphasized the need for "careful planning to insure sound development," and continued: "Such development should be timed, whenever possible, to assist in leveling off peaks and valleys in our economic life." Thus, approval was extended to the general idea of countercyclical scheduling of public works that would be started sooner or later anyway, and planning outlays were increased,[43] although in the current situation a speed-up was not considered to be necessary. The statement on the desirability of certain programs which were not included suggests perhaps a shade less restriction than the statement in the August 1953 Midyear Review of the Budget that construction rates were being stretched out. But, if so, the estimates for the major water resource agencies for fiscal 1954 were affected only to a small extent.

Proposals for Future Action

Confidence that the readjustment would be brief and self-correcting and that measures already taken would suffice was expressed in the *Economic Report*. But the administration also warned against complacency, stating that "there is no room for certainty in these matters." As a precaution, a number of "actions that we should take within the current year to build a stronger economy" were called for (p. 75). Again, a brief examination of the relation of these proposals to the recession that was then under way indicates pluses and minuses.

The first of two types of precautionary action was described

[43] *Hearings of the Joint Committee, 1954,* and Special Analysis F on Public Works in the *Budget, Fiscal 1955, op. cit.,* pp. 1-39 ff.

as "bold steps to protect and promote economic stability." These actions would (1) modernize unemployment insurance; (2) broaden the base and benefits of old-age and survivors insurance; (3) permit a longer carry-back of losses for tax purposes; (4) grant the President broad discretionary authority over terms of governmentally insured and guaranteed loans and mortgages; (5) establish a secondary home mortgage market; and (6) improve the planning of public works programs.

The administration's recommendations on unemployment insurance, as Flash has pointed out, were much the same as proposals that had been considered for several years in the Labor Department and elsewhere.[44] The major recommendation—extended coverage and the establishment of a federal loan fund for states in need— was basically a long-range reform, since the short-run effects of increased coverage probably would have been perverse. Employer taxes presumably would go up soon after enactment of the legislation, while benefits could be paid only after a period of covered employment. Another proposal, that the waiting period for employers to get experience ratings be cut from three years to one year, would have reduced this perverse effect—but only partially and only after one year. Other proposals for increasing the amount and duration of benefits were in the form of recommendations for state action.

The OASI recommendations were more expansionary. The administration repeated its July recommendation to expand coverage, which by itself would be deflationary in the short run. But, having failed to get a postponement of the payroll tax increase which went into effect on January 1, 1954, the administration proposed a substantial liberalization of benefits without a further tax increase to pay for them. This particular combination of proposed changes may have been partly a response to the recession, since it was pointed out that, during the transition in 1954, the increased OASI benefits would more than offset the net addition to tax payments under the proposed unemployment compensation system.

Extension of the operating loss carry-back from one to two years was made a feature of the tax code revisions subsequently

[44] Flash, *op. cit.*, pp. 296-99.

passed in August 1954. This provision was apparently added in part because of the recession, since it was not one of the proposals which Treasury officials the preceding summer had said were being studied. However, it was a permanent reform, not a temporary arrangement.

With respect to the government's home loan guaranties and insurance, as noted earlier, the administration did not use its existing discretionary authority. Moreover, it is not clear that, with the large volume of home building started in 1954 anyway, there would have been much additional stimulus from discretionary alteration of insurance terms.

The proposal to establish a secondary home mortgage market referred to the administration's plan to secure the participation of private capital in the Federal National Mortgage Association (FNMA), previously financed wholly by the federal government.[45]

As already noted, the administration emphasized public works planning at the same time it was reducing outlays for actual construction. The President's program, in January 1954, included a proposal for repayable planning advances to local governments in an effort to build up a shelf of planned nonfederal projects. However, under the program as enacted later that year, these advances become repayable on the initiation of construction, and the administration made no proposal for ways to implement actual construction if and when needed.

The other type of precautionary measures included four actions "to stimulate the expansive power of individual enterprise." These would (7) revise tax laws to increase incentives; (8) improve credit facilities for home building, modernization, and urban renewal; (9) strengthen the highway system; and (10) facilitate "the adjustments of farming to current conditions of demand and technology."

The proposals for increased tax incentives closely resembled suggestions that Treasury officials had made the previous year and subsequently developed in cooperation with the House Ways and Means Committee, which had held extended hearings on them. It has been pointed out that the Treasury was prepared to push essentially these proposals no matter what the state of the economy.[46]

[45] See Grebler, op. cit., p. 11.
[46] E. Cary Brown, op. cit., p. 169.

However, the fact that the administration was now reconciled to a substantial net loss of revenue from the reforms—which was previously uncertain—may be attributed partly to the recession.[47] Elsewhere (p. 81), the *Economic Report* stated that steps to speed up the processing of individual income tax refunds, and possibly to initiate current-year refunds of operating loss carry-backs, were being considered.

The administration's proposal for new kinds of credit facilities for housing was in the form of federal insurance of private funds, and was designed to increase the flow and improve the distribution of the supply of private loanable funds. Since new federal credit was not involved, this would not be a net expansionary action unless the funds made available for insured loans would otherwise have been hoarded.

Although the President's budget request for new highway authorizations in fiscal 1955 was kept at the fiscal 1954 level and the expenditure estimate showed little change, a proposed expansion was transmitted to Congress later. Again, the recession may have helped shape the size of the request, but it was clear then and later[48] that the Eisenhower administration favored increased federal spending in this area for reasons of long-run growth and development.

The farm proposal referred to the administration's hope for reduced federal outlays for farm price supports, and this probably would not have had much value as a counterrecession action.

One policy which was not recommended in 1954 is worth mentioning by way of contrast with proposals made in other recessions: In the 1954 *Economic Report,* it was argued (correctly in the writer's judgment) that an increase in the minimum wage would have uncertain and perhaps perverse effects in a recession year. Although Flash reports an incipient interest at this time on the part of the Labor Department in raising the minimum wage,[49] the Presi-

---

[47] According to Flash, *op. cit.,* pp. 274-76, contracyclical ends were an important reason for CEA Chairman Burns' support of these proposals in the administration's deliberations.

[48] A committee of private citizens was appointed by the President during 1954 to study the nation's highway needs and a few years later a greatly stepped-up federal program was initiated under the Highway Act of 1956.

[49] Flash, *op. cit.,* pp. 300-01.

dent reiterated a few weeks later that this was not the time for an increase.[50]

Finally, the *Economic Report* listed (pp. 112-13) a "very formidable" arsenal of weapons available "in case of need." These included Federal Reserve credit controls; debt management techniques of the Treasury; existing presidential authority to alter terms of FHA-insured mortgages; the flexible administration of budget expenditures; taxation; public works; accelerated depreciation for defense plants; and newly recommended agricultural price supports. According to the *Report,* if additional powers were needed to cope with the economic situation, Congress would be asked for them promptly.

Expenditure Flexibility Compared to Tax Cuts

The possibility of flexible administration of budget expenditures in general, and public works in particular, apparently played a key role in the confidence exhibited by the administration. As pointed out above, the staff of the Budget Bureau had started in July 1953 preparing studies of budget flexibility at the request of the CEA Chairman. The Budget Director, in his own testimony before the Joint Committee on the Economic Report, presented a brief summary of these findings.[51] He estimated that perhaps $3 billion a year could be added to government expenditures by administrative action alone. This amount excluded military outlays, atomic energy, and foreign military assistance programs, except for military public works which were included. He specifically pointed out that little administrative flexibility was available for civil public works, but the reasons given implied that this was mainly because supplemental appropriations would be required. By implication, additional amounts could be added to other programs also by supplemental appropriations and, of course, rescheduling outlays for defense would also add to the total.

This is not the place for a detailed analysis of these findings.

[50] *Public Papers, 1954,* p. 224.
[51] *Hearings of the Joint Committee, 1954,* pp. 32-34.

However, a paper presented to an NBER conference in the fall of 1953, and drawn from the same basic materials,[52] lends itself to a few tentative conclusions. First, civil public works, with or without supplemental appropriations, were a minor source of estimated potential flexibility, as was the case with federal grant-in-aid programs. Second, a major portion of purely administrative flexibility lay with certain lending operations, such as FNMA and the Export-Import Bank. Such programs would be stimulating to the economy if monetary and credit markets were demoralized, but under less extraordinary conditions would be essentially equivalent in aggregate impact to a general easing by the monetary authorities. Third, defense programs had more administrative flexibility than the rest of the budget combined.

The *Economic Report* expressed the view that the budget "permits more flexibility than is commonly appreciated." With respect to public works, it (p. 103) described a large backlog of needed projects—federal, state, and local; mentioned the large amount of advance planning already completed; described steps already taken, and others under way, to coordinate planning at the federal level; and proposed a program of federal aid to state and local planning. The opinion was expressed that outlays for federal public works could be stepped up "by one-half or more within a year," and state and local outlays to a similar extent if financial arrangements were adequate. In testifying before the Joint Committee on the Economic Report shortly thereafter, the CEA Chairman repeated the position taken in the *Economic Report* that there was considerable flexibility in expenditures for public works.[53] Estimates gathered later, and discussed briefly below, suggest that the CEA greatly overestimated the potential flexibility in public works outlays.

From February 1 through 18, the Joint Committee on the Economic Report held its annual hearings on the President's 1954 *Eco-*

[52] Samuel M. Cohn, Comment on David Lusher's paper, "The Stabilizing Effectiveness of Budget Flexibility," in *Policies to Combat Depression,* Conference of the Universities-National Bureau Committee for Economic Research (Princeton University Press, 1956).

[53] *Hearings of the Joint Committee, 1954,* p. 30. (In the following discussion of the *Hearings,* page references are inserted in the text.)

nomic Report. Some members of the Committee expressed concern that a recession might require action or supplemental appropriations later when Congress was not in session. Former CEA Chairman Nourse warned that an early upturn was not in sight, and that the recession could prove much more serious than the preceding one. Several other witnesses at the Joint Committee's hearings recommended more vigorous action to deal with the decline (pp. 32-33).

The administration line at these hearings, however, consistently was that the current situation did not call for action, but that the administration was ready to move when it did. When the Joint Committee Chairman, Jesse Wolcott, suggested giving the President authority to invoke a program of accelerated depreciation, if and when economic conditions warranted, Secretary Humphrey replied in the negative (p. 61), stating that the administration's recommendations for faster depreciation were long-term incentives.

The President's attitude on public works during the early weeks of February is reported by Donovan.[54] At the February 5 cabinet meeting, he announced that CEA was coordinating agency reports on public works projects to insure that work could be started promptly if needed, and he designated July 1 as a tentative date by which time the government should be prepared to act. He said he was ready to ask Congress for supplemental appropriations for a few immediate projects if any cabinet member recommended it, and suggested the possibility of a federal government guarantee of toll-road bonds to stimulate highway construction.[55] The Secretary of the Interior, Douglas McKay, not only recommended initiation of several power projects, but pointed out the importance of getting adequate funds to carry through existing projects. Treasury Secretary Humphrey, however, opposed a broad public works program until it was known whether operations already under way would turn the tide. The day after that cabinet meeting, CEA Chairman Burns reported to the President that, on the basis of the facts then

[54] *Op. cit.,* pp. 214-15.

[55] A few days later, the President announced that apportionments of highway grants would be stepped up by $225 million above the amounts contemplated in the budget. And since additional congressional authorization would be needed, he proposed earmarking the 2-cent federal gas tax for highway financing purposes.

available, the government was justified in taking action to strengthen the economy as had been recommended in the 1954 *Economic Report*, but not in launching a program to fight a real depression. Donovan was struck by the muted emphasis on budget balancing in this and subsequent cabinet meetings: "This goal had been emphasized before and was to be emphasized very strongly again. But with the fate of the economy in the balance, it was submerged under the determination of the President and of the Cabinet generally to undertake an expensive public works program if necessary and to prevent a serious depression at any cost."

The President assured the audience at his February 17 press conference that the administration was alert to the unfolding economic situation, that it would not hesitate to act if necessary, but that he did not want the government lashing out wildly in all directions. He implied that March was the key month. If the March statistics did not turn up, he said, it would probably mean that measures were needed—possibly larger tax concessions than the administration had already recommended for reform purposes.[56] In the meantime, during February, the Chairman of CEA did request another survey by the Bureau of the Budget of federal construction —this time of public works projects that could be undertaken quickly if a decision were made to do so.

The reaction of the Joint Committee on the Economic Report to the President's 1954 economic findings and proposals was made public on February 26. The Committee as a whole expressed confidence that "any serious further recession can be avoided and that this increase in private demand can take place in the interests of economic stability and growth *if the available tools are used in a timely and courageous manner.*"[57] The passage went on to say, however, that Committee members differed "as to the relative emphasis which should currently be given to the encouragement of investment expenditures and to the encouragement of expanded consumption." The Committee said its confidence was reinforced by the willingness of the government "to pursue programs which will

[56] *Public Papers, 1954*, p. 269.
[57] *Joint Economic Report, 1954*, p. 4. (Italics added; page references to this report appear in the text in the following paragraphs.)

advance the objectives of the Employment Act." But it also referred to "elements of uncertainty in the current situation," including perhaps smaller underlying backlogs of demand than at the time of the 1949 recession, and the danger of interactions between declining defense spending and reduced private outlays (p. 5).

The Joint Committee expressed approval of a number of presidential proposals. It supported increased OASI benefits both for reasons of equity and because this could make "a direct contribution in helping to bridge the transition to lower defense production levels." And it agreed with the proposed liberalization of unemployment compensation "whether or not one believes that the recently rising trend in unemployment will soon right itself." Presidential discretion on terms of government-insured housing loans was supported (p. 11) because government "aid to housing must be flexible and readily adaptable to changing economic conditions."

With respect to public works (p. 14), however, the Committee found "little confirmation for the hope that Federal public works might be speeded up administratively alone in any important way." It warned against overrating public works as a ready tool; questioned the picture of flexibility presented in the President's *Economic Report,* because that would depend on prompt action by Congress and other authorizing bodies; seemed to endorse the principle of federal assistance for state-local public works, by expressing doubt if there would be flexibility otherwise; but specifically recommended for the time being only stepped-up planning.

The Committee's report endorsed the idea of flexing depreciation over the cycle, and it announced appointment of a Subcommittee on Economic Stabilization to follow economic developments and the need for tax action on a day-to-day basis (p. 16). Also included in the *Report* (p. 48) were suggestions made by the Committee's staff for possible additional actions if necessary. Among these were further easing of money and credit markets, tax reductions beyond those contemplated in the President's program, and public works. But these, since they would unbalance the cash budget, "should be undertaken only after it is clear that the adjustment will either not be self-correcting or will bring hardships to the people if left to run its course."

From a policy viewpoint, the major issue raised in the *Joint Economic Report* concerned tax cuts. Seven Democratic minority members of the Committee submitted supplemental views (p. 20), which called for a cut of $5 billion in the individual income tax by raising personal exemptions from $600 to $800, and a drastic reduction of all excise taxes on "necessities and semi-luxuries" in order to stimulate consumption.

While the recession supplied a good reason for tax cuts, it was not the only explanation of the strong congressional backing for tax reduction at this time. Since the administration's recommendations for tax reform, including accelerated depreciation and a tax credit and exclusion for dividend income, were rather pointedly aimed at investors, it is not unreasonable to suppose that, in an election year, Congress wanted matching tax concessions more obviously benefiting consumers. Considerable Democratic support had built up for a bill, introduced early in the session by Senator Walter George of Georgia, to increase personal exemptions in two steps from $600 to $1,000; and, on February 19, Senator Paul Douglas had written to the President urging his backing of this proposal to head off a possible depression.[58]

The Democrats were not the only advocates of tax cuts; the Republican Speaker of the House, Joseph W. Martin, Jr., was actively pushing reduction of excise taxes. And the administration was not in a strong bargaining position since, unless Congress acted to extend them, several of the excise taxes and 5 points of the corporate income tax would expire automatically on April 1, 1954. Without the revenue from these taxes, the administration felt it might not be able to afford the recommended tax reforms which it believed were important for investment and the long-run health of the economy. By March, it was becoming clear that the administration would have to concede some additional revenues as the price for getting congressional extension of these taxes. Between the alternatives of a Republican-backed measure to cut excise levies by $1 billion, and the Democratic proposal for higher individual income tax exemptions, it was not hard to choose. The latter was anathema to the President and to the Secretary of the Treasury.

On March 15, 1954, in a radio and television address to the nation,[59] the President defended his tax reform proposals on the basis of equity and incentives to save and invest. He repeated his

[58] Donovan, *op. cit.*, p. 216.
[59] *Public Papers, 1954*, pp. 316-17.

request for extension of the corporate rate but, significantly, said nothing about extension of the excise rates which he had also been recommending. He vigorously opposed proposals to step up individual income tax exemptions, not only on grounds of revenue, but because "The $1,000 exemption would excuse one taxpayer in every three from all Federal income taxes. The share of that one-third would have to be paid by the other two-thirds. I think this is wrong." Speaking against the "professionally faint-hearted" who wanted tax cuts because of the recession, the President warned that "viewing with gloom is only to be expected in the spring of an election year," and said tax cuts beyond those he had proposed would be inflationary. After Congress cut the excise taxes, the President said, at his March 31 press conference, that he accepted the bill "wholeheartedly"—although it reduced revenues from what he had recommended. "There is one school of thought that believes that cutting of excise taxes can have such a great effect in stimulating of business that the revenues will not be hurt as much as we estimate."[60] Given the variety of motives and the particular circumstances surrounding the 1954 reduction of excise tax rates, it cannot be labelled clearly as a deliberate counterrecession action on the part of either the legislative or executive branch. However, the recession obviously constituted an additional argument that carried some weight with both.

At cabinet meetings during March and April the President showed increasing concern over the economic situation. Donovan reports that Eisenhower was "deadly serious" at the March 12 meeting over the latest unemployment statistics, and distressed by the fact that, although "plans had been prepared for countering a decline in the business cycle—when one came to look for recommendations as to when these plans should be put into effect, one looked in vain." When Treasury Secretary Humphrey warned against drastic action that could not easily be cut off, and recommended waiting until April or May to give the picture a chance to clarify, the President pointed out that timely action would forestall more drastic action later. Then, at the March 19 cabinet meeting, Burns reported some favorable signs, but recommended suspending judgment for a while longer. President Eisenhower argued for immedi-

---

[60] *Public Papers, 1954,* p. 364.

ate action to counter the decline and head off the Democrats; Vice President Richard Nixon agreed; and even Secretary Humphrey agreed that projects which in any case would be started eventually might well be started immediately. The President asked to have the current CEA studies on possible immediate actions expedited.[61]

Despite this concern, the President told the press on March 24 there was still no indication that the transition from wartime to peacetime economy was getting out of hand, that measures already adopted or recommended would be inadequate, or that a "slam bang emergency program" was called for.[62]

The list of possible immediate actions requested by the President was discussed at the March 26, April 2, and April 9 cabinet meetings. Included on the CEA list were further easing of credit by the Federal Reserve, liberalizing mortgage requirements, altering tax depreciation policy, and stepping up government procurement. Secretary Humphrey agreed that the administration ought to get additional measures started, and the President backed the recommendation of Commerce Secretary Sinclair Weeks for faster action on a newly agreed-on program to stimulate the ship-building industry by constructing tankers. The President stated that recommendations on the CEA list which could be undertaken by the executive branch without congressional action should be started without delay, but he cautioned on the need for care in public announcements. Chairman Burns agreed on the importance of public confidence. Three days after the April 2 cabinet meeting, the President in a radio and television address reported that the March statistics showed signs the recession was leveling off, but that the government was ready to act if necessary. Public construction and further lowering of taxes were "plans in reserve" but—again—a "slam bang emergency program" should not be started until necessary. When he received a cautious prediction of an upturn from Burns at the April 9 cabinet meeting, the President's reaction was that uncertainties should be resolved in accordance with the principle that there is more risk in doing nothing than in doing something.[63]

Meanwhile, staff work on public works planning was stepped up.

[61] Donovan, *op. cit.*, pp. 215-16.
[62] *Public Papers, 1954*, p. 339.
[63] Donovan, *op. cit.*, pp. 217-19.

A small group of experts in public works planning was established in CEA in April, and a Coordinator of Public Works Planning added to the Council staff.[64] Shortly afterwards, the Coordinator, General John S. Bragdon, a classmate of the President's, was placed directly on the White House staff. On April 21, the Bureau of the Budget completed and sent to the Chairman of CEA the study he had requested in February on federal public works projects that could be started quickly. The survey had been discussed by the staff of the two agencies in the interim, and the Bureau had carefully reviewed agency submissions with respect to the criterion agreed on—that projects could be started within two years or less. The projects had then been classified by agency, cost, geographic distribution, status of plans, time required for starting, duration of work, and order of priority. The total cost (including some projects not then authorized by the Congress) came to over $6 billion.[65]

A rough estimate of the potential flexibility implied by this total might be made as follows: If one-third of the total were started the first year and two-thirds the second, and as much as 10 percent of total project costs were incurred the year of starting (somewhat optimistic considering the heavy weighting in the total for water resource projects for which first-year expenditures average much less), then construction put in place in the first year might have been increased by about $200 million. Contracts, which have some economic impact in advance of expenditures, might have been slightly higher than this. However, this falls far short of the estimate in the President's 1954 *Economic Report* that spending could be speeded up by one-half within a year. Civil public works construction was running at an estimated $1.8 billion in fiscal 1954.

At the April 30 cabinet meeting, the President again endorsed the principle of speeding-up work on approved public works projects, and noted that, since such projects contributed to the country's future economic strength, they should be regarded as investments rather than expenditures. The CEA Chairman again reported some favorable economic indicators.[66] The President passed along the information that, in recent reports, the favorable factors outweighed the unfavorable at his May 5 press conference. But he

[64] See *Hearings of the Joint Committee, 1955,* p. 23.
[65] Information obtained from Bureau of the Budget archives.
[66] Donovan, *op. cit.,* p. 219.

added, "Just as I cautioned against too pessimistic an outlook some weeks ago, I would caution against looking at this thing through too rosy glasses now."[67]

A Six-Month Speed-up of Expenditures

A decision to speed up the expenditures budgeted for fiscal 1955 was made at the May 14 cabinet meeting. That day, Secretary of the Treasury Humphrey read a pessimistic letter he had received from a businessman, and said the administration should push Congress for early enactment of legislation already recommended that would help the economy within the next six-month period. The CEA Chairman again pointed to various activities which could be expedited without congressional action. The President directed a speed-up of worthwhile projects where the agencies had money available, and said the administration's policy on expenditure reduction should be applied only to nonessentials, not worthwhile projects.[68]

In response to the President's remarks at this May 14 cabinet meeting, it was decided that a budgetary policy of the administration would be to increase expenditures on useful projects as rapidly as possible, wherever this could be done within the overall limits of expenditure totals already planned for fiscal 1955. The Bureau of the Budget promptly made a program-by-program review listing potential increases in expenditures or orders which could be effected by the end of the July-September quarter of 1954, and which could be reversed in time to have no effect on expenditures already budgeted for fiscal 1955 as a whole. Items requiring legislation or supplemental appropriations were ruled out. Because it was not planned to make the speed-up attempt public at that time, it was specifically decided that Congress would not be asked to hasten action on regular appropriations, supplementals, or legislation already requested for other reasons, even where such action might hasten spending.[69]

[67] *Public Papers, 1954*, pp. 450 ff.
[68] Donovan, *op. cit.*, pp. 219-20.
[69] This and later information on the speed-up of fiscal 1955 expenditures was gathered mainly in conversations with former officials of the Council of Economic Advisers and the Bureau of the Budget; in some cases it was supplemented by information supplied by officials of the Defense and Agriculture departments and other federal agencies.

The decision that no new legislative proposals would be made, or old ones amended, ruled out a number of suggestions. These included a new program of federal construction grants for nonfederal public works, advancing the effective date for proposals already made to liberalize social security benefits, and an extension of the direct loan authority of the Veterans Administration (VA) which was scheduled to expire (Congress subsequently enacted the last without being asked).

It is questionable whether supplemental appropriations, even if not ruled out, could have been enacted and work started in time to have increased expenditures very much in the July-September period. Activities for which supplementals might have been requested included mainly construction on small public works projects and repair, improvement, operation, and maintenance of existing facilities of various civilian agencies. It was also decided that it would not be necessary to exercise the President's discretionary authority over FHA maturity and down payment terms. Although net budget expenditures were not involved, and additional discretionary authority had been vigorously requested by the administration (and was included among the provisions of the pending Housing Act of 1954), there was no evidence of a shortage of funds in mortgage markets. The total speed-up being considered in expenditures toward the end of May 1954, assuming prompt enactment by Congress of the 1955 appropriations (which had been requested in January 1954), was in the neighborhood of $1 billion, of which about three-quarters was for Department of Defense military programs.[70]

While a number of the speed-up actions were contingent on the early enactment of regular annual appropriations, supplementals, or legislation already requested for other purposes, there were few obstacles to speed-up on this account. A potential increase estimated for stockpiling medical and survival supplies by the Federal Civil Defense Administration became academic when the regular

---

[70] As mentioned later, this total included a few items for which expenditures were not likely to be recovered in time to leave the total for fiscal 1955 unaffected. The increase in estimated obligations (orders) corresponding to the above expenditure increase was larger—about $2.25 billion—of which 85 percent was for military functions of the Department of Defense.

appropriation was not enacted until September; and a cut in appropriations was a possible limiting factor for the Department of the Interior. But all other regular appropriations involved in the speed-up were enacted before the start of fiscal 1955 or immediately thereafter. Also, legislation awaited for speed-up purposes, such as the Housing Act of 1954 and the "trade-in and build" tanker program, in most cases was enacted.

The new Budget Director, Rowland Hughes, pointed out in a letter to the President, on May 21, that the proposed speed-up was within the existing expenditure plans of the administration for fiscal 1954 and 1955. Further, since these plans called for a downward trend, the temporary speed-up would not mean an increase in the level of federal spending—only that the downward trend would not be as sharp as it would have been. Also on that day, Hughes sent memoranda to agency heads describing the speed-up policy, listing the Bureau's suggestions for speed-up, and inviting them to suggest other possibilities.

In subsequent discussions, the agencies added some items, deleted others, and sought certain relaxations from the general rules on the speed-up. For example, the possibility of increasing FNMA mortgage purchases was considered, but the agency doubted this could be done without raising the total expenditures for the year, and it was not tried. Basically, the following agencies were responsible for programs in which speed-ups were attempted in 1955.[71]

1. The Department of Defense—which at all stages of the operation accounted for the great bulk of estimated potential speed-up in both orders and expenditures—laid plans for obligating its 1955 appropriations as early in the fiscal year as possible, and Assistant Secretary Thomas P. Pike was appointed to supervise the speed-up. Steps which were expected to have an expansionary impact included holding back on scheduled slowdowns of orders for selected hard goods and delaying scheduled termination of contracts; requesting contractors to step up production and delivery rates; placing orders for the 1955 shipbuilding program earlier than planned; speeding up award of contracts on military public works and the tempo on going construction; in-

[71] The fiscal aspects of the speed-up programs are evaluated later in this chapter.

creasing budget apportionments for operation and maintenance and asking the services to accelerate deferred maintenance projects; purchasing supplies for industrial and stock funds earlier than usual; and placing long-range charter contracts for private tankers. The recovery of expenditures for a number—in fact a preponderance—of these items could not reasonably be expected within the same fiscal year. But this violation of the supposed ground rules was tacitly overlooked for the most important agency in the whole speed-up attempt.

2.   The Commerce Department's projects included the tanker program and other civil ship construction; highway grants; airport grants; Washington National Airport; air navigation facilities; and forest highways. Although the Department doubted that it could increase airport grants by September 30, it was asked to try to do so. And it was given permission to make earlier than usual apportionments to the states of highway grant funds—although, if such funds were to have an effect, they clearly could not be reversed within the fiscal year.

3.   Interior Department speed-up plans were for Park Service roads, trails, parkways, buildings, and utilities; Bureau of Reclamation construction, operation, and maintenance; Bonneville Power Administration; Bureau of Indian Affairs buildings, roads, and trails; and Alaskan roads, railroads, and public works. When Interior's appropriation turned out to be less than the requested amount, the Department added public works in Alaska to this list, but cut the estimated total amount of the speed-up by half.

4.   The Agriculture Department planned a speed-up on forest roads and trails; direct procurement of grain storage facilities, and issuance of occupancy guarantees for private facilities; flood control and watershed protection; research facilities; farm housing loans; and loans by the Rural Electrification Administration (REA). Its target for the speed-up, initially set at September 30, was extended to December 31, 1954; and its annual total was raised in line with increased Congressional appropriations for such programs as the REA loans.

5.   The Office of Defense Mobilization (ODM), because of a recently approved change in stockpile goals, was exempted from the rule that annual totals should not be affected, and planned an

increase in obligations over nine, instead of three months.

6. Other items in the speed-up attempt were construction, operation, and repair or improvement of buildings or facilities by the General Services Administration, Post Office Department, Corps of Engineers (civil functions), U. S. Information Agency, and the St. Lawrence Seaway authority.

The timing of the speed-up has certain interesting aspects. As early as February 5, 1954, the President seemed to have given approval of a speed-up to his Cabinet, and his remarks on April 2 were interpreted by at least some members as a request to this effect. Yet it was not until May 14 that an acceleration of spending became a coordinated government policy. Although tankers and highways had been given a push, there had been no coordinated effort aside from planning and listing possible actions.

In part, this lag is evidence of the difficulty in shifting the direction of federal fiscal policy. It takes time, first, to recognize the need for change and, second, to mobilize the government's policy machinery. The decision for a speed-up came when, in contrast to earlier months, there were some favorable economic indicators mixed in with the unfavorable—when the possibility that the economy had already made the turn had been explicitly acknowledged. However, this was not a universal opinion, and concern over the health of the economy lingered in some quarters for months to come. Also, before May, the full magnitude of the defense cutbacks was still not universally appreciated. But it does not appear that the administration was suddenly worried in May that things might really get out of hand; otherwise it probably would not have been so determined to have the speed-up expire automatically after the first quarter of fiscal 1955.

An additional factor is suggested by the "next six-month period" that Secretary of the Treasury Humphrey at the May 14 Cabinet meeting considered so critical. Congressional elections were short of six months away, and the Republicans were being charged with inaction. It is not feasible, and probably not necessary, to separate the recession motive from that of the fall congressional elections. It was a thinly guarded secret, judging from newspaper speculation at the time, that "Pike's Peak" (the Defense Department's affectionate phrase in honor of the Assistant Secretary appointed in the fall of

1954 to the task of increasing defense orders) was concerned with the geographical distribution of unemployment as well as its total.

The administration's attention in May was not focused exclusively on the recession. The question of a balanced budget also came up at the May 21 Cabinet meeting. Budget Director Hughes, in projecting the budget picture, stated that little further reduction in nondefense outlays would be possible, and that further reduction in anticipated deficits would have to come out of defense spending. The President "warned sharply," says Donovan, against loose talk about a balanced budget, pointing out that balanced budgets had not been promised by any particular date, that the administration was moving in the right direction in cutting out nonessential expenditures, and should thereafter fight for adequate—and, if necessary, higher—taxes to meet necessary expenses. The CEA Chairman reported some hopeful news on the business front, Donovan notes, and said the economy might be swinging into an upturn.[72]

Although Burns again had optimistic news from the CEA at the June 4 Cabinet meeting, the President felt the government was not doing enough. He made the point—as he had in April—that the government should err on the side of doing too much, rather than too little, and asked Burns to prepare a presentation on additional actions that could be taken. The resulting recommendations, presented on June 11, included measures which again stressed housing, building, interest rates, and highway construction. President Eisenhower proposed a luncheon with influential congressmen who, he said, might understand the political, if not the economic, benefits of the housing program. Although the President urged the department heads to do what needed to be done quickly, and asked for reports at the next Cabinet meeting, this marked the end, according to Donovan, of urgency in the Cabinet over recession.[73]

Recovery and a Shift in Emphasis

The President, in a July 22 news release revealing the final fiscal 1954 budget totals, expressed pride that the deficit was less than estimated in January. Although receipts were down $3 billion (of

[72] Donovan, op. cit., p. 220.
[73] Ibid., p. 221.

which only a minor portion could be attributed to the 1954 effect of unbudgeted tax cuts), expenditures were down even more. Donovan reports "a note of elation" in the Cabinet the next day when CEA Chairman Burns reported that economic indicators showed definitely that the decline had come to an end.[74]

Although the trough in gross national product came in the second quarter of 1954, unemployment reached its maximum rate of a little over 6 percent of the labor force a quarter later.[75] The GNP increased by $34 billion (annual rate)—almost 10 percent—within a year after the trough, and unemployment declined by May 1955 to slightly over 4 percent of the labor force. This rate was considerably higher than unemployment before the recession, and one which persisted until the recession of 1957-58.[76]

Expansion after mid-1954 was pushed by the strong rise in residential construction which had started in the second quarter, and a strong rise in consumption starting in the fourth. The latter, sparked by purchases of automobiles, reached boom proportions in 1955. Federal spending dropped less steeply after the middle of 1954, and remained virtually level from the fourth quarter of 1954 through the third of 1955. Liquidation of business inventories ceased in the final quarter of 1954, and was changed to accumulation starting in the first quarter of 1955. Surveys of business plans for investment in plant and equipment gave little hint in early 1955 of the boom that was evident within a few months, and the monetary authorities later criticized themselves for not having reversed earlier the policy of monetary ease pursued during the contraction.

Starting in July 1954, the Bureau of the Budget sent letters to the heads of executive agencies giving ceilings and general policies for guidance in preparing submissions for the fiscal 1956 budget. New obligational authority was to be lower in 1956 than in 1955, with reduced levels of government employment and operations; and, to pave the way for this, agencies were to reduce obligation and ex-

[74] *Ibid.*, p. 222.

[75] See Hickman, *op. cit.*, pp. 121-31, for an analysis of the expansion which started in 1954.

[76] The unemployment rate before and after the 1953-55 recession and recovery may not be precisely comparable because of a change in the Census Bureau's sampling methods in January 1954. But this can hardly account for a difference as large as that between 4.1 percent and 2.6 percent.

penditure rates in the second half of fiscal 1955.[77] Other policies for fiscal 1956 included increased efforts to find reductions and savings and to eliminate unnecessary activities. No new civil public works were to be started for 1956; going construction was to be continued at minimum economic rates; maintenance and repair were to be held at minimum safe levels; new commitments for loans and credit programs were to be restricted; and excess inventories were to be sold or liquidated. However, investigations and advance planning of public works were to be stepped up to a point where "the Federal Government would be ready to effectively accelerate its public works programs, at a desirable time." With respect to both "general investigations and surveys and such preliminary plans as are necessary to determine the suitability of projects for authorization," the letter said "high priority should be given to relatively small projects having a wide geographical dispersion, which are urgently needed and economically feasible, and on which construction could be started quickly and could be completed at an economic rate within 18 months or less."[78]

The Housing Act of 1954 (P. L. 83-560) was signed August 2. Among other features, the act increased the size of mortgages eligible for FHA insurance; gave the President some discretionary authority to reduce down payments and increase maturities; and repealed FHA and VA control over fees and charges imposed by lenders upon builders (discounts). As indicated previously, several of the provisions had been described in the January 1954 *Economic Report* as helpful to the economy in a recession year, and the President had later considered asking for speedy congressional approval of the bill for the same reason. However, it is clear that countering the recession was not the paramount intent of either the executive or legislative branch. Of the various provisions of the act, the liberalization of eligibility for FHA insurance could have been

[77] These plans failed to materialize. New obligational authority enacted for fiscal 1956 turned out to be $6 billion more than enacted for 1955 (which was in turn about $1 billion higher than the administration's recommendations in January 1954). While budget expenditures in 1955 fell about $1 billion below the estimates of January 1954, actual 1956 expenditures rose about $2 billion over 1955. (See *Budget*, various fiscal years.)

[78] U.S. Bureau of the Budget, Budget Procedures Memorandum 57, July 19, 1954.

expected to have the major short-run impact on new residential construction. Grebler, who has made an extensive analysis of the forces shaping mortgage market behavior in 1954, concludes that the strong housing boom of that year was a classic response to a generally easy money market and received relatively little additional impetus from the Housing Act of 1954.[79]

On August 10, the President signed two bills (P.L. 83-574 and P.L. 83-575), which were substantially what the administration had proposed, providing a government push in modernizing the commercial tanker fleet. One authorized the Secretary of the Navy to enter long-term lease agreements for fifteen new tankers that would be constructed, purchased, owned, and operated privately, and authorized direct government procurement of five others. The other bill authorized, under the Secretary of Commerce, government payments of trade-in allowances on older tankers to be applied against the construction cost of new commercial flag tankers. The recession had been one argument of the Secretary of Commerce in favor of this program, and an acceleration of earlier plans was included at his suggestion in the general speed-up attempt. In signing these bills the President pointed out that they would "mean jobs in American shipyards," and said he had given instructions that new construction be spaced so "as to avoid undesirable peaks and valleys in construction and employment."[80]

The President's developing attitudes toward the budgetary situation and the desirability of holding down expenditures as recovery of the economy became more apparent are indicated in a number of statements made during the next few weeks. For example, at his August 11 press conference, the President reiterated his desire for economy in expenditures (p. 696). An August 12 press release on the State of the Economy at Midyear (p. 707) fell just shy of declaring a moratorium on the recession, which the President described as very small by historical standards anyway. Recent indicators of improvement in the economy were cited, and confidence

---

[79] Grebler, *op. cit.,* pp. 16-36, especially pp. 29-30; and George F. Break, *The Economic Impact of Federal Loan Insurance* (National Planning Association, 1961), pp. 72-73.

[80] *Public Papers, 1954,* p. 295. (Page numbers in the following text refer to this report.)

expressed in the future. On August 23, in vetoing a post office and civil service pay raise bill, the President complained particularly about the failure of Congress to provide revenues to meet its cost (pp. 744-47). And, on August 28, when signing the bill to increase the debt limit (P.L. 83-686), the President said the increase might prove inadequate, but that the administration would make every possible effort to carry on the government's activities within the limit (p. 770).

Also on August 28, in signing bills that increased veterans benefits (P.L. 83-695 and P.L. 83-698), the President promised that the administration would "continue to watch closely changes in economic conditions and, when warranted by reason of such changes," would "seek appropriate adjustments in compensation and pension laws" (pp. 771-72).

The Social Security Amendments of 1954 (P.L. 83-761), signed September 1, gave the President most of what he had requested in the form of increased coverage, stepped up monthly benefits, a liberalized formula for computing benefits, and a liberalized retirement earnings test. The Bill to Extend and Improve the Unemployment Insurance Program (P.L. 83-767) was signed the same date. Coverage was extended to approximately 1.5 million workers in establishments with four or more employees and to 2 million federal civilian employees. In signing the bill, the President spoke of economic security in the abstract rather than the legislation's short-run economic impact—appropriately, since the short-run effects of extending social insurance coverage are ordinarily contractionary.

The Rivers and Harbors and Flood Control Act of 1954 (P.L. 83-780) authorized $1.1 billion of new water resource projects. On September 3, the President said he signed the bill in spite of the fact that a number of projects were included for which inadequate local cost-sharing had been specified and others had been inadequately planned (p. 823).

In September,[81] the estimate of defense expenditures was down sharply from the January 1954 estimates. This reduction was enough to reduce the total expenditure estimate, in spite of in-

---

[81] *Midyear Review of the 1955 Budget* (September 14, 1954).

creases in most other areas of the budget. It reflected primarily a re-estimate based on later information rather than a deliberate attempt further to reduce expenditures. In fact, as described above, the Department was trying to increase orders and expenditures on a temporary basis, although no reference to this speed-up was made in the *Midyear Review*. Congress had made reductions in defense appropriations below the President's request but these would have their main impact after fiscal 1955. Most other expenditure estimates and appropriations were marked up from January—foreign aid and interest on the public debt being the only significant reductions aside from national security. Total new obligational authority was higher if anticipated supplementals are included.

Indicative of the administration's public stance in the fall of 1954 is the fact that estimates for outlays on resource public works in the current fiscal year were still down from the preceding year. This was made possible, the *Midyear Review* said, by "not starting various uneconomic projects in accordance with new and tighter standards, by completing some projects started in earlier years, and by carrying forward going projects at minimum economic rates."[82]

In January 1955, the economic proposals in the presidential messages specifically disclaimed any motive of stimulating further recovery. They were geared instead to growth, to economic security, or to particular depressed areas that were not taking part in the expansion then under way. The President's letter transmitting his *Economic Report* said that the transition from contraction to recovery had already taken place, and that high and satisfactory employment would be reached within the year.

Estimates of both receipts and expenditures for fiscal 1955 were down slightly from those in the September *Midyear Review* with little change in the anticipated deficit. Further efforts being made to reduce expenditures, together with higher revenues from an expanding tax base, the President said, should make possible some tax rate reductions "next year." In the meantime, there was still a deficit and an increase in the public debt anticipated for fiscal 1956, and the administration was therefore requesting a postpone-

[82] *Ibid.*, p. 27.

ment of the lowering of corporation income and excise taxes scheduled for April 1, 1955.

Hearings before the Joint Committee on the Economic Report, on January 28, 1955, dealt with fiscal policy. Most witnesses were cautiously optimistic and agreed that recovery was under way, but several recommended slightly more expansionist policies than the administration had proposed.[83] The subsequent findings, issued March 11,[84] noted that the Committee as a whole agreed with the President's recommendations to extend corporate and excise tax rates for another year. In supplemental statements, the Democratic members recommended watchfulness and preparedness to reduce individual income taxes if the expectations expressed in the President's *Economic Report* failed to materialize. For all practical purposes, however, concern with the recession was then at an end.

In assessing past developments, the President's 1955 *Economic Report* (pp. 18 ff.) listed a number of government activities which it credited with having slowed the decline or stimulated recovery. These actions—many also listed in the 1954 *Economic Report*—were:

1.   The automatic stabilizers, which reduced tax collections and increased expenditures for unemployment benefits and farm price supports.

2.   Confidence inspired by the Secretary of the Treasury's announcements on tax policy in September 1953.

3.   The reduction in individual income taxes and elimination of excess profits tax on January 1, 1954, only partly offset by higher social security contributions on the same date.

4.   Federal Reserve monetary ease.

5.   The confidence inspired by the January 1954 program proposals for tax revision, housing and urban renewal, OASI expansion, highway grants, public works planning, agricultural policy, and presidential discretion on housing terms.

6.   The excise tax cut and the loss of revenue from the structural tax changes in the 1954 Revenue Act.

[83] *Hearings of the Joint Committee, 1955,* pp. 317 ff.
[84] *Joint Economic Report, 1955.*

7. Aid to the hard-pressed shipbuilding industry through the tanker program.

8. Aid to zinc and lead mining through the stockpile program.

9. The expediting of refunds of overpaid taxes.

10. Prompt announcement of highway allocations to states.

11. The channeling of contracts to labor surplus areas.

12. A boost in the allowable rate of accelerated amortization on facilities needed for the mobilization base.

13. Expansion of the area development activities of the Department of Commerce.

Conspicuously absent was any reference to the general attempt to speed up expenditures initiated the previous summer.

Fiscal Effects of Discretionary Expenditure Actions

Available data on obligations and expenditures make no distinction between amounts attributable to the fiscal 1955 speed-up attempt and amounts which would have occurred without it. Hence, it is impossible to measure directly the extent to which the speed-up was successful—or, if successful, the extent to which it was reversed in time to leave fiscal year totals unaffected as originally planned.

The estimates of fiscal effects which are summarized in Table 22 were derived by a combination of methods. The actual annual totals were compared with annual totals estimated by the administration beforehand, and the monthly pattern during fiscal 1955 was compared with that in other years. The estimates also draw on judgments about leads and lags, and on conversations with government officials. Where there were ranges, the upper end was generally used to avoid understating the fiscal impact. The following discussion omits reference to a number of individually small items for which no fiscal effect from the speed-up can be discerned.

Taking the Department of Defense first, a comparison of the quarterly pattern of obligations for procurement and research during fiscal 1955 with the typical monthly pattern of other years indicates that a within-year shift of sizable proportions took place,

TABLE 22. Estimated Federal Expenditure Increases under the Speed-up in Fiscal Year 1955[a]

(In millions of dollars)

AGENCY	CALENDAR 1954		CALENDAR 1955		FISCAL 1955 TOTAL
	July-Sept.	Oct.-Dec.	Jan.-Mar.	Apr.-June	
Department of Defense, military	—	100	400	−100	400
Corps of Engineers, civil	20	10	10	− 10	30
General Services Administration:					
Stockpiling activities[b]	40	40	20	− 50	50
Construction, modernization and repair	1	1	1	1	4
Department of Commerce:					
Highway grants	10	10	10	10	40
Ship construction, civil	4	4	4	4	15
Forest Service	1	1	1	1	4
Total	75	165	445	−145	545

[a] Estimated by comparison of annual totals with advance estimates and comparison of within-year pattern with that of other years.

[b] Under directives issued by the Office of Defense Mobilization.

although the bulge came more in the October-December quarter of 1954 than in July-September. Whether this shift was accomplished without affecting the annual total of obligations is more difficult to state. Department of Defense obligations for military functions fell short of the original estimates made in January 1954 by almost $7 billion.[85] While it is possible that orders would have been still lower without the speed-up, it seems more likely that most of the speed-up in the first half of the fiscal year was offset by reductions in the second half, at least so far as orders are concerned.

A comparison of the quarterly pattern of defense expenditures in fiscal 1955 with other years, and also deliveries measured by the

[85] Annual budget documents and the 1955 *Midyear Review* show the following for military functions of the Department of Defense, fiscal 1955:

	Estimate			*Actual*
	January 1954	*September 1954*	*January 1955*	
	(In billions of dollars)			
Obligations	38.0	...	34.4	31.1
Expenditures	37.6	35.5	34.4	35.5

TABLE 23. Estimated Effects of Antirecession Defense Speed-up on Obligations and Expenditures, Fiscal Year 1955

(In billions of dollars)

Quarters	Obligations	Expenditures
July-September 1954	0.5	—
October-December 1954	2.0	0.1
January-March 1955	—1.0	0.4
April-June 1955	—1.5	—0.1
Fiscal year total	—	0.4

national income and product accounts, indicates a much smaller rescheduling of either expenditures or deliveries than of obligations. Also, as would be expected, the expenditure effect came after the obligation effect, principally in the January-March quarter of 1955. Moreover, given ordinary lags of expenditures behind obligations, expenditures could not have been cut back fast enough to leave the total for the fiscal year unaffected, even if this were the case with obligations. Assuming that the speed-up and its reversal did not affect the total of obligations for the year, and making reasonable allowance for lags and seasonal patterns, the estimated effect of the 1955 defense speed-up is given in Table 23.

The speed-up in nondefense outlays had a smaller impact. In January 1955, it was estimated that $21 million would be obligated in fiscal 1955 under the new program for trading in and building tankers. By June 30, 1955, three contracts covering fourteen obsolete tankers had been signed, and another for two more tankers was under consideration, but obligations incurred by the federal government came to only $8 million for the entire year.[86] Although the tanker program was slow to get started, other outlays for merchant ship construction subsidies were accelerated so that total expenditures in this category increased about $15 million—about a doubling—above the original estimates.

In revising objectives for the stockpile of strategic and critical materials in the spring of 1954, the administration hoped to aid producers in depressed industries and to decrease dependence on

[86] *Annual Report of the Secretary of Commerce, 1955*, p. 38; and *Budget, Fiscal 1957*, p. 470.

overseas supplies in the event of emergency. Objectives were raised for aluminum, nickel, molybdenum, tungsten, and other minerals. A supplemental appropriation of $380 million, requested and enacted by Congress for fiscal 1955, placed this item in a somewhat different category from the speed-up items, which were not supposed to affect annual totals. Later, in response to the Bureau of the Budget's request that orders be placed as early in the fiscal year as possible, the Office of Defense Mobilization—among other actions—issued purchase directives for lead and zinc. By January 1955, estimates for the year were about $360 million higher than the January 1954 forecast. However, expenditures fell back again in the first half of calendar 1955, and the fiscal year as a whole wound up only $50 million above the original estimates.

Estimates of expenditures for stockpiling and defense production expansion in fiscal 1955, compared to actual expenditures in 1954 and 1956 are as follows:[87]

Fiscal years	In millions of dollars
1954, actual	1,045
1955:	
Estimate, January 1954	893
Estimate, September 1954	1,100
Estimate, January 1955	1,251
Actual	944
1956, Actual	588

Assuming the January 1954 estimate accurately represented prerecession plans and assuming a level trend within the fiscal year as the norm, actual outlays ran about $40 million ahead of original estimates in the third and fourth quarters of 1954, about $20 million ahead in the first quarter of 1955, and then fell $50 million below the norm in the second—winding up fiscal 1955 with $50 million more than the January 1954 estimates. These differences reflect the revisions in program goals as well as the antirecession speed-up.

Although the Agriculture Department said it was taking steps in May 1954 to accelerate the planned purchase of facilities for

---

[87] Annual budget documents and the 1955 *Midyear Review, op. cit.*

grain storage, expenditures estimated for this purpose in fiscal 1954 did not take place until fiscal 1955. The Department estimated, on the basis of the congressional increase in REA appropriations by about $115 million, that it could further increase expenditures in the speed-up attempt. However, loans for the fiscal year fell short of even the January 1954 estimate by about $30 million. Public works expenditures by the Forest Service were $3.5 million above the original estimates, compared to an increase of $5 million in appropriations over the administration's request. Agricultural research facilities fell short of the estimate made in January 1954 before the speed-up by over a half.

Federal-aid highway grants wound up the year about $40 million higher than the estimates made in January 1954. It is not possible to state how much of this was due to the $300 million increase in appropriations over the January request—which had been hinted at in January and would probably have been requested anyway—and how much to the earlier than usual apportionment to the states. Outlays for airport grants, navigation facilities, and D.C. and Alaska airports finished the year slightly below original estimates, and showed no within-year speed-up.

There is little evidence of actual speed-up in figures for the Department of the Interior. Public works expenditures for the Park Service, the Bureau of Reclamation, and the Bureau of Indian Affairs were close to the original estimates for the year. Those for the Bonneville Power Administration and Alaska public works fell considerably short of the January 1954 estimates. The within-year pattern for the Department shows no significant difference from that of other years.

Civil public works expenditures by the Corps of Engineers did better. These wound up the year about $30 million higher than the original estimate, although there had been no increase in appropriations. They showed a within-year shift as well, with outlays in the first quarter of the fiscal year higher, and in the final quarter lower, than would have been expected from the pattern of other years.

The 1955 *Economic Report,* as noted earlier, listed a boost of the allowable rate of accelerated amortization on facilities needed for mobilization as one of the steps that was helpful during the recession. However, in reporting on fiscal 1954, the Secretary of the

Treasury made no mention of any such step, and the figures he gave on the amount and number of applications received and certificates issued for special amortization did not suggest any speed-up.[88] On the contrary, the sharp reduction in calendar 1953 was followed by further reductions in 1954, with certificates issued dropping more than applications received.

The speed-up of tax refunds was only moderately successful. The policy consisted of paying partial refunds in advance of final agreement on some disputed returns.[89] An examination of cumulative percentages[90] shows a lag through April compared to the previous year. Acceleration in May and June brought refunds to a total perhaps $75 million above what they would have been on the previous year's schedule (with corresponding reduction in the second half of the year).

Conclusions—1953-1955

The cutback in federal spending, primarily defense purchases, was a major—if not the major—cause of the 1953-54 recession. At the same time, however, the decline was cushioned and the recovery speeded by reductions of tax rates—reduction of individual income tax and the excess profits tax which became effective on January 1, 1954, and of excises in April 1954, and the further reductions for individuals and corporations embodied in the Revenue Code of 1954.

With the possible exception of excise taxes, these reductions were not put into effect primarily to counteract the recession. They had been previously scheduled, or planned earlier as part of the administration's campaign to reduce the size of the federal budget, or to reform the tax system from the standpoint of equity and incentives for investors. In all likelihood, they would have taken place without a recession. However, the recession constituted an important additional argument for the tax cuts, and it may have served to increase the revenue concession associated with the excise tax

[88] *Treasury Report, 1955,* p. 235.
[89] *Commissioner of Internal Revenue, Annual Report, 1954.*
[90] See Table 25 in Chapter VI.

reductions and the August tax reforms. The reduction in individual income tax on January 1, 1954, was partially offset by the increase at that time—also scheduled beforehand—in social security payroll tax rates.

More important, the tax reductions came later than the expenditure reductions and, when they did come, were considerably less than offsetting. This can be measured approximately by the implicit federal surplus at high employment as pictured in Table 24. At the trough, in the second quarter of 1954, the implicit federal surplus—the surplus that would have obtained under existing tax rates and expenditures had tax yields not been depressed because of the drop in income—came to $3 billion. This compares to an actual deficit of $7 billion at the prerecession peak. Moreover, the accruals recorded in Table 24 for the first half of 1954 include amounts for tax reduction under the 1954 Revenue Code not enacted until August, and probably not entirely anticipated beforehand in private spending plans. (By the same argument, the accruals in Table 24 probably understate the boost to recovery in the second half of 1954 attributable to the 1954 Revenue Code.)

The $11 billion reduction in federal expenditures during the contraction was so large that the federal government was able to reduce its actual deficit during the period of declining incomes and revenues—a dubious accomplishment, unique among postwar recessions.

From the vantage of hindsight and from the specific standpoint of stabilizing employment, perhaps the administration's major error was in not allowing the excess profits tax and individual income tax cuts to take place on July 1, 1953, rather than six months later. This was the date already scheduled for expiration of the excess profits tax and the date strongly pushed for individual income tax cuts by key congressional leaders—although not, it must be admitted, because they advocated budget deficits to stabilize employment. It took a strenuous effort by the administration to get the six-month postponement.

The decline in defense spending turned out to be much greater than originally anticipated, and as late as January 1954 was still seriously underestimated. Nevertheless, a cutback in defense spending, even of the smaller size contemplated in May 1953, probably

TABLE 24. Factors Affecting Federal Surplus, 1953-55 Recession and Recovery[a]

(In billions of current dollars at seasonally adjusted annual rates)

Item	1953 II-P	1953 III	1953 IV	1954 I	1954 II-T	Change Peak to Trough	1954 III	1954 IV	1955 I	1955 II-R	Change Trough to Terminal (R)
Surplus at prerecession peak	−7.0	−7.0	−7.0	−7.0	−7.0	...	−7.0	−7.0	−7.0	−7.0	...
Factors not due to recession											
Increased receipts, high employment, constant prerecession tax rates	...	0.8	1.5	2.2	3.0	3.0	3.8	4.5	5.2	6.0	3.0
Plus: OASI payroll tax rate increase	...	...	...	1.4	1.4	1.4	1.4	1.5	1.5	1.5	0.1
Less: tax reductions—											
Individual income, January 1, 1954	...	...	...	3.0	3.1	3.1	3.1	3.2	3.2	3.3	0.2
Excess profits (expiration)	...	...	...	1.6	1.6	1.6	1.6	1.6	1.6	1.6	—
Excise	...	...	...		0.5	0.5	1.0	1.0	1.0	1.0	0.5
Revenue Code of 1954:[b]											
Individual income	...	...	...	0.4	0.4	0.4	0.7	0.7	0.7	0.7	0.3
Corporate income	...	...	...	0.8	0.8	0.8	0.8	0.8	0.8	0.8	—
Less: expenditure increase											
Purchases, goods and services:											
National defense	...	−1.2	−2.9	−5.7	−9.0	−9.0	−10.7	−12.8	−12.9	−11.4	−2.4
Other	...		−1.8	−0.3	−2.8	−2.8	−2.6	−2.6	−2.6	−2.4	0.4
Transfer payments to persons	...	−0.1	0.2	0.4	−0.7	−0.7	0.9	1.7	2.1	2.6	1.9
Transfer payments abroad	...	−0.7	−0.5	−0.5	−0.7	−0.7	−0.5	−0.5		0.4	0.3
Grants to state and local governments	...	−0.7	0.5	0.5	0.2	0.2	0.2	0.5	0.5	0.4	0.2
Net interest paid	...	0.1	0.1	0.2	0.2	0.2	0.2	0.1	0.1	0.1	−0.1
Subsidies less current surplus of government enterprises	...		0.1	0.1	0.2	0.2	0.4	0.7	0.6	0.8	0.6
Subtotal = prerecession surplus adjusted for factors not due to recession	−7.0	−3.4	−3.8	−2.9	3.0	10.0	3.8	5.4	5.6	4.2	1.2
Less: discretionary antirecession expenditures[c]											
Department of Defense	...	...	...	...	...	...	...	0.5	1.5	0.5	−0.5
Stockpiles, public works, other	...	...	...	...	...	...	0.3	0.3	0.2	0.2	−0.2
Subtotal = implicit high employment surplus	−7.0	−3.4	−3.8	−2.9	3.0	10.0	3.5	4.6	3.9	4.9	1.9
Less: effect, built-in stabilizers											
Corporate profits tax accruals	...	1.2	5.5	4.8	4.5	4.5	4.4	3.1	1.5	0.9	−3.6
Excise taxes	...	0.2	0.7	1.4	1.3	1.3	1.4	1.1	0.8	0.2	−1.1
Employment taxes	...		0.1	0.3	0.4	0.4	0.4	0.4	0.3	0.1	−0.3
Individual income tax accruals	...	0.3	1.0	1.7	2.0	2.0	1.2	0.8	1.0	0.6	−1.4
Unemployment compensation	...	0.1	0.5	0.9	1.4	1.4	1.4	1.3	0.6	0.4	−1.0
Other adjustments[d]	...	−0.4	−0.2	1.4	1.2	1.2	0.2	−0.2	1.1	0.8	−0.4
Total = actual surplus (national income account basis)	−7.0	−5.6	−11.8	−10.6	−5.4	1.6	−5.1	−2.3	0.8	3.5	8.9

a See Appendix D for sources and methods.
b Affected calendar-year 1954 liabilities although not enacted until August 1954.
c See Table 23.
d In addition to adjustments explained in Appendix D, there is an adjustment here for the overlapping involved in calculating both tax rate reductions and the effect of built-in stabilizers on the basis of high employment and prerecession rates.

could not have been digested by the economy—in the absence of tax cuts—without a setback. In this failure to schedule tax cuts earlier, some lingering concern about inflationary tendencies, uncertainty about the response of the economy to removal of direct controls carried over from the Korean War, and the independent importance attached to balanced budgets per se—all played a role. Since unemployment remained low, even by Korean War standards, up until September 1953, concern over potential inflation in the first half of 1953 was not completely unreasonable.

Discretionary counterrecession expenditure actions were slow to be initiated, were not all announced to the public, and were modest in scope—being limited at first to a within-year shift of government expenditures. While considered early in 1954, the general speed-up of expenditures was not actually initiated until May. The attention given to arranging for the speed-up to be reversed after six months suggests that the administration was fairly confident that a turning point in the economy was imminent, and that the purpose of the speed-up was to hasten, or strengthen, the recovery rather than to initiate an otherwise doubtful turning point. The timing of the speed-up and other circumstantial evidence suggest that, in addition to the recession, the fall congressional elections were a factor in stimulating these actions. There is nothing inherently wrong in this—it may, in fact, represent an example of a desirable influence of representative government on the behavior of its elected officials.

The speed-up attempt appears to have had no significant effect until the October-December quarter of 1954, and to have reached its peak impact in the first quarter of 1955. On the other hand, the increases, once initiated, helped stimulate recovery—the amounts added to defense spending were not negligible. The administration's willingness to undertake this action in the face of indications that an early upturn was likely perhaps may be regarded as a moderate advance over 1949 for the principle of compensatory fiscal policy.

The expenditure speed-up was reversed by the second quarter of 1955, but not in time to leave the fiscal year expenditure totals unaffected as originally planned. One lesson suggested by the 1954 experience with discretionary actions is that the potentialities of a

within-year speed-up of expenditures are—outside of defense programs—very limited. With few exceptions, the speed-ups achieved
in nondefense spending were in programs where planned annual
totals were lifted, such as in stockpiling and highways, and the defense speed-up also probably was not completely offset within the
same fiscal year.

Some progress may also be recorded for the response of Congress. It did not try to tailor expenditures to declining revenues, as
it had in 1949. And it exhibited somewhat greater acceptance than
in 1949 of arguments for compensatory fiscal policy in discussions
of possible tax cuts and in the reports of the Joint Committee on
the Economic Report.

As in 1949, concern over the maintenance of confidence in the
private sectors of the economy was a major factor shaping the administration's behavior. This concern is reflected in the administration's various descriptions of what it had done, was doing,
and could do if necessary—which, on examination, appear to be
slightly exaggerated in terms of direct income effects. This same
concern led to leveling the charges of "gloom and doom" at the
political opposition, and was definitely a factor in the delay and
modesty of discretionary expenditure actions.

The answer to the question of how prepared the government
was in case of a more serious decline is not entirely clear. Preparation of reserve actions started even before the downturn was detected in the statistics, and these were given considerable attention
in both the public and internal activities of the Council of Economic
Advisers. Nevertheless, the failure of the administration to prepare
Congress and the public for possible tax cut proposals would seem
to leave a rather large hole in such plans. Political debate was vigorous, both over those proposals for tax reduction that were sent
forward by the administration for reasons other than the recession
—even though they had been discussed for some time—and over
proposals in Congress for increased exemptions from individual
income tax. The vigor of that debate casts doubt on the speed with
which tax proposals made for purely stabilization purposes, without
extensive earlier discussion, could have been enacted.

Turning to the budget totals during the period of recession
and recovery, the actual federal surplus on a national income ac-

count basis reached a rate of $3.5 billion in the second quarter of 1955, compared with a deficit of $7 billion at the prerecession peak two years earlier. A switch of this magnitude—$10.5 billion—cannot be totally unrelated to the fact that unemployment in 1955 was substantially higher than in 1953 before the recession. Compared to unemployment of 2.6 percent of the labor force in 1953, unemployment in the middle of 1955 was still at a rate of 4 percent, where it subsequently remained. In view of the emergence of inflationary trends in wholesale prices in the latter half of 1955 and in consumer prices toward the middle of 1956, it is not argued here that this fiscal policy was inordinately restrictive. Perhaps partly because of these price trends, the 4 percent unemployment rate was widely regarded as reasonably full employment. But the sizable boom which developed in business and consumer outlays for durables in 1955 and 1956 was not generally anticipated in 1953 and 1954 when these fiscal policies were being formulated. In two later recessions, as will be seen, considerably less restrictive budget policies met with a far less favorable response by the economy.

Thus it appears that, in the 1954-55 recovery—somewhat as in that of 1949-50—a potentially too-tight fiscal policy was redeemed by the emergence of inflationary pressures from unexpected quarters.

CHAPTER VI

Recession and Recovery, 1957-1959

BEFORE IT WAS OVER, the recession which started in the middle of 1957—the third since 1948—impelled a Republican administration and a Democratic Congress into an unprecedented attempt to outdo each other in adding to the expenditure side of the federal budget. But the recession started in a period of nagging inflation, which persisted well into the period of decline; and the Eisenhower administration, which had gained respect for the inherent strength of the economy from its bout with the 1954 recession, tried initially to ride out the storm. Also playing a role in the slow response to contraction was the budgetary situation in the first half of 1957.

Budgetary Crisis

Even as it was being unveiled to the public, the fiscal 1958 budget, which President Eisenhower transmitted to Congress in January 1957, was criticized by his Secretary of the Treasury, George M. Humphrey, as too large. Proposed new spending authority and expenditures were up from the 1957 fiscal year by almost $3 billion. With an increase in revenues estimated at roughly the same amount, a surplus of $1.8 billion was forecast for fiscal 1958

188

—about what was expected for the year then under way. Predicting a "hair-curling" depression unless spending was brought under control, Secretary Humphrey expressed the hope that Congress would be able to cut the budget. And a few days later, the President at his press conference gave an impression of agreeing with Mr. Humphrey more than he did with the budget.[1] He promptly ordered the Director of the Bureau of the Budget to resurvey the expenditures of each department and agency in an effort to find additional savings.

Secretary Humphrey's alarm was toned down slightly on January 16, 1957, in a "Statement in Support of the President's Budget Message for the Fiscal Year 1958."[2] But in Congress in the weeks that followed, as reported in the *New York Times*,[3] Democrats vied with Republicans in their criticism of the budget, egged on by the press and public. A number of Democratic congressmen accused the administration of trying to shift the responsibility for curbing spending to the Congress (Jan. 25, 1957). And Senate Minority Leader William F. Knowland forecast $2 billion of congressional cuts (Feb. 10). The Chamber of Commerce asked for $5 billion in cuts (Feb. 4 and March 17); and the National Association of Manufacturers upped the ante to $8 billion (Feb. 17 and March 14). Democratic Senator Harry F. Byrd urged $5 billion in cuts to curb inflation; called the budget a "luxury budget padded with increased spending"; and forecast "disaster" if the budget was passed in its current form (Feb. 11 and March 22). Congressional mail was reported running heavily in favor of expenditure cuts (March 10 and April 2).

In March 1957, over Republican protests, Congress adopted House Resolution 190 calling for substantial reductions in the fiscal 1958 budget, and asking the President to tell Congress where this could best be done. In the meantime, from a stabilization point of view, the Joint Economic Committee and its staff both concluded in the report published at the end of February that economic condi-

[1] National Archives and Record Service, *Public Papers of the Presidents of the United States, 1957* (1959), pp. 72 ff. (Cited hereinafter as *Public Papers, 1957,* or with indications of subsequent dates.)

[2] *Annual Report of the Secretary of the Treasury, 1957,* p. 226. (Cited hereinafter as *Treasury Report, 1957,* or with an indication of subsequent dates.)

[3] The dates of the following references to the *New York Times* are given in the text.

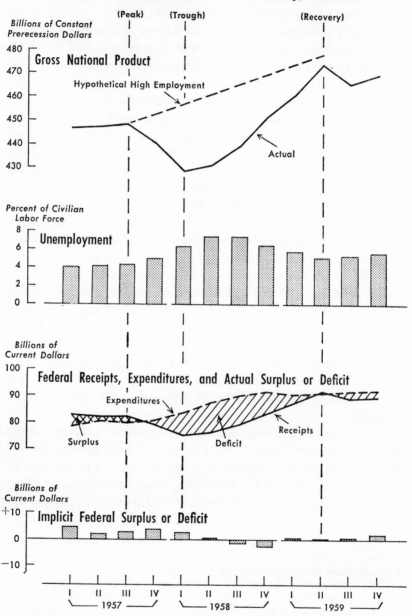

Chart 4
Gross National Product, Unemployment, and Federal Receipts and Expenditures, Quarterly, 1957-59

Billions of Constant
Prerecession Dollars

(Peak) (Trough) (Recovery)

Gross National Product

Hypothetical High Employment

Actual

480
470
460
450
440
430

Percent of Civilian
Labor Force

Unemployment

8
6
4
2
0

Billions of
Current Dollars

Federal Receipts, Expenditures, and Actual Surplus or Deficit

Expenditures

Surplus

Deficit

Receipts

100
90
80
70

Billions of
Current Dollars

Implicit Federal Surplus or Deficit

+10
0
−10

I   II   III   IV   I   II   III   IV   I   II   III   IV
└── 1957 ──┘   └── 1958 ──┘   └── 1959 ──┘

Source: Appendix D.

190

tions called for continued government restraints on the economy.[4]

The results of the administration's resurvey of the budget were sent to the Speaker of the House on April 18. The President listed possible reductions of $1.4 billion in spending authority. However, he made it clear that reductions in actual expenditures would be much smaller; that some of the authorizations would have to be restored in the following year; and that, with the apparent exception of some stretch-out in construction, the reductions were based on later estimates of workloads rather than program changes. In fact, the President specifically opposed cutting the defense budget below his recommendations; pointed to the many sectors of the budget where liability was fixed by law; and said in effect that significant reductions other than those proposed were not possible because program levels would be affected.[5]

Thus, rather belatedly, the President implicitly defended the substance, if not the estimates, in his budget. But Congress continued to show such zeal for reduction that the President felt compelled to deliver, on May 14, a radio and television address defending his amended budget, including the administration's controversial proposal of federal aid for school construction (p. 341). A little later, the President appealed for Senate restoration of the deep cuts the House of Representatives had made in the defense budget (p. 397). Meanwhile Senator Byrd called for the ouster of Budget Director Percival F. Brundage.[6]

Given these attitudes on the budget; the slender surplus that had been estimated for both fiscal 1957 and 1958; two years of reasonably satisfactory employment and considerable public discussion about the evils and seeming inevitability of inflation; and statements by various analysts that the inadequate use of fiscal restraints during the previous two years had placed too large a share of the anti-inflationary burden on monetary policy—given all this, it is small wonder that the large unbudgeted bulge in defense spending

[4] *Joint Economic Report,* Joint Economic Committee, 85 Cong. 1 sess. (February 1957). Cited hereinafter as *Joint Economic Report, 1957,* or with indications of subsequent dates. The name of the Joint Committee on the Economic Report had been shortened in 1956.

[5] *Public Papers, 1957,* p. 301. (In the following paragraph, page numbers in the text refer to this volume.)

[6] *New York Times,* May 21, 1957.

which occurred toward the end of fiscal 1957 caused considerable consternation on the part of the President and his administration.

Congress usually has followed the practice of full-funding with respect to military equipment—that is, it appropriates the entire estimated cost of a particular weapon system, or a large part of it, even when procurement is expected to stretch out over several years. There exists among military people the attitude that, once Congress has granted an appropriation, the actual time when it is subsequently used should be determined by technical military considerations. This is an understandable position, although one making for a certain amount of volatility in defense outlays. In any event, there had been little attention paid up to that time to the rate at which the military departments were signing contracts, and, although the administration had made its desires known with respect to expenditure results, it was in a poor position to enforce them. In response to rising defense orders, aircraft employment had increased sharply—reaching a peak in the spring of 1957 considerably above the levels of the Korean War—and deliveries to the Air Force rose faster than expected. By May 1957, it was clear that defense outlays for fiscal 1957 would run substantially ahead of the January estimates. Under federal budgetary procedures, the legislature has often displayed its frustration at being unable to control the actual rate of expenditure of appropriated funds. But on this occasion, even the executive branch was frustrated.

On June 1, 1957, Secretary of Defense Charles E. Wilson ordered the Air Force to cease its practice of "phased buying." According to this practice, instead of using appropriations for the full cost of a certain number of weapons, the Air Force used its funds for components of a larger number, thus giving the administration and Congress little alternative to further appropriations for the remaining essential components. A public controversy ensued, but the Air Force eventually agreed to the change. Meanwhile, Secretary Wilson ordered an across-the-board cut of $500 million in military contract awards. But these steps came too late to have much effect on disbursements in fiscal 1957. By the time the smoke cleared on June 30, 1957, defense outlays for the fiscal year were about $2.5 billion higher than the estimates made as recently as January.

As it turned out, a substantial shortfall in foreign aid expenditures and a large unbudgeted repayment to the Treasury by the Federal National Mortgage Association (FNMA), together with higher than anticipated budget receipts, permitted the administration to show a surplus for 1957 anyway. But a series of steps were taken to get defense spending back under control, and these took effect just about the time that the economy was, as became clear later, on the verge of recession. At the end of June 1957, both a stretch-out of weapons production and restrictions on overtime work by defense contractors were announced for the avowed purpose of cutting expenditures. And, in July, a series of Army and Air Force manpower cuts were announced to take effect over the coming year, starting immediately.[7]

The Joint Economic Committee's Subcommittee on Fiscal Policy had held hearings during the first half of June 1957,[8] at which witnesses were questioned on the economic impact of a (presumably hypothetical) substantial reduction in federal appropriations and spending in 1958. The economists who testified generally stressed the need for continued high defense spending. And, although there seemed to be general agreement that the economy had slowed down recently, most expressed the view that signs of recession were not such as to justify tax cuts in the face of an uncertain international situation.

The Contraction

The cyclical peak, as measured by either the gross national product (GNP) or the more detailed method of the National Bureau of Economic Research (NBER), came in the July-September quarter of 1957. From peak to trough, GNP declined by 3.4 percent from a seasonally adjusted annual rate of $448.3 billion (current dollars) in the third quarter of 1957 to $432.9 billion in the first quarter of 1958. With price levels generally rising during the contraction, the decline was somewhat greater in real terms (4.3 per-

[7] *New York Times,* June 28, July 17, and July 25, 1957.

[8] *Fiscal Policy Implications of the Economic Outlook and Budget Developments,* Hearings before the Subcommittee on Fiscal Policy, Joint Economic Committee, 85 Cong. 1 sess. (1957).

cent), making this the sharpest of the four postwar recessions. Unemployment rose from 4.3 percent of the labor force in the third quarter of 1957 to its postwar peak of 7.4 percent a year later.

The largest component of GNP change from peak to trough was business investment in inventories, which had been declining slowly for over a year and, after the third quarter of 1957, switched sharply to liquidation. Defense spending, as a result of the administration's economy efforts (congressional cuts in appropriations would not have had an effect this soon), declined by about $1 billion (annual rate) in October-December 1957, but began rising again in the first quarter of 1958. As Hickman points out,[9] expenditure figures understate the economic impact of the defense pinch because defense orders fell by more than expenditures. Nevertheless, declining defense was certainly a far less depressing factor than it had been in the 1953-54 contraction, even after allowance for partially offsetting tax cuts in the earlier contraction.

Disposable personal income was cushioned by the prompt and vigorous response of the built-in fiscal stabilizers, and by the corporate sector's absorption of a large part of the decrease in final demand. Consumer outlays declined little in total, with purchases of durables falling, nondurables holding steady, and services rising.

Because this was the first recession in the postwar period which was largely free of war influences, and because business fixed investment played an earlier and somewhat larger role in the decline, the 1957-58 recession frequently has been described as a "classical" or "text-book" example of business contraction. That it was arrested within two quarters, and before any deliberate correctives other than monetary ease were in effect, lent support (after the episode was history) to a growing belief that the economy is less susceptible to serious prolonged depression than it once was. Nevertheless, there were dark moments for officials before the 1957-58 recession was over.

Business news was spotty in July and August 1957, and the financial press began to ask whether the economy was headed for recession. The *New York Times* reported on July 3 that Secretary

[9] Bert G. Hickman, *Growth and Stability of the Postwar Economy* (Brookings Institution, 1960), p. 153.

of the Treasury Humphrey told the Senate Finance Committee he could see some "leveling off" because of the tight curbs on credit, but he doubted this would result in recession. In early August, the new Secretary of the Treasury—Robert B. Anderson—informed the chairmen of the House Ways and Means Committee and Senate Finance Committee that the administration would try to live within the existing debt ceiling of $275 billion.[10] Given the touch-and-go situation with respect to projected receipts and expenditures, this decision on the debt limit meant that expenditures would have to be controlled closely. On August 9, a cut of 5 percent in advance "progress payments" to defense contractors was announced, to take effect September 1; in the same month, a series of arsenals and bases were closed down or announced for closing. Also on August 9, a round of increases in the discount rate from 3 percent to 3½ percent started at some of the Federal Reserve banks. At the time, there were rumors of a rift between the New York Bank and the Board of Governors in Washington over whether an increase just then was proper. The New York and Chicago Federal Reserve banks waited two weeks before going along with the change.

By September 1957, recession talk was increasingly linked with the defense cutbacks, a number of analysts blaming the cutback in progress payments for the unfavorable business outlook. That defense contractors could reasonably doubt whether they would be paid in full on delivery may seem strange. But the complaints to this effect were so strong that the new Secretary of Defense, Neil H. McElroy, felt it necessary to issue a statement assuring contractors that the government was not planning to avoid payment altogether.

Inflation, however, was still worrying the administration. And the White House announced on September 14 that the President was beginning regular meetings on the inflation problem with the

[10] The administration may have been convinced, on the basis of private conversations, that an increase in the debt limit would be strenuously opposed in Congress. This would not have been unusual, however, and need not have been overriding if the administration really believed an increase was necessary. The other important element in the situation was that, the administration having decided that defense spending should be held down, but not having altogether convinced the military services of this necessity, a tight debt limit would constitute an important additional reason for economy.

Chairman of the Federal Reserve Board, William McChesney Martin, Jr., Secretary of the Treasury Anderson, Chairman Raymond J. Saulnier of the Council of Economic Advisers (CEA), and White House Assistant Gabriel Hauge. In fairness it should be noted that, while evidence of the recession was accumulating, so far there had been no sign of let-up on the price front. The persistence of "cost-push" inflation in the face of declining demand was being discussed as a major public problem in private as well as official quarters. Moreover, the leading indicators and diffusion indexes leaned on heavily by CEA Chairman Saulnier, after having signaled "recession" in May 1957, turned up again, and did not turn down decisively until late in 1957.[11]

In October 1957, after Congress adjourned, the *Midyear Review of the 1958 Budget* was issued. It showed, for the first time since 1953, a reduction in spending authority below the amounts initially recommended by the President. The Democratic-controlled Congress had not stopped at the President's suggestions, but had made numerous additional reductions, including a cut of $3 billion in defense appropriations.[12]

October marked a policy turning point in several ways. For one, the Russian sputnik heralded an early reversal of the defense cutback. For another, the Federal Reserve policy switched to active monetary ease through open market purchases of government bonds in order to take pressure off bank reserves.[13] The *New York Times,*

[11] See Charles J. V. Murphy, "The White House and the Recession," *Fortune,* Vol. 57 (May 1958), for a discussion of the administration's gradual recognition of the recession.

[12] Although the *Midyear Review* did not include an anticipated supplemental request for defense appropriations, this does not necessarily establish official administration acceptance of the congressional cuts. This was a Bureau of the Budget publication, not a presidential document, and the rule followed was to include anticipated supplementals only if needed to meet expenditures required by law. The fact is that President Eisenhower and members of his administration had ambivalent attitudes. They did not want a real reduction in the defense effort, and the President had earlier protested against the House cuts, but neither did they want an unbalanced budget or the embarrassment of asking for an increase in the debt limit.

[13] Testimony of the Chairman of the Board of Governors of the Federal Reserve System, *Hearings on the Economic Report of the President, 1958,* Joint Economic Committee, 85 Cong. 2 sess. (1958). (Cited hereinafter as *Hearings of the Joint Committee, 1958,* or with indications of subsequent dates.)

on September 3, had reported that "government economists" viewed any new upsurge in the economy as dependent on tax cuts. And at least one staff recommendation is known to have been received at policy levels in October proposing consideration of a tax reduction to stimulate the economy as part of the President's program then under preparation for the coming January annual messages.[14] Responding to a question at his October 30 news conference, the President acknowledged that unemployment had increased and there was no doubt the economy was "taking a breather." However, there were mixed trends, he said, and the government was watching developments very closely. He did not think a need for tax or spending changes was indicated.[15]

By November, discussion in the financial press and in business publications had switched to speculation over how severe the recession would be, and whether it would be over by mid-1958. By then, the fact that the cutback in defense orders had temporarily carried below levels programmed for the longer run—together with the post-sputnik revision of these levels—promised an early sharp rise in defense orders. On November 13, the President in a radio-television address said needed increases in defense outlays could not be fully offset by economies in domestic programs. He warned that national security should not be sacrificed in worship of a balanced budget, although a balanced budget was important "over the long term." On January 7, 1958, immediately after Congress reconvened, and a week before transmission of the regular budget for fiscal 1959, the President sent Congress a request for supplemental defense authorization amounting to $1.3 billion for fiscal 1958.

In retrospect, the defense economies turned out to be ill-timed. But the defense cutback was mild and short-lived by 1953 standards. Furthermore, there would have been some decline in defense orders and some drop in aircraft employment at about that time, whether or not the administration felt pressed by short-run budgetary considerations. Several years later, in describing the run-up in aircraft employment which culminated in the spring of 1957, Assistant Secretary of Defense Charles J. Hitch told the Joint Economic

[14] Information received in conversation with former CEA and Bureau of the Budget officials.
[15] *Public Papers, 1957*, p. 228.

Committee: "Actually, there was no solid long-term basis for this increase in aircraft industry employment. The defense programs then contemplated could not by any stretch of the imagination support for very long such a high level of employment in that industry."[16] Moreover, the decline in defense orders probably would have ended about when it did regardless of sputnik, because orders had been brought into line with longer range plans.

Finally, Congress was even more zealous at that time than the executive branch in cutting expenditures, defense outlays in particular, although the reduced appropriations had a much slower effect than the administration's actions.[17]

The 1958 Program of the President

The State of the Union Address, January 9, 1958,[18] was largely devoted to two issues which far outweighed all others—national security and peace. The President acknowledged some decline in output and employment in the closing months of the year, but said there were "solid grounds for confidence that economic growth will be resumed without an extended interruption." Continuing, he said the government, "constantly alert to signs of weakening in any part

[16] *Hearings of the Joint Economic Committee, 1961,* p. 620.

[17] Some accounts of the 1957 defense slowdown emphasize the role of the tight public debt limit. (See Hickman, *op. cit.,* p. 153; A. E. Holmans, *United States Fiscal Policy, 1945-1959* [London: Oxford University Press, 1961], pp. 263-64; Marshall Robinson, *The National Debt Ceiling* [Brookings Institution, 1959], pp. 38-46; Walter W. Heller, "Why a Federal Debt Limit?", Proceedings of the Fifty-first Annual Conference on Taxation, National Tax Association [1959], pp. 252-53.) But this view puts the cart before the horse. The administration had decided to hold down defense before it decided not to seek an increase in the debt limit. It is quite possible, of course, that had the administration pressed for an increase in the teeth of the economy drive then taking place in Congress it would not have been successful. But since the administration did not, it seems at least as reasonable to regard the role of the debt limit, in this case at least, as more symbolic than real—a reminder of the importance attached to budgetary balance and fiscal prudence as independent policy goals. The issue is of some consequence, since the conventional view of the 1957 defense slowdown would seem to imply that a great blow for budget flexibility could be struck by simply eliminating public debt limits. Without endorsing the principle of debt limits, budget flexibility appears to be a good deal more difficult than this.

[18] *Public Papers, 1958,* pp. 2 ff.

of our economy, always stands ready, with its full power, to take any appropriate further action to promote renewed business expansion."

A few weeks later, the President's *Economic Report* said[19] GNP had been declining and unemployment rising in the closing months of 1957. It forecast a further decline of plant and equipment outlays—although the magnitude and duration of the decline were uncertain—and said foreign demand was expected to exert a moderately contractive influence for the time being. On the brighter side, it pointed out that personal income and consumer expenditures had declined but little; the rate of inventory reduction might be no greater than had already taken place; residential construction and state and local government outlays were expected to rise; and defense orders and expenditures would also increase. All in all, the *Economic Report* stated (pp. 49-50), "these considerations suggest that the decline in business activity need not be prolonged, and that economic growth can be resumed without extended interruption."

The reversal of monetary policy starting in mid-October and certain actions on housing credit taken in January 1958 were described in the *Economic Report* (p. 8) as deliberate steps to counter the decline. The Federal Housing Administration (FHA) had reduced down-payment requirements twice during 1957, but these steps were characterized—accurately—as efforts to moderate the impact on housing of general measures to restrain inflation (p. 7). In this connection, the *Report* also focused attention on the dilemma for policy makers posed by the fact that consumer prices had been rising strongly throughout 1957, with no sign of faltering:

If fiscal and credit policies are sufficiently stern to keep the price level from rising, there are risks of economic dislocation, an unnecessarily slow rate of economic growth, and extreme and inequitable pressures on some who are not themselves contributors to the inflation of costs and prices. On the other hand, if economically unwarranted increases in wage rates or prices are validated by credit and fiscal policies, a persistent decline in the value of the dollar results (p. 9).

[19] *Economic Report of the President, 1958.* (Cited hereinafter as *Economic Report, 1958,* with indications of subsequent dates.) Page numbers in the following paragraphs also refer to this report.

The administration's January recommendations for further expansionary action were also rather sparse. Included in the President's program at that time was a proposed change in the tax law affecting small business and a longer lease on life for the Small Business Administration. Also requested were increases in FHA commitment authority and permissible size of insured loans, but this proposal could have been safely forecast no matter what the state of the economy. Moreover, a major motive for this and similar proposals made by the administration—such as an increase in the permissible interest rate on home loans guaranteed by the Veterans Administration (VA) and the elimination of discount controls—was said to be the use, where possible, of insurance and guarantee programs as a substitute for direct federal loans.

The President's Budget Message[20] expressed confidence that the economy would soon turn up because of rising defense orders, increased state and local outlays, technological advances, expanding consumer needs and desires, and "government policies." What these government policies were is difficult to discern. Elsewhere, the message listed among principles shaping the budget fiscal soundness; economy in expenditures; and, in periods of high business activity, a balanced budget and debt reduction—implying that, for the budget year starting six months later, business activity was expected to be at a high level. Proposed defense expenditures were up about $1 billion from the current year. Economy was emphasized with respect to nondefense outlays, for which increases and decreases were roughly offsetting.

The federal government's share of the expense of certain grant-aided state and local government programs was to be reduced. Direct federal lending activity was to be decreased by raising interest rates or using federal guarantees of private loans. In the natural resource field, the budget policy was to curtail, or stretch out, construction where this could be done "without impairing the value of investments previously made." Because continuing work on going projects would require increased expenditures, no new water re-

[20] *Budget of the United States Government for the Fiscal Year Ending June 30, 1959* (January 1958), pp. M-5, M-9-M-10. (Cited hereinafter as *Budget, Fiscal 1959*, with indications of subsequent dates.)

source projects were to be started. The general aid-to-education proposals of the previous year, which had been rejected by Congress, were replaced by less controversial, and less costly, proposals to aid science education. Revision and reduction of taxes were described as desirable "when possible." In the meantime, a one-year extension of corporate and excise tax rates, scheduled for reduction July 1, 1958, was recommended to help balance the budget.

The current "readjustments" in the economy were blamed for the downward revision of revenue estimates and the small deficit estimated for the 1958 fiscal year. The assumption of an early sharp recovery in the economy, according to the administration, permitted a revenue estimate for fiscal 1959 that would be high enough—in conjunction with proposed increases of $700 million in postal rates, the extension of corporate and excise tax rates, and other proposed legislation—to produce a small surplus. While necessarily based on an assumption of something less than full employment, the estimate of fiscal 1959 revenues subsequently turned out to be too optimistic by over $6 billion.

The seeming inconsistency between revenue estimates and the tone of the President's *Economic Report* is partly attributable to "fiscal politics." There was discussion at the time of the possibility that showing a balanced budget would forestall expenditure cuts—cuts which would have been a perverse reaction to recession.[21] Inconsistency between the *Economic Report* and the President's

[21] Consider the following exchange when CEA Chairman Saulnier testified before the Joint Economic Committee on January 27, 1958 (*Hearings of the Joint Committee, 1958*, p. 9):

"Mr. Saulnier: One of the comforting implications of optimism in these matters is that by and large, optimism about the future encourages one to do the things that will help make the optimistic expectation come true.

"Senator Douglas: In other words, by blowing on the thermometer you raise the temperature.

"Mr. Saulnier: Not at all, Sir. These questions about revenues to be raised 18 months ahead are matters about which there can be fairly wide difference of opinion. All I am saying is that when you make your judgement as to what figure seems to you best within that range, that if you lean towards the optimistic view, you may be encouraged in certain respects to do things that will help your optimism to be realized."

Also see the account of Saulnier's participation in the budget process given by Murphy, "The White House and the Recession," *op. cit.*

policy proposals in the *Budget* perhaps may be explained partly by the much longer lead time involved in preparing the *Budget*. Recognition of recession dawns slowly, in small increments, and it is not easy to translate economic forecasts into a coordinated expenditure policy on short notice. More basically, however, the difference demonstrates again the way in which long-range program goals often conflict with short-run stabilization needs. The proposals to transfer certain costs from the federal government to the states and to individuals reflected the general thinking of the administration, and also was consistent with freeing resources for expected needs of the defense and space research programs.

The absence of proposals for tax reduction, however, is harder to explain. It might seem that a tax cut at that juncture would have been eminently consistent with the administration's general philosophy and its specific recommendations for the coming year. True, the defense situation posed uncertainties which perhaps could not be fully covered in the allowance for contingencies, and there was good reason to believe that Congress would not go along with various economy proposals, of which the increase in postal rates, at least, had sizable budgetary implications. On the other hand, one way to enhance the acceptability of economy proposals is to tie them to tax reductions.

Partly accounting for the absence of proposals for tax cuts were the rather strange guidelines apparently held by the President's chief fiscal advisers. George M. Humphrey was probably reflecting what he thought was administration policy—not only his own views —when, in January 1957, while still Secretary of the Treasury, he said that, if a program of strict economy in expenditures were adhered to, "we can, a year hence, give consideration not only to some further payment on the public debt but also to further tax reductions. This, of course, must be conditioned upon continuation of our present prosperity."[22] And, six months later, in June 1957, Budget Director Percival Brundage had given an even more stringent rule which, if taken literally, would rule out tax cuts except under a most unlikely combination of circumstances. Tax reductions should be undertaken, he said, "only when our budget

---

[22] *Treasury Report, 1957*, p. 226.

surplus and the economic outlook justify them."[23] Also noteworthy in this connection are the CEA Chairman's attitude toward tax cuts. According to an account given by a *Fortune* magazine reporter,[24] Saulnier, prior to the sputnik, had hoped that proposals for tax cuts could be timed to counteract the recession, but he regarded sputnik as having effectively eliminated the use of tax cuts as an antirecession tool. While all these individuals, on other occasions, had expressed less difficult rules for tax cuts, it seems clear that the administration had no definite plan of action.

Whatever its reasons, the administration was to pay dearly for its failure to recommend tax reduction in January. Without its own counterrecession program, it proved impossible for the administration to resist proposals for increased expenditures put forward on a piecemeal basis by Congress (and executive agencies) as the business news and outlook grew bleaker.

One of the more interesting aspects of the 1958 recession is the extent to which the Eisenhower administration was carried along by the force of events. It accepted, indeed embraced, actions and policies to stimulate the economy which were contrary to its expressed wishes and advance injunctions, and for which its spokesmen later expressed regret. Thus, at an early stage, when still opposed to antirecession actions, the administration specified benchmarks for performance of the economy that would be considered satisfactory and would not require government action. Although the recovery started sooner, and proceeded more briskly, than required by these benchmarks, the administration endorsed various expenditure increases without waiting to test its forecasts. Moreover, this apparent loss of nerve came in spite of frequent statements that confidence was more important to recovery than government action and strong opposition to "pump-priming" as a matter of principle. Perhaps most interesting of all, the President and other administration spokesmen specifically expressed a preference for actions stimulating private activity rather than public, but when the time came accepted a variety of increases of government expenditures and opposed tax cuts.

[23] *Fiscal Policy Implications of the Economic Outlook and Budget Developments, op. cit.*, p. 267.
[24] Murphy, *op. cit.*

The Great Debate—January to March

The period from January through early March 1958 was given to debate rather than action. The evolution of congressional and administration attitudes went through several stages.[25] At the outset, Congress received the budget in a different spirit from its predecessor. Opposition to nondefense expenditure cuts was reported (Jan. 15) among congressional Republicans, and even the Appropriations Committee was reported (Feb. 15) to feel that the President had gone too far in cutting domestic outlays.

During January, the President's statements implied there was no immediate need for action to fight recession, and at Republican party meetings, blamed politics for recession talk. He indicated on January 15 at his news conference (p. 96) that if something happened to unbalance the budget, he would prefer a moderate deficit to increased taxes, stating that "it would be a bad time to raise taxes, because you want the economy to have a little needle, a needle rather than a check rein on it." At the same time, he described monetary policy as a powerful tool and said there was no need for other actions. At a Republican dinner on January 20, he apparently thought inflation still was a more potent political topic than recession—calling inflation a sinister threat to prosperity, warning of danger in the attitude that accepts inflation as inevitable or desirable—and made no reference to employment trends (p. 115). And on January 31, again speaking to Republicans (p. 138), he had unkind words for the "political Cassandras" who "pop up regularly to suggest that deep depression is just around the corner, and only panicky governmental intervention on a massive scale can stem the disaster."

Over the preceding half year, the Treasury had discovered that living within the public debt limit of $275 billion had reduced cash balances at times to "distressingly low" levels,[26] and with expendi-

[25] The main sources drawn upon in the discussion of this three-month period are *Public Papers, 1958* (to which page numbers in the text refer) and the *New York Times* (for which dates are given in the text).

[26] *Treasury Report, 1958*, p. 245.

tures expected to rise and receipts to fall, the administration sought a $5 billion (temporary) increase in the limit as soon as Congress reconvened in January 1958. Despite a reported move in the Senate Finance Committee to trim the amount, the increase was enacted in February. During January, Secretary of the Treasury Anderson had publicly said he was opposed to tax cuts at the time, but that the administration would act to prevent the slump from worsening —with tax cuts if necessary.

During February, the debate increased in intensity.[27] Senate Democrats and the Democratic Advisory Council attacked the administration for failure to act against the recession. Meanwhile, the President forecast an upturn "toward the middle or just after the middle of the year," and said that a tax cut could be used if business did not turn up as fast as expected (p. 147). On the Democratic side, Senators Hubert H. Humphrey and Mike Mansfield urged that action be taken, and former President Truman deplored the lack of leadership in the fight against recession. Secretary of Commerce Sinclair Weeks accused the Democrats of gambling with prosperity for political advantage.

On February 12, 1958, prompted by January unemployment statistics that were worse than expected, the President released a prepared statement on the economic situation, forecasting that the decline would slow by March and recovery would begin "later this year." An accompanying "fact sheet" listed steps already taken, and the President promised to take additional useful public works and buildings "off the shelf" if needed. The fact sheet consisted, for the most part, of details on the administration's program in the January budget, plus a previously unannounced plan of $100 million in borrowing authority for construction in the District of Columbia over a five-year period. Also cited was the President's directive of the previous day for the Postmaster General to present to Congress a three- to five-year program of post office modernization. The administration still was not willing to deliberately unbalance the budget, as indicated by the fact that the post office modernization was made contingent on enactment of the January recommenda-

[27] See, especially, the *New York Times* of February 1, 3, 7, 10, and 13, 1958.

tion for a postal rate of 5 cents for out-of-town mail (pp. 151-52)—a proposal which had little chance of being accepted.

In mid-February, eleven Democratic governors sent a telegram asking the President to open an antirecession drive (Feb. 14). Republican Senator Jacob K. Javits spoke up for an antirecession program; and Arthur F. Burns, former chairman of the CEA, was reported in the *New York Times* to believe that the recession would continue until the government intervened on a larger scale (Feb. 16). President Eisenhower, replying to the Democratic governors, took the position that only a loss of confidence could turn the recession into a deep and protracted decline, and pointed out the responsibility of persons in positions of trust and authority to act so as to strengthen, not weaken, confidence (pp. 169-70).

The tempo of criticism of the administration's reaction to recession stepped up. The AFL-CIO charged the administration with seeking to tranquilize the public; the Democratic National Committee attacked Eisenhower's "Hoover-like approach"; and former President Truman asserted that five years of Republican misrule had brought the country to the brink of depression. On the other side, Republican congressional leaders, after a White House briefing, opposed tax cuts or "spending orgies" in view of the expected upturn (Feb. 17, 19, 22, and 23).

The signal for a change came when the President, on February 24, 1958, speaking to the National Food Conference, advocated pushing worthy, approved federal projects. His comments had the earmarks of the kind of extemporaneous expression of opinion he had made at cabinet meetings in 1954, which his administration had failed to act upon for several months. Having been made publicly this time, his remarks promptly became administration policy. At the same time, the President warned against getting trapped into spending that had no useful purpose except to hand out something, and said the country needed confidence more than federal government projects (p. 175). Next day, Budget Director Brundage, speaking in New York (as reported by the *New York Times,* Feb. 26), expressed his personal preference for tax cuts over new public works starts, and the Joint Committee on Internal

Revenue Taxation released a staff study of the revenue effects of alternative types of tax cuts.[28]

President Eisenhower told his news conference, February 26, 1958, an upturn in job opportunities in March would be taken as a signal of the beginning of the end of the recession, but he was not necessarily forecasting even a gradual upturn in March—merely an upturn by midyear. In answer to one question, the President denied that tax cuts should be considered only as a "last resort," but a little later he asserted "certainly you don't want to go into a tax cut until that is necessary to bring about an upturn." He explained the meager initial economic impact of new public works starts, and the superiority in this respect of accelerating work on projects already under way. He reiterated his belief that the time had come to accelerate useful projects already in process, and repeated the favorite administration theme that confidence was an important determinant of the level of economic activity (pp. 188, 190, and 192).

After several weeks of hearings, the Joint Economic Committee was ready on February 27 to release its own report on the economic situation.[29] The majority favored further actions to ease credit, a selective increase in expenditures, but no tax cut unless it appeared that the other measures would be inadequate to stop the recession. Democratic Senator Paul H. Douglas, however, filed a dissent recommending immediate tax cuts.

The debate continued into March. Republican National Committee Chairman Meade Alcorn labeled the Democrats as "panic mongers" trying to weaken the economy, but Republican Senator Javits spoke out in favor of stepped-up federal spending (March 1 and 4). On March 5, President Eisenhower pointed out that the private economy had a way of steering its own course and that the federal government was not, and could not be made, the most important factor in the economy. He acknowledged at that news conference that there was no specific proposal for a tax cut "on the shelf," and the proper kind of tax cut would have to be decided if and when the time came (pp. 199-200).

[28] *Alternative Plans for Tax Relief for Individuals,* Staff Report of the Joint Committee on Internal Revenue Taxation, 85 Cong. 2 sess. (February 25, 1958).
[29] *Joint Economic Report, 1958.*

Combating Recession

Finally, the ice was broken, on March 8, 1958, in the form of separate presidential letters to the Senate and the House minority leaders, William Knowland and Joseph Martin.[30] In them, the President said that the proper role of government in the growth and vigor of the economy "must necessarily be to stimulate private production and employment, not to substitute public spending for private spending, nor to extend public domination over private activity." He opposed the recent upsurge of "pump-priming" schemes and talk which evidenced "lack of faith in the inherent vitality of our free economy."

The letters went on to list certain steps being taken by the administration and other steps proposed for congressional action —all described as "orderly accelerations of programs that are genuinely needed in the public interest, have long been planned, and are already approved." The administrative actions listed were an acceleration of civil public works projects; the release of $200 million from the President's discretionary fund for FNMA special assistance mortgage purchases; the award of more defense contracts to labor surplus areas; an increase in the discount allowance on VA-guaranteed mortgages; and a liberalization of lending rules by Federal Home Loan Banks to savings and loan associations. Proposed for congressional action were supplemental appropriations for the coming fiscal year to allow the speed-up in public works to continue into fiscal 1959; a three-year suspension of expenditure limitations in the Highway Act to permit apportioning an additional $2.2 billion of federal funds to the states over a three-year period; and a temporary extension of the duration period for persons who exhausted their unemployment benefits.

Since highway grants are paid from a trust fund financed wholly by earmarked highway user charges, increased expenditures would also require legislation to increase highway tax rates, divert general fund revenues, or provide borrowing authority for the trust fund.

[30] *Public Papers, 1958*, pp. 208-11.

But the President failed to suggest at this time any means for financing the highway speed-up. This issue was not resolved until the following year, and its resolution involved a sharp reversal of the net expansionary stimulus from the highway program.

By early March 1958, then, the administration—without waiting to test its forecasts—moved to increase expenditures. The fact that various bills for new public works were being pushed strongly in Congress on grounds of reducing unemployment played no small part in this decision. The administration's action did not noticeably diminish congressional activity on this score, and by the end of the session, over 25 such bills had been introduced. Some came dangerously close—from the administration's point of view—to enactment.

A few days later, on March 12, a budget amendment was transmitted asking for $25 million to be immediately available for loans for small reclamation projects, and on March 14 the January request for funds for hospital construction grants was amended. The latter raised the fiscal 1959 request to the level already enacted for 1958. This, it is safe to assume, was the minimum Congress would have added without being asked.

The Senate, prodded by Senator Lyndon B. Johnson, joined the parade by passing, on March 14, a concurrent resolution asking that military construction programs also be accelerated as rapidly as possible (within existing authorizations) in the interest of reducing unemployment. The House gave its approval five days later.[31]

On March 18, 1958, the President described to a Republican Women's Conference steps already undertaken as projects that were useful and needed in themselves, which would start quickly and provide employment quickly, and would not drag out so long as to compete with the needs of private enterprise when recovery came. Considering inclusion on the administration's list of a three- to five-year post office modernization program, a three-year suspension of highway expenditure limitations, and a speed-up of urban renewal (in which projects typically last five to seven years), the President's emphasis on speed and reversibility probably indicated merely a preference for his particular proposals over alternatives being dis-

[31] Senate Concurrent Resolution 69, 85 Cong. 2 sess. (1958).

cussed in Congress. Significantly, the President went on to pledge any measure—even tax reduction—if "such action should prove desirable and necessary—that will assist healthy economic recovery."[32] His conditions for further action no longer included the requirement that they be necessary to initiate a turning point.

The following day, in letters to the Administrator of the Housing and Home Finance Agency (HHFA) and the Secretary of Agriculture (released simultaneously to the press), the President initiated five more steps to speed up expenditures within the previously expressed ground rules that appropriations and authorizations were already available:

1. Reserves were being released on $100 million in balances of authorizations for the public facility loan program, and the HHFA was to broaden loan eligibility and take steps to accelerate the starting of new projects.

2. Starts on college housing were to be expedited where planning was completed or substantially completed, again liberalizing loan eligibility where necessary.

3. Urban renewal projects were to be expedited, broadening the types of construction eligible for authorized financing where necessary.

4. In cooperation with local authorities, steps were to be taken to speed construction of public housing under annual contributions contracts.

5. The Rural Electrification Administration (REA) was to encourage faster construction by REA borrowers and loans to REA consumers for purchase of electrical equipment.

That same day, the Senate Democratic Policy Committee pledged speedy action on the administration's antirecession measures in a "nonpartisan" spirit.

Additional administrative actions were announced on March 20. The Secretary of Agriculture said loan criteria were being liberalized, and loans encouraged by the Farmers Home Administration for farm homes and buildings and by the Commodity Credit Corporation (CCC) for on-farm grain storage facilities. The Secretary of Commerce announced fiscal 1959 allocations to states for airport construction. This announcement was earlier in the year than usual, although the amounts were as budgeted in January. The Federal Housing Administration issued instructions that local fee appraisers be used to supplement FHA's salaried staff in the processing of the heavy volume of applications for appraisal. And the Small Business Administration reduced its underwriting fee on deferred participation loans.

On March 25, Congress received the administration's plan for temporary extension of regular unemployment benefit periods by 50 percent, to be administered by the states and financed by interest-free federal advances repayable within five years. The following day, the President asked Congress to authorize advance procurement of supplies and equipment by civilian agencies, to be charged against planned appropriations for 1959. At the same time, the Bureau of the Budget instructed agencies to speed the placement of planned orders under already available authorizations, and the General Services Administration (GSA) raised its limits on stock levels. The Department of Defense, however, was specifically excluded from both orders.

The President discussed taxes at his March 26 news conference.[33] He did not exclude tax cuts as a possibility, but said this was such a serious step that he was not going to be stampeded into it. He then revealed that the Secretary of the Treasury had reached an agreement with the Democratic congressional leaders that nothing would be done on taxes before bipartisan consultation. Expressing his belief that the economy was then at, or near, bottom, the President said his hesitancy on tax cuts was based on the possibility of substantially increased expenditures—if various spending proposals being put forward were approved—and on the desire to avoid large and continuing deficits. "We have got to think of the years to come as well as the immediate month in which we are living."

The "gentlemen's agreement" on taxes by leaders of the legislative and executive branches was primarily a move to head off a threatening race between Republicans and Democrats over who would be able to claim the credit, in an election year, for cutting

---

[33] *Public Papers, 1958,* pp. 234-36.

taxes.[34] Although Treasury Secretary Anderson described it later as an act of prudence and restraint, some administration officials, at that time, were known to favor explorations with Congress of ways to cut taxes, rather than ways not to. Some members of both the executive and legislative branches felt that further action might be required, and that available flexibility on the expenditure side of the budget was rapidly being exhausted. The negotiations reportedly uncovered a fundamental cleavage in tax philosophy, with Secretary Anderson leaning toward investment incentives such as depreciation liberalization and the Democratic chairman of the Ways and Means Committee, Wilbur Mills, toward splitting the first bracket of the individual income tax.[35] To some extent then, the agreement may have reflected recognition on both sides that debate over the proper way to cut taxes would be bitter and time-consuming, which should be avoided unless absolutely necessary. In any event, the agreement put an end to tax cuts for the duration of the recession and recovery.

On April 1, 1958, the President signed S. 3418, an act "to stimulate residential construction," with misgivings about some of its features.[36] He endorsed the temporary extension of the loan guarantee program for World War II veterans, liberalization of FHA down-payment terms, and several other provisions, but vigorously objected to the authorization of $1 billion for FNMA special assistance purchase at par of FHA-insured and VA-guaranteed mortgage loans on new houses costing $13,500 or less. The President argued, probably correctly under prevailing conditions of easy money, that this would merely substitute public for private funds.

A series of public announcements in early April set forth some of the current plans and expected accomplishments under the various speed-ups. On April 2, the Department of Health, Education, and Welfare (HEW) announced that state, local, and private contracts for medical research facilities, hospitals, and waste treatment plans would be given priority in the allocation of federal funds to projects which could be started quickly. On April 4, the White

[34] Murphy, *op. cit.*

[35] Information obtained in conversation with former CEA and Treasury Department officials.

[36] *Public Papers, 1958*, pp. 257-58.

House announced various actions initiated under the recent housing legislation to stimulate home building. On April 5, GSA announced its plans to channel orders to areas of labor surplus; and, on April 8, the Post Office Department announced a speed-up of private construction of post offices under lease-purchase arrangements (with no mention this time of higher postal rates as a prerequisite).

Recovery Begins

The view that the decline was slowing and would soon end was put forward in late March and early April by various private sources, such as the monthly reviews of the Chase Manhattan Bank and the First National City Bank of New York. Although only dimly perceived at the time, April 1958 marked the cyclical turning point (as measured by the National Bureau of Economic Research). The trough in gross national product had actually been reached earlier—in the January-March quarter. However, preliminary Commerce Department estimates showing an increase in GNP in the second quarter were not available to policy officials until the end of May. Although for two more quarters consumer purchases of durables remained steady and business fixed investment continued to decline, total production and income rose sharply from the first quarter of 1958 through the first half of 1959.

Federal outlays increased during 1958 under a variety of anti-recession programs (described later) and for several programs not related to the recession, such as defense, farm price supports, and civilian and military pay raises. Residential construction played an outstanding part in the recovery, responding to generally easy money market conditions, reinforced by federal government mortgage purchases undertaken as an antirecession move.

By 1959, consumer durables and business plant and equipment were giving an additional lift to the recovery, which received a further impetus in the second quarter of 1959 from inventory building in anticipation of the impending steel strike. The unemployment rate of 5.1 percent reached in the second quarter of 1959 held only temporarily, and subsequently turned out to be as close as the economy was to come for some time to the prerecession rate.

On April 8, 1958, the White House released a statement that the March pickup in jobs[37] and the leveling off of unemployment indicated that the decline in economic activity was slowing down.[38] Ignoring possible anticipatory effects, none of the discretionary actions—with the exceptions of the January change in housing rules and some speed-up in tax refunds—had been in effect in time to affect the March employment figures. The following day, as reported in the *New York Times* of April 10, Budget Director Maurice H. Stans forecast a large deficit for the next few years as a result of the antirecession measures, and warned against further spending increases.

An interagency group of staff economists meeting under CEA auspices cautiously forecast in mid-April that GNP in the second quarter would be up slightly from the first quarter, marking the end of the decline. But the group felt that recovery would be slow enough, and the risks of further decline large enough, that further policy action was not likely to be inflationary and might be helpful to the recovery. Although not unanimous, the group's recommendation of cuts in excise taxes and a temporary reduction in individual income tax rates was sent forward to policy levels in several agencies.[39]

During April, the President and Congress continued to have differences on the state of the economy and the kind of legislation which was needed. A Rivers and Harbors and Flood Control authorization bill was vetoed by the President on April 15 on grounds that it authorized too many projects not adequately investigated, others which were deemed unsound, and still others for which inadequate local cost sharing was provided. The President did not agree that the bill would help counter the recession, pointing to the long lead time in starting construction from scratch, and the $5 billion of other authorized projects on which planning was much further advanced. Instead, he asked Congress to act quickly

[37] As measured by payroll statistics of the Bureau of Labor Statistics; nonfarm employment as estimated by the Census Bureau was down.

[38] *Public Papers, 1958,* p. 293. (In following paragraphs, page numbers in the text refer to this report.)

[39] Information based on conversations with former officials of the Council of Economic Advisers.

on legislation requested in January raising the authorization limits on certain projects already under construction where 1958 and 1959 requirements would exceed authorized amounts. This veto aroused sharp criticism of administration indifference to unemployment; and eleven days later the President sent letters to the Republican congressional leaders dividing the projects in the vetoed bill into two lists—those requiring modification before being acceptable, and those that should be passed right away.

The Highway Act of 1958 (P.L. 85-381), giving the President his requested suspension of expenditure limitations for three years, was passed on April 16, but it gave the President an additional antirecession program he had not requested. This was a $400 million authorization for grants to states for ABC (primary, secondary, and urban) highway projects which could be placed under contract by December 1, 1958, and completed within one year. The President objected to the two-thirds share of project cost to be borne by the federal government—a departure from the traditional 50-50 federal-state arrangement on ABC projects—and the provision for temporary federal advances covering most of the states' one-third share. Nevertheless, he signed the bill because, he said, the objectionable features were temporary and he hoped there might be a prompt impetus to employment (p. 322). The funds were allotted to the states the following day.

On April 16, the Senate passed—over strong objections by the administration but with the support of a number of Republican senators—a bill (S. 3497) to step up the public facility loan program of the Community Facilities Administration. Although this bill was labeled by its supporters as an antirecession move, the administration objected strongly to a measure which probably would not be temporary, and which it disliked in principle, arguing that it would be too slow-starting to have any value as an antirecession device. In any case, the bill never came to a vote in the House.

In late April, in order to aid the railroad industry—described as hard hit by the recession—the Commerce Department proposed to Congress revised rate policies for the Interstate Commerce Commission (ICC) and a new program of federal loan guarantees for equipment and rolling stock (pp. 395-96). A few days later, the Secretary of the Interior proposed a new program of subsidy payments on domestically mined copper, lead, zinc, fluorspar, and tungsten covering the difference between the market price and a fixed "stabilization" price on a designated "normal" level of output. In contrast to most other administration expenditure proposals in 1958, Interior's proposal failed to gain congressional approval.

The President advised his news conference on April 23 that the indices for three weeks had suggested a flattening out, although the recession was not over. And on May 14, he implied that no additional public works could be decided on, funded, and started in time to have any effect on the recession.

Taxes, however, continued to receive major attention, both in administration and congressional circles, during the following weeks. On May 1, the Treasury Department announced that personnel had been reassigned and temporary help employed in an extraordinary effort to speed refunds of 1957 overpayments on income taxes. The President, who earlier had noted that his major objection to a tax cut was that defense requirements would remain high for many years, on May 14 said a final decision on tax cuts would have to be made soon, since certain excises and the corporate income tax rate were scheduled for reduction on June 30 (pp. 401-02).

In the meantime, Senator Douglas had not given up hope for a tax reduction. He had been presiding over hearings in the closing days of April at which a parade of witnesses—many of whom thought the decline would soon end—recommended temporary tax cuts to speed recovery.[40]

The administration expressed its final decision not to seek tax cuts on May 26. Presidential letters sent to the congressional leaders renewed the January request for continuing corporate and excise taxes at existing rates, stating:

This renewed recommendation is made after consultation by the Secretary of the Treasury with leaders of both political parties in the Congress. Consideration of fiscal measures will continue to be made in

---

[40] *Fiscal Policy Implications of the Current Economic Outlook,* Hearings before the Subcommittee on Fiscal Policy, Joint Economic Committee, 85 Cong. 2 sess. (1958).

the light of the developing economic situation and with full regard to both the short and long-range effects of any proposal.

The Administration deeply appreciates the thoughtful and full co-operation with which the leadership of both parties in the Congress has worked with us in these matters (p. 424).

The Democratic congressional leaders immediately announced support for the President's opposition to tax cuts. In June, however, a move developed in the Senate, led by Senator George A. Smathers of Florida, to eliminate the excise taxes on freight transportation. Although Senator Smathers (and others) have been perennial advocates of reductions in transportation excises, the argument that such reductions were necessary to alleviate the depressed condition of the railroad industry carried somewhat greater weight in a recession year. As a result, when the excise and corporation income tax extension (P.L. 85-475) was finally enacted on June 30, the bill eliminated the 3 percent tax on freight transportation, the tax of 4 cents a ton on hauling coal, and the 4.5 percent tax on transportation of oil by pipeline, all effective August 1, 1958; but other taxes were extended at existing rates. Loss of revenue from the eliminated taxes would amount to an estimated $500 million on a full-year basis.

Toward the end of May, the heavy volume of applications for FHA mortgage insurance had about exhausted the $26 billion limit on outstanding insurance and commitments, and the agency had to start limiting new commitments. On June 4, a $4 billion increase in authorization was enacted (P.L. 85-442), and FHA was able to move ahead again. On the same date, the temporary unemployment compensation bill (P.L. 85-441) was signed much along lines originally suggested by the President, except that state participation was to be voluntary.

An Unbalanced Budget

Knowledge that economic recovery was underway became rather general by June 1958, although there remained some doubts about its vigor, and attention turned to the budgetary consequences of what had been done. On June 2, the President's news conference

for the first time in several months brought forth no questions on
the recession or on tax cuts. Instead, a question was asked about
the size of the deficit. The President expressed hope that, with re-
viving receipts from recovery and with "some little bit more sense
in the new appropriations we make," progress towards a balanced
budget could be made. However, he said the size of the prospective
deficit precluded soon or sudden achievement of a balanced
budget.[41]

Two actions, which for practical purposes marked the end of
fiscal efforts to counteract the 1958 recession, were taken in July.
On July 3, the President signed a revised Rivers and Harbors and
Flood Control Bill authorizing $750 million for new navigation,
beach erosion, and flood control projects, and raising limitations
on previously authorized projects by $870 million. The bill, he said,
contained practically none of the objectionable features of those he
had vetoed in the past two years. On July 15, the President signed
H.R. 11451 authorizing construction of two "superliner" merchant
ships. He had previously supported this authorization, but objected
to the provisions for mortgage financing by the federal government
rather than federal guarantee of private financing. He recommended that no appropriations under this authorization be made
until fiscal 1960 (p. 548).

It had become clear that expenditures in fiscal 1959 would run
considerably higher, and receipts considerably lower, than estimated in January, and that the temporary $5 billion increase in the
public debt limit enacted in February would be totally inadequate.
Therefore, on July 28, the President requested increase in the permanent debt limit, to $285 billion, plus an additional $3 billion
of temporary debt authority (pp. 571-72).

The extent of the administration's concern with budgetary considerations at the time is indicated by the President's veto of the
Independent Offices Appropriation Act on August 4 for the sole
reason that it included a general fund payment of $500 million to
the Civil Service retirement and disability trust fund (pp. 581-82).
This intragovernmental payment would not have affected the cash
budget, and would have had no economic significance. It would,

[41] *Public Papers, 1958,* pp. 513-14. (In following paragraphs, page numbers in
the text refer to this report.)

however, have increased budget expenditures, the deficit in the administrative budget, and the public debt subject to limitation. On August 6, 1958, in response to a question about the inflationary consequences of the prospect for deficits "for the next five years," the President told his press conference that he had been concerned about the problem of inflation "a few months back where everybody wanted to spend more money and decrease taxes." (P. 587.)

By the time Congress adjourned on August 24, 1958, there was widespread recognition that a strong recovery was underway. The Federal Reserve, with an eye on the cash deficit still to be financed, had moved to increase discount rates starting August 15.

In October 1958, the *Midyear Review of the 1959 Budget* revealed that the slender half-billion dollar surplus estimated in January 1958 had been converted into a deficit of over $12 billion. Reduced income levels had trimmed about $7 billion from estimated receipts, and the recession could also be blamed for higher expenditures for housing, unemployment, and public works. But pay increases were higher than budgeted and postal rates smaller than requested—these, and a variety of other legislative changes not primarily due to the recession, also took their toll. The largest increase was for farm price support payments, not significantly due to recession, but rather to extraordinarily large crops. Another major addition to the January estimates, $1.4 billion, was an increase in the U.S. subscription to the International Monetary Fund. This payment had previously been planned for a later time but, with fiscal 1959 so far in the red anyway and with the prospect of a much smaller deficit or even a balanced budget in 1960, it could be paid as easily in June 1959 as in July. The transaction had no immediate economic impact.

Defense expenditure estimates were also sharply higher. The budget in January 1958 had included a special allowance of $500 million for unspecified defense contingencies. The President had sent up amendments to his budget in April for additional missiles, missile submarines, and strategic aircraft; Congress had amended the amendments; and the revised defense expenditure estimate in October took care of the $500 million contingency allowance plus another $500 million.

Concern with the forthcoming elections and the record peacetime deficit as revealed in the *Midyear Review* touched off recrimination as to who had been responsible.[42] For example, Representative Richard M. Simpson blamed Democratic leaders Lyndon Johnson and Sam Rayburn for leading the fight for more spending, and credited the Republicans with saving $9 billion by cutting bills approved by Democratic committees (Oct. 4). The Democratic Advisory Council blamed the administration for the deficit (Oct. 5). The Democrats were charged by Vice President Nixon with fiscal irresponsibility (Oct. 5); by Republican National Committee Chairman Alcorn with lack of fiscal integrity (Oct. 7); and by President Eisenhower with being "champions of spending," "spendthrifts," and "extremists on spending." (Oct. 23, 28, and Nov. 1). But House Speaker Rayburn held President Eisenhower responsible for the record peacetime deficit (Nov. 8). Amid speculation during December 1958 of how large the forthcoming 1960 deficit would be, Clarence Cannon, Democratic Chairman of the House Appropriations Committee, announced he would seek to end unnecessary spending and to balance the budget (Dec. 11). Several weeks before transmission of the budget, the President took the unusual step of announcing that the budget for fiscal 1960 would be balanced at approximately $77 billion, $2 billion below the latest expenditure estimate published for the current 1959 fiscal year (Dec. 23).

Thus, in the course of a little over one year, budget and fiscal attitudes of policy officials had swung from one extreme to another and back. Although production and unemployment had not recovered prerecession rates, concern with these was all but over. The stage was set for a renewed economy drive. It began to take hold before the end of 1959 and, by early 1960, that drive restricted the levels of economic activity enough to be a definite factor in precipitating another recession.

Effects of Discretionary Antirecession Actions

In 1958, as in other recessions, the general attitudes of both the executive and legislative branches toward spending were affected, with the recession providing an additional argument for public

[42] For the examples which follow, dates inserted in the text refer to the *New York Times*.

expenditure proposals primarily favored for other reasons. For this reason, it is impossible to make a precise separation between the effects of antirecession measures and other proposals. Moreover, in the expenditure data for a given program, any antirecession speed-up is usually merged with, and thus indistinguishable from, ordinary outlays. The estimates in the following pages were derived by a combination of methods: comparison of final expenditure data with earlier estimates, and examination of within-year trends compared with other years and use of a Bureau of the Budget staff report covering the 1957-58 recession.[43]

Administrative Actions

Among steps taken by the administration that did not require action by Congress (except for some supplemental appropriations), the following items appear to have been primarily antirecession in purpose:[44]

1. Speed-up in construction rates on direct federal public works projects already under way—primarily water resource projects.

2. Encouragement of faster private and state and local government action on urban renewal, college housing, community facilities under federal loans, public housing, airports, hospitals, and construction supported by loans to REA cooperatives. In some of these cases, funds that had been held in reserve were released or apportioned to the agencies for spending earlier than they might have been in the normal course of events. In other cases, the action consisted of exhortation only.

3. Speed-up within fiscal 1958 of agency procurement of supplies, materials, and equipment.

4. Speed-up early in calendar 1958 of processing and payment of tax refunds.

5. Liberalization of FHA and VA housing credit rules and speed-up in processing FHA loan applications.

[43] Bureau of the Budget, "Staff Report, Federal Fiscal Behavior During the Recession of 1957-58," January 13, 1961, multilithed. (This is not an altogether independent source, since the author of the present study was also responsible for some of the estimates and judgments in the Budget Bureau report.)

[44] *Ibid.*

6. Release of budgetary reserves in various FNMA special assistance mortgage purchase programs.

7. Liberalization of eligibility rules for Farmers Home Administration loans.

8. Emphasis on labor surplus areas in procurement contracts placed by the Department of Defense and the General Services Administration.

From an examination of public works programs nominally subjected to administrative speed-up—including grant-aided state and local government programs as well as direct federal public works —it appears that perhaps $50 million to $100 million may have been added by the antirecession effort to fiscal 1958 public works outlays, and from $150 to $200 million in fiscal 1959. The 1958 figure represents water resource projects of the Corps of Engineers and the Bureau of Reclamation; in 1959, the Corps accounted for about half the estimated total and the Bureau of Reclamation, Forest Service, and renovations and repairs by GSA accounted for most of the remainder. Minor amounts may also have been added in 1959 for airport construction grants, National Park Service construction, and the Bureau of Indian Affairs. Interestingly, the speed-up seems to have gone into reverse in the July-September quarter of 1958. Water resource construction in that quarter was below the corresponding quarter of 1957 and, making allowance for seasonal influences, below the second quarter of 1958 both in expenditures and in work put in place.[45] It thus appears that the public works speed-up in the last quarter of fiscal 1958 was in part at the expense of outlays that would otherwise have come in the first quarter of fiscal 1959.

Public works programs specifically advertised as being speeded up, but for which federal expenditures fell below the estimates made in January 1958, include: hospital construction grants, public facility loans, college housing loans, public housing, grain storage facilities, waste treatment grants, and health research facilities grants. Total civil public works (excluding expenditures from the highway trust fund) also fell below advance estimates. Although

[45] See *Monthly Treasury Statement,* various issues, and Department of Commerce, *Construction Reports,* various issues.

Congress asked for an administrative speed-up in military construction, there is no evidence that this took place. Expenditures in fiscal 1959 fell below the January 1958 estimate by more than $100 million.

The administrative speed-up within fiscal 1958 of procurement of supplies, materials, and equipment can be assumed to have had little effect on the economy. (This judgment follows from the meager success in advance procurement of fiscal 1959 supplies, materials, and equipment, for which legislation was required and which is discussed later.)

Refunds of individual income tax were more successfully speeded up in 1958 than they had been in the 1954 recession. From comparison of the cumulative percentage of calendar year refunds paid by the end of each month (Table 25), it appears that refunds in March and April 1958 were about $600 million higher, and in May and June about the same amount lower, than they would have been if the pattern of the previous year had been followed. The welfare aspects of a speed-up of this kind are certainly favorable,

TABLE 25. Refunds of Individual Income Tax, Recession Years Compared to Preceding Years[a]

(Cumulative percentage of total paid by end of month and dollar amount for year)

End of Month	Prerecession 1953[b]	Recession 1954[b]	Prerecession 1957	Recession 1958	Prerecession 1960	Recession 1961
January	1.7	1.9	0.8	−1.3	−1.5	0.4
February	12.6	11.2	5.3	3.8	7.2	11.0
March	43.3	39.6	21.6	24.8	36.3	46.1
April	74.6	67.0	52.4	67.1	65.6	70.6
May	82.5	85.5	81.5	90.5	87.6	90.5
June	87.6	90.0	91.6	93.5	92.0	93.9
July	90.9	92.5	94.1	95.5	94.4	...
August	92.9	94.6	96.2	97.0	96.2	...
September	93.5	94.8	97.6	98.3	97.8	98.5
October	95.9	95.9	98.6	99.1	98.9	...
November	97.8	97.6	99.4	99.7	99.6	...
December	100.0	100.0	100.0	100.0	100.0	100.0
Amount (in millions)	$3,070	$3,293	$3,484	$3,801	$4,280	$4,765

a Data from U. S. Treasury Department.
b Figures include refunds of internal revenue other than individual income taxes. However, these do not significantly affect the monthly pattern.

particularly for those whose refunds stem from unemployment during the previous year. But the effects on aggregate demand are probably small. First, even a sizable accretion to aggregate demand one month, if offset by a corresponding reduction two months later, would hardly change the duration or general severity of a recession. Second, while most of the economic impact of refunds is probably delayed until cash payment, some anticipatory effect in the month or two before is not unlikely. To the extent this happens, speeding up the cash payment of refunds does not advance the effective date of economic impact unless anticipations are similarly modified.

The 1958 housing boom featured a rise of 40 percent in residential construction between the second quarter of 1958 and the second of 1959, and was one of the strong factors in the recovery. Although not affecting budget totals, administrative actions releasing housing reserves and affecting housing mortgage terms probably played some part in this expansion of private construction. However, administrative actions on housing terms were probably less significant than the April 1 down-payment liberalization on FHA loans, which required legislation. Moreover, changes in housing credit terms—either administrative or legislative—were probably much less important in the housing boom than the large increase in mortgage credit availability. And this increase was primarily the result of Federal Reserve easing actions, with an assist from FNMA special assistance purchases of low-cost mortgages, a legislative antirecession item which is discussed later.

The liberalization of eligibility rules for farm housing loans added an estimated $10 million to expenditures in fiscal 1959. However, lending activities in general, which are excluded from budget totals on a national income account basis, probably have a smaller impact on aggregate demand dollar-for-dollar than most other forms of federal outlay. While most federal outlays directly increase both incomes and net wealth in the private sector, lending operations do not have direct income effects and, so far as net wealth is concerned, increase equally liabilities and assets of the private sector.

In procurement programs, the effects on aggregate demand, if any, of emphasis on labor surplus areas would also appear to be minor. Since the same price is supposed to be paid in all locations, total government and private expenditures are the same (unless re-spending propensities are higher in labor surplus areas). This does not deny that a change in the geographical distribution of income may be desirable in some political or social sense. But the impact on the contour of recession and recovery may be safely considered nil.

Legislative Actions

Legislative antirecession actions were more significant than the purely administrative ones in 1958. Of the many items of legislation during 1958 for which the recession was perhaps a factor, four were clearly antirecession in their major purpose:

1. Temporary extended unemployment compensation (P.L. 85-441, June 4, 1958) provided federal funds with which states could pay benefits to unemployed individuals who exhausted their benefit rights for half again as long as they were able to collect under the regular state unemployment compensation systems.

2. The legislation on advance procurement (P.L. 85-386, April 24, 1958) authorized agencies other than the Department of Defense to order (or buy) in 1958, if possible, up to 50 percent of amounts proposed in the January budget for 1959 supplies, materials, and equipment, to be charged against 1959 appropriations when finally enacted.

3. The Highway Act of 1958 (P.L. 85-381, April 16) increased: (a) 1959 authorizations for interstate, ABC (primary, secondary, and urban), and forest and public lands highways; (b) 1960 and 1961 authorizations for interstate highways; and (c) 1961 authorizations for forest and public lands highways. In addition, it provided for an advance to 1959 of ABC authorizations to be repaid from 1961 and 1962 authorizations. To make apportionments to the states against these various authorizations possible, it waived, with respect to apportionment of the 1959 and 1960 authorizations, the pay-as-you-go requirement of the basic highway legislation.

4. The Housing Act of 1958 (P.L. 85-364, April 1) authorized, among other things, a reduction in minimum down pay-

ments on FHA-insured mortgages; $1 billion for special assistance purchase by FNMA of mortgages on new homes costing $13,500 or less; and an increase in the interest rate limit on VA-guaranteed loans. Other provisions, such as renewal of VA's expiring direct loan program, may also have had some counter-recession aspects, but would probably have occurred anyway.

The fiscal impact of these measures is estimated in Table 26.

The temporary extension of unemployment compensation undoubtedly had a prompt and sizable economic impact during the recovery. Although transfer payments in general probably have a smaller total impact on aggregate demand per dollar of outlay than government purchases of goods and services, the extended unemployment compensation was probably relatively efficient in this respect since it went to individuals with presumably high re-spending propensities. The original program was to terminate April 1, 1959,

TABLE 26. Estimated Impact of Major 1958 Antirecession Legislation on Budget or Trust Fund[a]

(In millions of dollars)

Legislation	Fiscal Year Increase in Expenditures			
	1958	1959	1960	1961 and later
Temporary extended unemployment compensation	48	447	—13	—482
Advance procurement, 1959 supplies and equipment	6	—6	...	...
Federal aid to highways:				
ABC (primary, secondary and urban)	...	262	241	—103
Interstate and forest and public lands highways[b]	...	20	156	334
FNMA special assistance mortgage purchases, low-cost housing[c]:				
Purchases	...	657	186	...
Repayments[d]	...	—4	—14	—839
Total, budget and highway trust fund	54	1,376	556	—1,090

[a] Bureau of the Budget, "Staff Report, Federal Fiscal Behavior During the Recession of 1957-58," January 13, 1961, multilithed.
[b] Based on increase in 1959 and 1960 interstate authorizations. Increase in 1961 interstate authorizations assumed not to be antirecession in purpose.
[c] Excludes secondary market (trust fund) operations of Federal National Mortgage Association (FNMA) which, perhaps partly because of this legislation, acted in a partially offsetting fashion.
[d] Excludes interest receipts.

but was subsequently extended to continue benefits for claims filed prior to that date. The (interest-free) repayments by the states to the federal government are due by 1963, which may or may not be good timing from a stabilization standpoint. Since not all the states participated (a number choosing to enact special programs financed with state funds instead), there seems to be no way to waive the repayment requirement. The net economic stimulus from the unemployment insurance system was sharply reversed, starting in the second half of 1959, for several reasons. A number of the states began to anticipate the repayment requirements by raising payroll tax rates. Also, there were the automatic (lagged) tax rate increases under experience-rating provisions of state laws, the termination of benefits under the temporary unemployment compensation program, and the drop in benefits under regular state programs.

The effort at advance procurement in fiscal 1958 of 1959 supplies and equipment for nondefense agencies had little success. Only a short time elapsed between conception of the program and the enabling legislation, which was quickly followed by instructions to the agencies. Nevertheless, only $6 million of expenditures was shifted forward into fiscal 1958. There is no record of how much speed-up was achieved within fiscal 1959, but it appears safe to assume it was small. Moreover, anything added to demand during the early stages of recovery in this manner was deducted before the end of the recovery. As stated in the Budget Bureau *Staff Report:*

> Agency reasons for falling short of advance estimates included lack of storage space, insufficient time, long-term commitments, and several others which support the general impressions that (1) short of a dire national emergency it is extremely difficult to change established agency procedures and practices on very short notice, and (2) procurement items of significant magnitude are apt to require a long lead-time.[46]

Of course, exclusion of the Department of Defense from this speed-up meant excluding the bulk of government outlays for supplies, materials, and equipment.

Following enactment of the highway legislation, state plans covering the whole of the increase of $400 million in 1959 authorizations for primary, secondary, and urban highways were sub-

[46] *Op. cit.,* p. 18.

mitted, and were approved by the Bureau of Public Roads by December 1958. Construction by the states was about 95 percent completed by the original target date of December 1, 1959.[47] Most states accepted the option of interest-free federal advances to cover two-thirds of the state cost of the project (the state cost amounted to one-third of total cost; the federal cost to two-thirds.) This brought federal expenditures in 1959 and 1960 to $503 million, of which $103 million would be recoverable later from 1961 and 1962 ABC authorizations. The increase in interstate authorizations was expended more slowly. It is not clear whether this legislation increased construction by the amount of federal outlays or by something less. Total highway construction increased during the relevant time period, but by less than the amount of federal grants. The $503 million in federal ABC expenditures nominally supported $600 million in construction. But most state plans which were approved by the deadline were at an advanced stage prior to the speed-up, suggesting that at least some projects would have been undertaken with state funds anyway.

The reimbursement feature helped give reversibility to the economic impact of the highway speed-up. More important, however, the speed-up was initiated with an inadequate balance in the trust fund to see it through to completion. As a result, by July 1959, it was necessary to postpone 1961 apportionments for which the pay-as-you-go rule had not been waived. Legislation enacted in the fall of 1959 increased the gas tax from 3 cents to 4 cents, and reduced 1961 interstate authorizations to below the level existing prior to the 1958 increase. In addition, because of the small trust fund balance, a special system of control over the within-year rate of state contracting was installed in fiscal 1960 to regulate expenditures. The net result of these restraints and uncertainties, which state highway officials began to anticipate in the first half of calendar 1959, was an immediate sharp drop in highway construction after the second quarter of 1959.

The FNMA program of special assistance purchase of mortgages on newly constructed low-cost houses appears to have been a relatively inefficient antirecession device, in that construction was probably increased by substantially less than federal outlays. While

[47] U. S. Bureau of Public Roads.

**TABLE 27. Federal National Mortgage Association Operations,
Calendar Years, 1957-59**[a]

(In millions of dollars, unadjusted for possible seasonality)

Operation	1957	1958		1959
	July-Dec.	Jan.-June	July-Dec.	Jan.-June
Budget fund				
Gross commitments:				
Antirecession	. . .	412	588	. . .
Other	310	211	102	187
Purchases:				
Antirecession	. . .	. . .	102	555
Other	48	98	164	245
Sales	—	4	12	1
Net purchases	48	93	253	800
Trust fund (secondary market)				
Gross commitments	425	126	136	280
Purchases	406	174	85	225
Sales	—	393	72	3
Net purchases	406	—219	13	222
Combined operations				
Gross commitments	734	749	827	467
Purchases	454	272	351	1,025
Sales	—	398	84	4
Net purchases	454	—126	266	1,022

    [a] Data from Housing and Home Finance Agency.

the whole $1 billion in special assistance (budget) funds was committed by the end of calendar 1958, builders stockpiled commitments received from FNMA, and a substantial portion remained unused until the 1959 building season. More important, the initial injection of funds came at a time when mortgage money was plentiful, and the competition for available mortgages active. The state of mortgage markets is indicated by the large volume of mortgages FNMA was able to sell under its secondary market (trust fund) operations which, as usual, were governed by general mortgage market conditions rather than antirecession motives.[48] To the extent that

    [48] See Table 27 in which FNMA operations during fiscal 1958 and 1959 are shown, for reference purposes.

the special assistance antirecession program—by reducing the supply of mortgages relative to the volume of funds seeking investment in this form—permitted larger sales under FNMA's secondary market operations than would otherwise have taken place, the net impact of the antirecession legislation was less than its nominal gross (budgetary) effect. And even the net effect on the supply of loanable funds might have been substantially achieved by more active monetary ease by the Federal Reserve. Inefficiency is also suggested by the fact that, while the bulk of special assistance purchases went into VA-guaranteed mortgages, the housing boom in the second half of 1958 and the first half of 1959 took place in the FHA and conventional sectors of the market. On the other hand, because construction occurs on the basis of advance commitments issued by FNMA, and prior to government mortgage acquisitions, the economic effects of this bill, whatever they were, were ended by the middle of 1959, in contrast to the carry-over of $186 million in budget expenditures into fiscal 1960.

One of the striking features in Table 26 is the high degree of recoverability or reversibility in the 1958 antirecession actions. And the reversal was, for highways and housing, quicker than indicated in Table 26 for the reasons given above. Thus (with the possible relatively minor exception of water resource public works), the stimulus from these legislative 1958 antirecession actions ended by the middle of 1959, and most of the major items not only ended but were sharply reversed.

Conclusions—1957-1959

In retrospect, the defense cutbacks in the second half of 1957 were badly timed from a stabilization standpoint. They reduced demand and had adverse effects on business expectations at a time when the economy was already starting into decline. But the cutbacks were certainly not a major cause of the recession. The defense drop itself was small—much smaller than in 1953, for example, even allowing for tax cuts in the earlier recession—and was quickly reversed. Nevertheless, the economy declined considerably more rapidly than in 1953-54.

Contrary to first appearances, the tight public debt limit was not a major cause of the 1957 defense cuts, although this was later used as one of the excuses. The decision to try to hold down defense spending was made at a time of widespread concern about the high level of the federal budget, and after the military services had demonstrated that their expenditures might rise unexpectedly unless kept under control. This policy was adopted before the administration decided to try to live within the debt limit without asking for an increase from Congress. It is not unreasonable to argue, in light of the 1957 experience, that the debt limit is more important as a symbol of fiscal prudence than as an operational constraint on expenditures. The reluctance to request an increase in the debt limit is a reminder that fiscal goals have importance of their own in the minds of public officials apart from the economic effects of government fiscal behavior. As in other recessions, such attitudes helped to delay official recognition of, and response to, the 1957-58 recession.

The persistence of inflation after the onset of decline, and uncertainty in the immediate post-sputnik period about what levels of defense and space research expenditure might be required in the period ahead, were also factors in the administration's delay in acknowledging the recession and proposing corrective actions.

Once the recession was acknowledged, the administration's initial response was that the inherent strength of the economy would keep the decline within tolerable bounds without the need for counterrecession action by the federal government. However, that position proved politically untenable. The administration's lack of a reserve plan of attack on recession, the meagerness of purely administrative actions when defense is excluded from a speed-up attempt, the fact that 1958 was an election year, and the organization of Congress by the rival political party—all combined to take the initiative for counterrecession action from the executive. As a result, the administration seemed to alter its strategy in midstream and to abandon any test of its forecast of early satisfactory recovery without government action.

The estimated fiscal effects of the 1958 discretionary antirecession actions, along with other factors affecting the federal budget during the period of recession and recovery, are shown in Table 28. Since the table is on the basis of the national income accounts, it

TABLE 28. Factors Affecting Federal Surplus, 1957-59 Recession and Recovery[a]

(In billions of current dollars at seasonally adjusted annual rates)

Item	1957 III-P	1957 IV	1958 I-T	Change Peak to Trough	1958 II	1958 III	1958 IV	1959 I	1959 II-R	Change Trough to Terminal (R)
Surplus at prerecession peak	2.6	2.6	2.6	...	2.6	2.6	2.6	2.6	2.6	...
Factors not due to recession										
Increased receipts, high employment, constant prerecession tax rates ••	...	1.1	2.2	2.2	3.2	4.3	5.4	6.4	7.5	5.3
Plus: OASI payroll taxes—										
Increase, taxable wage base	...	...	...	...	...	...	...	0.9	0.9	0.9
Increase, payroll tax rate	...	...	...	...	...	...	...	0.9	0.9	0.9
Less: tax reductions—										
Expiration, excise on freight transport	...	...	...	...	...	0.5	0.5	0.5	0.5	0.5
Liberalized tax on small business	...	...	0.2	0.2	0.2	0.2	0.2	0.2	0.2	—
Less: expenditure increase—										
Purchases, goods and services:										
National defense	...	-1.0	-0.6	-0.6	-0.4	0.1	-0.5	0.9	1.5	2.1
Other	...	0.4	1.3	1.3	2.2	3.5	3.8	2.0	2.1	0.8
Transfer payments to persons	...	0.5	1.0	1.0	2.0	2.1	2.3	3.3	4.2	3.2
Transfer payments abroad	...	0.2	...	...	0.1	...	0.4	0.3	0.2	0.2
Grants to state and local governments	...	...	0.6	0.6	1.1	1.3	1.5	2.2	2.1	1.5
Net interest paid	...	-0.1	-0.2	-0.2	-0.3	0.3	-0.1	0.2	0.4	0.6
Subsidies less current surpluses of government enterprises	...	-0.2	-0.1	-0.1	0.2	0.2	0.2	-0.1	-0.2	-0.3
Subtotal = prerecession surplus adjusted for factors not due to recession	2.6	3.9	2.4	-0.2	0.7	-0.5	-1.3	1.3	0.9	-1.5
Less: discretionary antirecession expenditures										
Highways, special ABC (primary, secondary, urban) funds	...	...	...	...	...	...	0.4	0.2	0.2	0.2
Highways, in authorizations, interest system	...	...	...	...	...	...	...	...	0.1	0.1
Public works speed-up	...	...	...	...	0.2	...	0.2	0.2	0.3	0.3
Temporary extended unemployment compensation	...	...	...	...	0.2	0.8	0.5	0.3	0.2	0.2
Subtotal = implicit high employment surplus	2.6	3.9	2.4	-0.2	0.3	-1.3	-2.4	0.6	0.1	-2.3
Less: effect, built-in stabilizers										
Corporate profits tax accruals	...	2.4	5.2	5.2	4.9	3.2	0.4	0.2	0.2	-7.2
Excise taxes	...	0.4	0.9	0.9	0.8	0.8	0.3	...	0.1	-0.8
Employment taxes	...	0.2	0.6	0.6	0.7	0.6	0.6	0.4	0.1	-0.5
Individual income tax accruals	...	1.3	2.7	2.7	3.3	2.7	2.3	1.1	0.3	-2.4
Unemployment compensation	...	0.7	1.3	1.3	2.2	2.1	1.8	0.6	...	-1.3
Other adjustments	...	0.2	0.2	0.2	0.5	—	-0.3	-1.0	-1.1	-1.3
Total = actual surplus (national income account basis)	2.6	-0.9	-8.1	-10.7	-11.1	-10.7	-8.1	-2.7	0.5	8.6

[a] See Appendix D for sources and methods.

232

leaves out one major 1958 antirecession program—purchases of mortgages by FNMA. But under the prevailing easy money market conditions, this program was inefficient and perhaps not an important additional factor in the recovery. The acceleration of individual income tax refunds and a few federal loan programs are also excluded; again, however, without seriously distorting the picture.

As Table 28 shows, the swing from surplus to deficit in the federal budget over the period of contraction was almost wholly the work of the built-in fiscal stabilizers. Discretionary antirecession actions were not in effect by the trough in the second quarter of 1958. And the increase in federal expenditures not related to the recession during the period from peak to trough was little more than the increase in receipts that would have taken place at continued high employment. This is indicated by the fact that the implicit federal surplus declined only slightly from the third quarter of 1957 to the first quarter of 1958.

The discretionary antirecession actions made their peak contribution in the last quarter of 1958—well after the cyclical trough in the first quarter of 1958—but had not been completely turned off in the second quarter of 1959. More important during the recovery than deliberate counterrecession actions were those taken for other reasons. Among such actions, outstanding were increased expenditures for post-sputnik defense programs and farm price supports and the reduction in transportation excises. The effect of such factors more than outweighed the increase in revenues that would have taken place at continued high employment, although partially offset by the substantial increase in OASI payroll taxes. As a result, the implicit federal surplus would have declined during the recovery period, even in the absence of discretionary antirecession actions. Taking account of the discretionary antirecession actions as well as the factors not due to the recession, the implicit surplus declined by $2.3 billion during the recovery.[49]

[49] The estimates of the implicit high-employment surplus shown in Table 28 are much lower than the "full employment estimates" presented by the Council of Economic Advisers in *Economic Report, 1962* (p. 82); the difference is especially great in the second half of 1958 and the first half of 1959. Conceptual differences between the estimates are mentioned in Chapter I (footnote 13, p. 14), and the high-employment benchmarks used in this study are described in Chapter I and Appendix A.

It is also interesting to contrast the behavior of the implicit surplus during this recession with its behavior in the previous one (Table 24, Chapter V). Spanning the whole period from prerecession peak to the terminal quarter of recovery, the decrease in the implied federal surplus in 1957-59 contrasts with a large increase in 1953-55.

Thus, to the extent that the 1958-59 recovery was less satisfactory than 1954-55, in that unemployment failed to decline by the second quarter of 1959 to acceptable levels, this was not because fiscal policy was less expansionary, at least up to the middle of 1959. The earlier abandonment in 1958-59 than in 1954-55 of the easy money policies instituted in the recessions may partly explain the different pattern. However, the economy seemed strikingly less vulnerable to fiscal restriction in 1955 than in 1959—so much so as to suggest a basic difference in the structure of income-spending relationships in the private economy in the two periods.

After the middle of 1959, the discretionary antirecession actions were not only turned off but sharply reversed. This was powerfully reinforced by the attempt to reduce government expenditures generally—in part a reaction to the deficit produced by the recession itself. The fiscal reaction after the recession was over may have been the worst feature of the fiscal policy response to the 1958 recession; and, significantly, that reaction was a matter of discretionary policy rather than built-in fiscal stabilizers. It is only fair, however, to recall that there was little dissatisfaction with the performance of the economy in 1959 in either government or private circles—perhaps because the protracted steel strike in the second half of the year obscured underlying trends. To the extent that the large belated cash deficit provoked the postrecession fiscal behavior, and a reaction to such deficits is likely to recur, there is a strong case for concentrating attention on (accrued) budget totals on national income and product accounts which more accurately reflect the economic impact of federal fiscal behavior, particularly the implicit surplus at high employment.

There is also a strong case for efficiency in antirecession actions—actions which have the maximum impact per dollar of deficit and, if possible, have their impact on the budget when there is still concern over the level of unemployment rather than later. The

1958 recession prompted, as did 1954, actions or proposals to help particularly depressed industries—railroads and mining in 1958, mining and shipbuilding in 1954—which probably would not deserve the same attention on grounds only of long-range efficiency.

The political difficulties that would be encountered in trying to put together an antirecession tax cut on the spur of the moment, as in the two earlier recessions, again were illustrated by the 1958 experience. The issues which naturally arise in a discussion of tax cuts—investment versus consumption, business versus individuals, upper-income versus low-income individuals—are major impediments to countercyclical tax policy, at least for mild recessions, unless there has been an advance attempt to reach a political consensus on the best ways to handle them.

The 1958 recession demonstrated greater political (if not economic) flexibility on the expenditure than on the tax side of the budget. This is inherent in the fact that expenditure programs can be modified one at a time in a more gradual fashion, and defended on other than stabilization grounds. Such flexibility is a great advantage to the policy official, since recognition of recession—first whether there is one, later how severe and the chances of self-correction—proceeds slowly and by little increments.

Policy officials in 1958 feared tax cuts would imply a public admission by government that the recession was serious and corrective action needed—an unpleasant admission that weighed less heavily against expenditure increases. In this connection, the 1958 experience suggests that it is bad strategy for government officials to announce publicly that tax cuts will only be used if a recession grows to serious proportions. It would have been difficult following the 1958 statements to later recommend tax cuts, if they had been needed, without producing the adverse psychological impact that the administration so much feared.

CHAPTER VII

Recession and Recovery, 1960-1962

THE 1960-61 RECESSION, with which both a Republican and a Democratic administration had to cope, was the shallowest of the four since World War II, but it began before recovery from the previous recession was really completed. The brief interlude between the 1958-59 recovery and the 1960-61 decline, together with the fact that business fixed capital investment started down again without having recovered its 1957 peak, renewed fears, once the recession was recognized, of secular stagnation. These fears were carried over from the 1930's into the early postwar period, but had been largely dissipated after seemingly successful bouts with three recessions in a row. As a result, the policies eventually proposed by the new Kennedy administration in 1961 were aimed at providing a greater stimulus to the economy than a temporary recession was thought to require. However, the stagnation thesis failed to win universal agreement. And the Democratic Congress, with one of its own party in the White House, was not under the pressure it had been in 1958 to show how reluctant the President was to spend, and was less generous with expansionary authorizations for nondefense expenditures. Partly for this reason, the 1960-61 recession did not bring forth much more in the way of actual fiscal expansion than in 1958.

236

Also, soon after the recession trough was passed, primary attention returned to fiscal responsibility and balanced budgets. There were important differences, however.

A Too-Tight Budget, Mid-1959 to Mid-1960

The effect of overly restrictive federal budget policy on the inadequate recovery from the 1958 recession has been discussed at length. Similarly, there has been much discussion of the fact that the 1960-61 recession began after the shortest expansion of any in the postwar period.[1] The federal surplus, on a national income basis in the first quarter of 1960 was $6 billion compared with a deficit of $11 billion in the second quarter of 1958. This meant that an increase of $17 billion in tax revenues relative to federal outlays had to be absorbed by the economy in the intervening period. However, the entire span, considered in this fashion, fails to show the important distinction between the discretionary changes and the automatic changes in response to rising levels of economic activity. From the second quarter of 1958 to the end of 1959, the swing toward a budget surplus was caused almost entirely by the built-in fiscal stabilizers. The implicit high employment surplus was little more at the end of 1959 than it had been in 1957.

But an economy wave had swept both the executive and legislative branches, even before the end of 1958, partly in reaction to the large fiscal 1959 deficit. On a national income basis, purchases of defense goods and services declined $1 billion from the second

---

[1] See for example, testimony of Joseph A. Pechman and Charles L. Schultze, *Current Economic Situation and Short-Run Outlook,* Hearings before the Joint Economic Committee, 86 Cong. 2 sess. (1961), pp. 112-14 and 114-22; testimony of Walter W. Heller and Herbert Stein, *Hearings on the Economic Report of the President, 1961,* Joint Economic Committee, 87 Cong. 1 sess. (1961), pp. 353-57 and 209-15; Arthur Burns, "Examining the New 'Stagnation' Theory," *Morgan Guaranty Survey,* May 1961, and the reply by the Council of Economic Advisers (at request of Joint Economic Committee), June 10, 1961, reprinted with Burns' further reply in *Morgan Guaranty Survey,* August 1961; *Joint Economic Report,* Joint Economic Committee, 87 Cong. 2 sess. (1961), Appendix pp. 119-25; and Robert Solomon, "Fiscal Aspects of the Cycle," paper presented to the Annual Forecasting Conference, New York Area Chapter of American Statistical Association, May 5, 1961, multilithed.

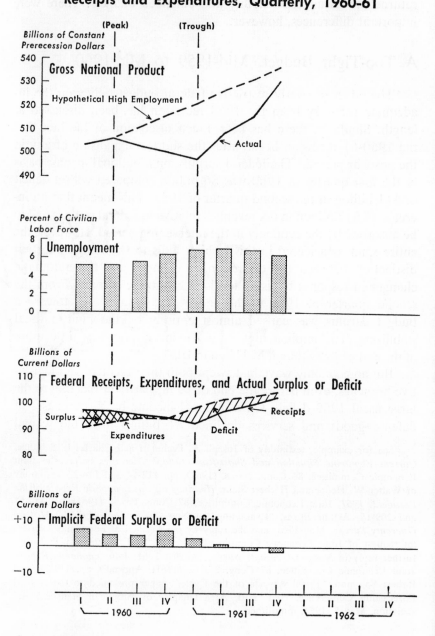

Chart 5
Gross National Product, Unemployment, and Federal Receipts and Expenditures, Quarterly, 1960-61

(Peak)   (Trough)

Billions of Constant
Prerecession Dollars

540

Gross National Product

530

Hypothetical High Employment

520

510

500   ← Actual

490

Percent of Civilian
Labor Force

8

Unemployment

6

4

2

0

Billions of
Current Dollars

110

Federal Receipts, Expenditures, and Actual Surplus or Deficit

100

Surplus   Receipts

90   Expenditures   Deficit

80

Billions of
Current Dollars

+10   **Implicit Federal Surplus or Deficit**

0

−10

I   II   III   IV   I   II   III   IV   I   II   III   IV
⌞— 1960 —⌟   ⌞— 1961 —⌟   ⌞— 1962 —⌟

Source: Appendix D.

238

quarter of 1959 to the second quarter of 1960 (seasonally adjusted annual rates), and federal grants—mostly for highways—declined another half billion. Net interest and transfers to persons rose over this period, producing an increase in total federal outlays (national income budget terms) of about $1.5 billion. But revenues at stable

TABLE 29. Gross National Product, Unemployment, and Federal Budget, Second Quarter 1959 to Second Quarter 1960[a]

(Dollar amounts in billions at seasonally adjusted annual rates)

Item	1959			1960	
	II	III	IV	I	II
Gross national product	488.5	482.3	488.3	501.5	506.4
Federal budget (national income basis):					
Receipts, total	91.6	89.1	89.6	97.0	96.9
OASI rate increase	...	...	...	2.0	2.0
Gas tax rate increase	...	...	0.4	0.7	0.7
Other	91.6	89.1	89.2	94.3	94.2
Expenditures	91.1	91.6	92.0	90.5	92.5
Surplus	0.5	—2.5	—2.4	6.5	4.5
Unemployment rate, seasonally adjusted (percent of labor force)	5.1	5.3	5.6	5.2	5.2

[a] Federal receipts and expenditures from U. S. Department of Commerce, *Survey of Current Business,* July 1961. Unemployment rate from U. S. Department of Labor, *Monthly Report on the Labor Force,* January 1962.

growth would have increased about $5 billion. Adding $700 million (annual rates) for the gas tax increase in October 1959, and approximately $2 billion for the increase in payroll tax rates for old-age, survivors and disability insurance (OASDI) on January 1, 1960, the implicit surplus would have increased by about $6 billion from the beginning to the end of fiscal 1960. The actual surplus, affected by the steel strike from July to October and special inventory accumulation before and after the strike, rose by $4 billion, as shown in Table 29. This sharp switch in fiscal policy, together with a drop in residential construction and the failure of plant and equipment outlays to rise as strongly as in the 1955-57 boom, proved too much for the economy. The 5.1 percent unemployment rate reached in April-June 1959 was the lowest achieved in the recovery.

A statement presented to the Joint Economic Committee in March 1961 by Herbert Stein[2] illuminates the role of fiscal policy in clamping down on the economy in 1960. Correlating unemployment rates with federal surplus on income and product account, Stein shows that, for the period 1955 through 1959, the federal budget (national income basis) consistently tended to strike a balance when about 5.2 percent of the labor force was unemployed.[3] His findings show a deficit at higher rates of unemployment and a surplus at lower, with a change of about $6 billion in the surplus or deficit for a change of 1 percentage point in the unemployment rate. In the first half of 1960, however, unemployment of 5.2 percent was associated with a surplus of over $5 billion; and in the second half of 1960, unemployment of 6.1 percent was accompanied by a surplus of $1.2 billion, rather than the $5 billion deficit implied under the previous relationships. In short, the implicit federal surplus in 1960 suddenly became too large by $5 billion to $7 billion. The arresting of expenditures and the increase in tax rates—amounting to $2.7 billion at annual rates but largely unnoticed because it affected trust fund receipts rather than the administrative budget—were important aspects of this development.

Fiscal policy in January 1960 was directed toward further tightening. The Eisenhower administration, as indicated in the President's economic message to Congress,[4] favored a large surplus and reduction in the public debt to restrain inflationary pressures, permit lower interest rates, and to strengthen confidence in the dollar at home and abroad. The President's budget proposed an increase of $4 billion more in receipts than expenditures. However, Congress showed far less enthusiasm for expenditure restraint in the 1960 election year than it had the year before, and appropriations were subsequently increased in virtually every category except foreign aid.

[2] *Hearings of the Joint Economic Committee, 1961*, p. 209.

[3] Stein's unemployment ratios were calculated prior to the 1962 revisions in seasonal indexes, and differ slightly from ratios referred to elsewhere in the present study.

[4] *Economic Report of the President, January 1960.* (Cited hereinafter as *Economic Report, 1960*, with indications of subsequent dates.)

Private forecasts at the end of 1959 and in early 1960 consistently pictured rising levels of economic activity during the year, although the possibility of a slower rate of rise in the second half was mentioned.[5] Witnesses before the Joint Economic Committee in February were almost unanimous in their support of a policy of continued high federal surplus as a means of restraining inflationary pressures. The Committee itself recommended policies it said were needed to promote more vigorous expansion in total demand and reduce the level of unemployment. The policies recommended were easier monetary and credit conditions, and a still larger budget surplus than proposed by the administration. The latter was to be achieved by "restructuring" the budget, with increases in defense and educational expenditures more than offset by economies in farm outlays, elimination of waste in defense practices, higher postal rates, and closing of tax loopholes.[6] Apparently the Committee on this occasion was differing less with the administration's general fiscal policies than with its selection of expenditures.

In retrospect, it seems clear that the magnitude of the wrench to the economy from the sharp tightening of budget policy in fiscal 1960 was excessive. The policy was caused in part by faulty diagnosis of the state of the economy, and not exclusively by a decision to balance the budget without regard to the health of the economy. The administration's policy was defended by Secretary of the Treasury Robert B. Anderson in December 1959 before the annual meetings of the American Finance Association.[7] He argued that budget deficits, appropriate for recession years, should be offset by surpluses in good years, with the budget balanced over the cycle rather than annually. And President Eisenhower's *Economic Report* took the position, in January 1960, that, with a strong upswing likely, a large budgetary surplus would speed growth by supplying investment funds to the private sector through public debt retire-

[5] *Hearings on the Economic Report of the President, 1960,* Joint Economic Committee, 86 Cong. 2 sess. (1960), especially pp. 127-42. (Cited hereinafter as *Hearings of the Joint Economic Committee, 1960,* with indications of subsequent dates.)

[6] *Joint Economic Report,* Joint Economic Committee, 86 Cong. 2 sess. (1960). (Cited hereinafter as *Joint Economic Report, 1960,* with indications of subsequent dates.)

[7] *Annual Report of the Secretary of the Treasury, 1960,* p. 282. (Cited hereinafter as *Treasury Report, 1960,* with indications of subsequent dates.)

ment. As already noted, the Joint Economic Committee and witnesses appearing before it in early 1960 were not of the opinion that fiscal policy was too restrictive.

The Contraction and Fiscal Politics

The decline which started in May 1960 proceeded more slowly and took longer to be diagnosed as "recession" than its predecessor. The steel strike which lasted over much of the second half of 1959, and which was commonly blamed for the unsatisfactory levels of economic activity at that time, was partly responsible for the slow diagnosis. The rate of expansion from the trough in the first quarter of 1958 up to the time of the steel strike had been extremely rapid. And, although the recovery in the second quarter of 1959 had been helped in part by inventory accumulation attributable to the anticipation of the strike, there were few who doubted that the strike settlement would be followed by renewed expansion. Further confusion surrounded the drop in inventory investment in the second quarter of 1960, since some of the first-quarter demand in this category was clearly attributable to the replenishment of inventories after the strike. A downward revision in the revenue estimates for fiscal 1961 was required by the time of the midyear review of the budget in October 1960. Nevertheless, the Secretary of the Treasury was still able, with some plausibility, to describe the adjustment taking place as a leveling during one quarter in gross national product (GNP), caused by inventory correction which would be reversed before the end of the year.[8]

The April-June quarter of 1960 turned out to be the peak quarter in GNP, and the reference cycle approach of the National Bureau of Economic Research (NBER) places the peak in May 1960. From this peak to the subsequent trough in the first quarter of 1961, GNP declined by 2.2 percent in constant (1961) prices, the smallest decline in any recession since World War II. The decline in GNP in current prices was $5.6 billion (annual rates), and this was more than accounted for by the switch from inventory accumulation at a rate of $5.4 billion in the second quarter of 1960

[8] Statement of Secretary Anderson, Treasury Department Press Release on *1961 Federal Budget Midyear Review,* October 4, 1960.

to liquidation at a rate of $4.0 billion in the first quarter of 1961. Important categories of final demand also fell, with purchases of consumer durables down by $5.9 billion and business purchases of durable equipment by $4.4 billion. These, however, were more than offset by increases in net exports, government purchases—federal as well as state and local—and consumer outlays for services.

Unemployment, at 5.2 percent of the labor force in the second quarter of 1960, was already high by postwar standards for relatively prosperous periods. But it rose to 6.8 percent by the trough in the first quarter of 1961, and averaged still higher—6.9 percent —in the April-June quarter. Judging from interest rates, which started to decline sharply early in 1960, monetary ease was initiated more promptly than in 1957.

The recession received little public discussion during the summer and fall of 1960. It was conspicuously ignored in public statements by presidential candidates of both parties, until late in the campaign, as well as by the incumbent administration. However, budget policy, particularly the defense budget, had been hotly debated all year. In January, leading Democratic senators questioned the adequacy of President Eisenhower's defense budget.[9] Governor Nelson A. Rockefeller of New York, an apparent contender for the Republican nomination for President, joined the critics in June (June 9). Immediately after the defense appropriation was passed in July, giving the President a billion dollars more than he had requested, Senator John F. Kennedy urged a $2.5 billion to $3 billion further increase, with a tax increase to pay for it if necessary (July 11). There were reports that the administration had impounded a large part of the additional appropriation but, in August, President Eisenhower denied that the money was impounded at that time (August 9-11).

Defense orders started climbing in the summer of 1960 and rose during the remainder of the year. Deliveries also increased, by $1.7 billion at annual rates from the second quarter of 1960 to the first quarter of 1961, thus providing an offset to the decline in GNP. The contracyclical influence is probably understated in a national income tabulation of deliveries, since part of the economic

[9] *New York Times,* January 19, 1960. For further references to the *New York Times* in this paragraph, dates referring to this newspaper are given in the text.

impact of defense orders is felt prior to delivery. Part of the further sharp rise in defense purchases in the second quarter of 1961 is also attributable to the increase in orders prior to the change of administration, but that quarter was also affected by an antirecession speed-up.

President Eisenhower maintained optimism to the end of his term. His Budget Message in January 1961[10] conceded there had been a "leveling out" in the latter part of 1960, but described the state of the economy in sanguine terms. A budget surplus, he said, was necessary in good times in order to offset the inevitable deficits during recessions. The President asserted that to ignore the principle of fiscal integrity is to undermine our strength as a nation through deficits and unmanageable public debt, which would result in inflation and the "cheapening of our currency." He further stated that "the problem of maintaining reasonable price stability will require close and continuing attention in the future." The President promised that his *Economic Report* would describe the trends which indicated that substantial expansion of the economy could be expected during calendar 1961.

However, the *Economic Report,*[11] as it had at a similar juncture in 1958, gave a slightly less rosy view of events. Toward the end of the document (p. 64), the administration's budget policy was stated, without a defense, this way: "Funds appropriated by the next Congress for the fiscal year 1962 should be held within the limits of expected revenues." The more outstanding tone of the *Report* was set in its opening words: "Employment, production, and income in the United States attained in 1960 levels well above those of 1959. The advances, however, were concentrated in the first half of the year; in the second half, production and employment declined and unemployment rose." Doubt was expressed that business fixed investment would contribute to higher demand in the immediate future. However, favorable factors included improvement in the net export balance; a material increase in federal, state, and local government outlays; "eventually" lower borrowing costs

[10] *Budget of the United States Government for the Fiscal Year Ending June 30, 1962* (January 1961). (Cited hereinafter as *Budget, Fiscal 1962,* with indications of subsequent dates.)

[11] *Economic Report, 1961.* (In the following discussion, page references to this *Report* are given in the text.)

for construction; personal consumption expenditures; and the fact that "major maladjustments" had not been created in the previous expansion. Thus, "an increase in general economic activity should not, accordingly, be long delayed," although reduction in unemployment might take longer. Stating that the basis for more fully realizing the economy's growth potential had been laid by the increases in productive capacity and in government policies which brought inflation under control, the *Report* forecast that "the economy can now look forward, provided public and private policies are favorable, to a period of sound growth from a firm base." (Pp. 42-44.)

Noting that there had been a surplus of $5.2 billion (seasonally adjusted and in national income budget terms) in the second half of the fiscal year 1960, the *Economic Report* said in recent months the surplus had been considerably reduced. "The restraining effect of the budget on the economy thus was substantially lessened in the course of 1960." Actions said to be helpful to the level of economic activity, listed in the *Report,* were certain steps taken by the Federal Housing Administration (FHA), the Federal National Mortgage Association (FNMA), and the Federal Home Loan banks during 1960 to ease the supply of housing credit, and relaxation of emergency controls over state highway contracting made possible by a trust fund balance that was larger than anticipated. The fact that fiscal 1960 procurement and construction were started earlier than usual because of earlier enactment of 1960 appropriations was also described in terms hinting that this was part of a deliberate antirecession policy. Thus, while the President's Budget Message seemed concerned exclusively with inflation and budgetary balance, the *Economic Report* admitted not only to a recession but to a number of fiscal actions that might have been partly antirecessionary (pp. 31-33, 43).

A Change of Administration

As 1961 started, however, the policies and proposals of the outgoing administration were of considerably less moment than those of President-elect Kennedy. His advisers, led by Paul A. Samuelson of the Massachusetts Institute of Technology, issued, in early

January, a task force report on the U.S. economy.[12] This report
turned out to be a good forecast of the attitudes and policies of the
new administration, at least for the early period following the inaug-
uration.

Stating frankly that the economy was in a recession, the task
force described what it said were first and second lines of defense.
The first line—based on an "optimistic model" of the economy, in
which GNP was assumed to decline at most for one or two more
quarters—called for increased federal expenditures and actions to
ease the supply of credit for residential construction. Illustrative expenditure increases were listed as defense, foreign aid, education,
urban renewal, health and welfare, improved unemployment compensation, useful public works, highway construction, depressed
area programs, and natural resource development programs. The
second line, to be resorted to if the economy threatened to continue
down longer or unemployment reached intolerable levels (7.5 percent of the labor force, the previous postwar peak, was mentioned
in this connection), called for a temporary tax cut.

Perhaps as important as the specific policy recommendations
contained in the task force report were the diagnosis of the economic situation and identification of constraints on policy. The views
of the task force appear to have greatly influenced later administration policies.

The task force took the view that unsatisfactory performance
of the economy was not a problem only of temporary recession,
but of recession superimposed on a tendency toward chronic slack
in the economy. As a result, in the words of the task force, "certain
expenditure programs that are worth while for their own sake, but
that inevitably involve a lag of some months before they can get
going, can be pushed more vigorously in the current situation because of the knowledge that the extra stimulus they later bring is
unlikely to impinge upon a recovery that has already led us back
to full employment."

Second, the balance of payments problem constituted an important new policy constraint not noticeably present in the earlier
postwar recessions. The *Economic Report, 1961,* of the outgoing

[12] Reprinted in *New York Times,* January 6, 1961.

administration stated (p. 39) that one of the major objectives of fiscal and monetary policies in 1960 had been the maintenance of confidence in the dollar as a "sound and reliable currency." The task force report, also alert to this problem, suggested that its existence enhanced the importance of fiscal policy relative to monetary policy in counteracting a recession. Since capital movements in response to international interest rate differentials would aggravate a balance of payments deficit, according to the task force, an antirecession program could plan only limited use of the easy money policies that would otherwise be appropriate. Another facet—that economic expansion, however produced, would tend to increase imports relative to exports—was given short shrift in the task force report: "It would be unthinkable for a present-day American government to deliberately countenance high unemployment as a mechanism for adjusting to the balance of payments deficit." Be that as it may, the addition of a balance of payments problem to problems already facing policy makers—including a possible conflict between policies to reduce unemployment and policies to avoid inflation—might be expected to tilt the scales to some degree against governmental action to stimulate the economy.

Third, the task force explicitly mentioned a possible tendency for price-wage inflation to appear before the economy returned to a high level of employment. There was no prediction that this would or would not later be a problem, but the report implied that, at least for the present, it could be set aside: "If recovery means a reopening of the cost-push problem, then we have no choice but to move closer to the day when that problem has to be successfully grappled with." This might require, it was indicated, new policies to deal more directly with productivity, wage rates, and price formulation, since the traditional anti-inflation weapons of tight money and budgetary surplus might produce too much unemployment.

Fourth, increases in federal expenditures were considered desirable, aside from short-run stabilization objectives. As the task force said of its first-line expenditure increases: "The following measures are not being advocated in the faith that they will help business from declining in the first months of the new year. Some of them will, at best, pay out money only after a considerable delay. They are advocated for their own sakes as builders of a better, fairer, and faster-growing economy." The task force's estimates for this first-line defense (some $3 billion to $5 billion more than the outgoing administration's expenditure plans, which were still to be announced) did "not purport to make up for the accumulative deficiencies in those vital areas."

Finally, uncertainty must be listed among the constraints on stabilization policy recognized by the task force: "At this time it would be urgently important to make sure that any tax cut was clearly a temporary one. With the continued international un-certainty and with new public programs coming up in the years ahead, sound finance may require a maintenance of our present tax structure and any weakening of it in order to fight a recession might be tragic." As in earlier recessions, the belief that defense expendi-tures in an uncertain world might have to be increased by some un-specified, but potentially inflationary, amount again influenced fis-cal policy formulation.

Expenditures for Recovery and Growth

The condition of the economy was President Kennedy's first topic in his State of the Union Message to Congress, January 30, 1961.[13] The problem was not merely recession, but "seven months of recession, three and one-half years of slack, seven years of di-minished economic growth, and nine years of falling farm income." The President did not forecast when the recession would end and he gave no target date for recovery. But stating that the adminis-tration would not "stand helplessly by" in the face of alarmingly unanimous forecasts of continued slack and only slightly reduced unemployment throughout 1961 and 1962, he promised proposals within fourteen days on a variety of programs affecting unemployed and low-income families and labor surplus areas, along with others to stimulate housing, provide incentives for business plant invest-ment, develop natural resources, and encourage price stability. Else-where in the message, proposals for federal aid to education and

[13] National Archives and Records Service, *Public Papers of the Presidents of the United States, 1961* (1962), pp. 19-28. (Cited hereinafter as *Public Papers, 1961.*)

for medical care for the aged were promised. Announcing that he had ordered a review of the entire defense program, the President said in the meantime he had initiated step-ups in defense programs for airlift capacity, Polaris submarines, and missile programs generally. Declining revenue prospects, the President pointed out, indicated a budget deficit in fiscal 1961 and 1962. But it was his intention to advocate a program of expenditures which, including revenues from a stimulation of the economy, would not "of and by themselves unbalance the earlier [Eisenhower] budget."

Three days later, the President in his Economic Message[14] indicated another constraint to be added to those implied or specified in the task force report—budgetary balance—which has been close to the surface in each postwar recession. The task force report had begged off having to say whether a budget balance over the course of the business cycle was possible, and in fact had suggested that deficits for most of the first half of the coming decade might be necessary. The President, stating his belief that budget surpluses in good years should more than offset deficits in poor years, again made the point that his proposals would not "by themselves unbalance the budget which was earlier submitted."

The Economic Message included a score or more steps recommended for congressional action or being initiated administratively. The message explained that the proposals were aimed not merely at recession, but at the tendency toward chronic slack and inadequate growth: "Many of these expenditures will automatically cease when high employment and production are restored. Other measures contained in this message propose necessary uses of national economic capacity and tax revenue for our long-range growth, and are essential even in the absence of recession." Continuing, he said, "Fortunately, the measures to overcome recession, to take up the slack, and to speed growth all reinforce each other." The President asserted that his proposals would be appropriate even though "minor improvements in business conditions" might occur without their adoption and cautioned that "speaking out of realism, not pessimism—we cannot rule out the possibility of further deterioration if we fail to act."

[14] *Ibid.*, pp. 41-53.

The Kennedy proposals can conveniently be grouped into those which required administrative action only and others requiring legislation. Actions already initiated or being initiated administratively were the following:

1. Treasury discussion with the Federal Reserve authorities on means to check declines in short-term interest rates and thus minimize the adverse balance of payments effects of an easy money policy.

2. Reduction of the maximum permissible interest rate on FHA-insured loans from 5¾ to 5½ percent.

3. Liberalization of FNMA secondary market mortgage purchase terms.

4. Request that the Federal Home Loan Bank Board help in the effort to reduce mortgage interest rates.

5. Reduction of interest rates charged on public facility loans, and assignment of priority in new loans to quick starting projects and to labor surplus areas.

6. Speed-up of commitments for new college housing loans, and attempts to move forward the starting dates on already approved projects.

7. Urging 297 mayors to hasten urban renewal projects already under way or about to begin.

8. Expansion of counseling and placement services under the U.S. Employment Service (USES).

9. Expansion of surplus food distribution.

10. Use of previously legislated but unused authority to initiate a pilot food stamp plan.

11. Study of improvements in school lunch programs.

12. Advanced payment of 1961 National Service Life Insurance dividend ($258 million) and study of a possible second dividend.

13. Immediate acceleration in all agencies, including defense, of construction and procurement with available funds, and an inventory of additional public works projects that could be started quickly with additional funds if later economic conditions warrant.

14. Immediate removal of restraints on state use of remaining highway funds scheduled for current year.

15. Improvement of machinery for channeling federal contracts into labor surplus areas.

The President asked for congressional enactment of these additional proposals:

16. Temporary extension of unemployment compensation for twelve months, with outlays to be repaid fully by a later increase in the limit on the taxable wage from $3,000 to $4,800.

17. A permanent strengthening of the federal-state employment security program, details to be furnished the Congress later.

18. A temporary program of aid to dependent children of the unemployed, pending a study of possible permanent reforms.

19. Distressed area redevelopment, embracing loans, grants, technical assistance, and programs for training and retraining workers.

20. Improvements in old-age and disability insurance to: (a) raise the minimum monthly benefit; (b) offer optional retirement for men at age 62; (c) liberalize the requirement for insured status; (d) increase benefits for aged widows; and (e) broaden disability insurance. These were to be financed by an increase in the tax rate on employers and employees of ¼ percentage point each (about $2 billion annually), the tax increase not to take place until January 1, 1963.

21. An increase of the minimum wage to $1.15 an hour immediately, and to $1.25 within two years, and an expansion of coverage to several million additional workers.

Here was the new administration's first line of defense as previewed in the earlier task force report. The President said proposals would be made later on tax incentives for investment, but specifically placed these in the "growth" category, and in fact promised proposals for closing tax loopholes that would offset any revenue loss. The list concluded with his assurance that: "if these measures prove to be inadequate to the task, I shall submit further proposals to the Congress within the next 75 days." This statement was taken by the press to mean that the President would reach a determination by April 15, 1961, on whether temporary tax cuts would also be appropriate.[15]

[15] See, for example, *Washington Post*, February 3, 1961, p. 1.

The President, and the authors of the task force report before him, appear to have been somewhat optimistic in proposing to combat both recession and stagnation without a tax reduction. The task force apparently thought that the implicit budget surplus was already several billion dollars too high; furthermore, revenues under existing tax rates would rise by about $5 billion a year with high employment growth, and an increase of approximately $2 billion in OASDI payroll taxes was scheduled for January 1, 1963. Unless there was a change in past relationships between private consumption and investment and high employment GNP, government expenditures would have to rise enough not only to correct the currently excessive implicit budget surplus but also to offset the increase in tax yields that would occur while high employment was being achieved.

But there were important obstacles to tax cuts. It might well have seemed to the new President, for example, that tax cuts would have seriously jeopardized congressional approval of controversial expenditure proposals—such as aid to education—about which he felt strongly. If this is part of the explanation of the absence of tax cut proposals, it repeated a recurring phenomenon in the postwar recessions—a direct conflict between policies appropriate in the short run for raising the level of employment, and policies proposed for other important, long-run purposes. Another part of the explanation is suggested by the later remarks of the principal author of the task force report. Commenting on the problems facing the administration in early 1961, Samuelson wrote that "whatever the economic merits of a tax cut, it seemed politically out of the question. The President had run on a platform that asked sacrifices of the American people. How then could he begin by giving them what many would regard as a 'handout'?"[16] Political constraints on presidential antirecession proposals, by way of public stands taken previously, also were nothing new in 1961, having been significant factors at comparable stages of the 1948-49 and 1953-54 recessions.

In any event, the President's proposals drew immediate dis-

[16] Paul A. Samuelson, "Economic Policy for 1962," *Review of Economics and Statistics,* Vol. 44 (February 1962), p. 3.

agreement from Republican congressional leaders. Reacting to the State of the Union Message and the administrative actions, House Minority Leader Charles A. Halleck objected to "spending programs that will cost billions of dollars," while Senate Minority Leader Everett M. Dirksen objected to their "puny" economic impact and simultaneously to the problem of "what you are going to use for money."[17]

During February, a series of special messages gave details and amounts on the President's earlier antirecession recommendations and conveyed additional recommendations for new or stepped-up programs. The most expensive new proposal was for federal aid to elementary and secondary education, to cost an estimated $500 million in fiscal 1962. Other recommended new programs or program increases were for medical care for the aged under social security, farm housing loans, veterans housing loans, farm ownership and operating loans, health research, public assistance, child welfare, science education, veterans compensation, and "modest but symbolic" increases for natural resource development. Agriculture proposals called for authority for the Secretary of Agriculture to impose tighter production and marketing controls, which it was claimed would eventually result in lower expenditures, but in the meantime a substantial increase in 1962 price support outlays would be required. Also, early in February, the administration revealed that refunds of individual income taxes would be accelerated "to stimulate the nation's economy" if taxpayers would cooperate by filing their returns early.[18]

On February 28, the President recommended an increase in highway authorizations of $12 billion to cover revised estimates of the cost of completing the interstate system by 1972 as originally planned, and an increase of $900 million a year in highway user charges to prevent the scheduled diversion of general fund revenues to the highway trust fund. Unless there was congressional action, the 1963 apportionments to be made in July would have to be cut below even the previously authorized amount.

By early March, Chairman Walter W. Heller of the Council of

[17] *Washington Post*, February 3, 1961, p. A-13.
[18] *Ibid.*, February 8, 1961.

Economic Advisers (CEA), testifying before the Joint Economic Committee,[19] was able to forecast an increase of approximately $3 billion in federal outlays (national income basis) within twelve months after enactment of the proposals made up to that time, excluding the (presumably temporary) effects of construction and procurement speed-up, and with housing and defense still to be heard from. (This increase was in addition to that of $2.5 billion or so for fiscal 1962 which had been implied in President Eisenhower's January budget.) Heller emphasized, even more than administration spokesmen had previously, that the current problem was not only recession, which he strongly implied might soon turn around, although no forecast was made on this score. (P. 314.) Also, and more troublesome, he said, was the problem of chronic slack, the possibility of slow recovery, and the size of the gap between actual and potential production. Low growth since the mid-1950's was explained in part by a retardation of investment and an aging of the capital stock. More basically, low growth, the large persistent "gap" between potential and actual output, and incomplete recovery from the 1958 recession all reflected inadequate aggregate demand: "The best stimulus to capital expansion is pressure on present capacity, and that has been noticeably lacking in most industries since the mid-fifties." (P. 339.) The high unemployment rate going into the recession, according to Heller, was not primarily due to structural changes in the composition of the labor force but rather to inadequate demand (pp. 378-82). Programs aimed at correcting the recession and at lifting the growth rate were "consistent and mutually reinforcing." (P. 341.)

Slow growth and inadequate demand, Heller's testimony indicated, were due in large part to overly restrictive federal fiscal policy. The revenue-raising power of the tax system had increased relative to actual government expenditures, and the budget tended to come into balance at too high a rate of unemployment (pp. 355-57). "This 'latent surplus' may also make the attainment of full recovery more difficult." (P. 349.)

There was a hint in Heller's testimony that the expenditure pro-

---

[19] *Hearings of the Joint Economic Committee, 1961*, pp. 358-59. In the following discussion of the Heller testimony, page references are given in the text.

posals made so far by the administration would not be enough: "Indeed, recent fiscal trends make clear that full recovery with the present tax structure would generate substantially more revenue than is required by the President's proposed programs, thus leaving a generous margin for retirement of debt and restraint of inflation. Whether this margin is consistent with the achievement and maintenance of full employment cannot yet be determined." (P. 357.) The President had promised further stimulatory action if necessary, Heller pointed out, which could include additional public works, housing measures, or tax cuts: individual income tax cuts would be particularly helpful in this connection. It is clear that the administration did not have any early target date for recovery. Timing and reversibility of expenditure increases, Heller said, would not be a problem. Since "the road to full recovery is a long one," he explained, "the expansionary effects of government programs will be welcome even if they occur well after the recession has been reversed." (Pp. 359-60.)

The President's housing message on March 9, in addition to steps announced previously, asked for new or expanded authorizations for FHA insurance, rental and cooperative housing, public housing, demonstration projects, housing for the elderly, urban renewal, urban and metropolitan planning, reservation of open lands in urban areas, public facility loans, farm housing loans, and guaranteed and direct loans for veterans.

The President's message on budget and fiscal policy, March 24, summed up the changes to that date. The President was able to demonstrate, by rather complicated calculations, that, possible defense revisions aside, his new nondefense recommendations would not of and by themselves unbalance the budget submitted by President Eisenhower in January. (The nondefense recommendations would cost an estimated $2.3 billion in fiscal 1962, after allowing for an induced revenue effect from these proposals of $900 million; the Eisenhower budget had a $1.5 million surplus.) However, the earlier estimates also had to be corrected for overestimation of revenues and underestimation of costs of certain programs. When this was done, the outlook for fiscal 1962, defense revisions aside, was for a deficit of $1.8 billion.

Defense program revisions outlined in the President's defense message of March 27 called for an increase of about $2 billion in new obligational authority over the January proposals. However, the effect on fiscal 1962 expenditures would be small, the previously announced speed-up in construction and procurement accounting for most of the change in the defense budget after January. The revised estimate of the fiscal 1962 deficit was $2.2 billion.[20]

Congress showed little enthusiasm for the President's request for tight controls on farm production and marketing under the discretion of the Secretary of Agriculture, and passed instead an "emergency feed grains" bill (P.L. 87-5, March 22, 1961), which provided for sharply increased price support levels for corn and other feed grains for the 1961 crop year, together with in-lieu payments for land taken out of production.[21] While the bill bore little resemblance to the administration's recommended approach to the farm problem, the President gave no evidence of discontent in signing the bill. This legislation had been rather frankly given a tag of "get the money out quickly" by some of its supporters, and was listed in the President's 1962 *Economic Report* (p. 103) as one of the actions taken in 1961 that helped restore recovery and growth. Advance commitments under the program were issued shortly after the bill's enactment, farmers signed up in unexpectedly large numbers, and by June 30 the program had added significantly to fiscal 1961 expenditures of the Commodity Credit Corporation (CCC). Even before the new feed grains legislation, price support levels had been lifted administratively under existing law for corn, cotton, butterfat and milk, soybeans, and most other price supported commodities for the 1961 crop year. And, on February 8, the President had ordered a speed-up of payments to farmers for storage of crops under price support loans. These actions were also listed in the 1962 *Economic Report* (p. 98) as conducive to recovery and growth, and it seems likely that expenditures were at least somewhat higher than they would have been were there no recession.

The Temporary Extended Unemployment Compensation Act of 1961 (P.L. 87-6) was enacted on March 24. It extended the

[20] Statement of Budget Director David E. Bell, *Hearings of the Joint Economic Committee, 1961*, pp. 504-61.

[21] The "emergency feed grains" program was extended for an additional crop year in legislation enacted later in the session (P.L. 87-128, August 8, 1961).

benefit period up to thirteen weeks for unemployed persons who, after June 30, 1960, but before April 1, 1962, exhausted their benefits under regular state programs (or under the programs of unemployment compensation for veterans and former federal employees). The cost was estimated at approximately $800 million for fiscal years 1961 and 1962 combined. This was to be financed initially by outlays from the federal budget and repaid by doubling (from 0.4 to 0.8 percent of taxable wages) the federal unemployment payroll tax on employers for calendar years 1962 and 1963. The tax increase would yield approximately $400 million annually. Although state participation was optional, there was a strong incentive for states to join because the tax increase was to cover employers in all states. Similar temporary extension of benefit periods for workers covered by the Railroad Unemployment Insurance Act was enacted (P.L. 87-7).

On April 6, 1961, the Small Business Administration (SBA) cut the interest rate charged on loans to small business firms and development companies in areas of substantial unemployment and revealed it had liberalized eligibility for such loans by relaxing its definition of small business. Also, 5,000 letters urging communities to take advantage of the loan program had already been sent out.

The President's recommendations on taxes were sent to Congress on April 20. The major feature was a sliding tax credit for business investment intended to stimulate growth. This would equal 15 percent of new plant and equipment investment in excess of current depreciation allowances, 6 percent of such expenditures below this level but in excess of 50 percent of depreciation allowances, with 10 percent of the first $5,000 of new investment as a minimum credit. The President argued against a flat across-the-board credit which would entail a revenue loss for investment that would be undertaken anyway, or which represented no new level of effort. He was not precluding later changes in depreciation rules, he said, but opposed accelerated depreciation as an investment incentive on grounds of equity and possible cost-price distortion and because it provided less incentive per dollar of revenue loss than the tax credit. The estimated loss in revenue from the President's proposal would be $1.7 billion in the first year. This cost was to be offset by tightened tax treatment of certain foreign-source income and of unnecessary business expenses; withholding of tax on dividends and interest; repeal of the dividend exclusion and dividend tax credit provisions of the 1954 code; and ending of capital gains treatment for gains from sale of depreciable property. At the same time, extension at current rates of corporation and excise taxes scheduled for reduction July 1, 1961, was requested, and an extension of the existing 2-cent per gallon aviation gas tax rate to also cover jet fuels.

According to the dating method employed by the National Bureau of Economic Research, the recession trough came in February 1961, and the first quarter also marks the trough in gross national product. While the administration's antirecession program being launched just about this time probably was not accompanied by knowledge of the precise dating of the trough, few observers felt the decline would last much longer. As indicated above, the administration's proposals were aimed as much, or more, at speeding recovery than at initiating a turning point. On April 21, Secretary of the Treasury Douglas Dillon expressed the opinion that the turning point might well have been reached early in March. But recovery was likely to be sluggish, he said, and the modest budget deficit in prospect for the following year was entirely appropriate in its stimulating effects on the economy.[22]

The gross national product rose sharply in the second quarter of 1961, a little less strongly in the third, surged again in the fourth, and advanced at a considerably slower pace after the turn of the year. Over the first three quarters of recovery, GNP rose by 8 percent, with inventories and virtually all categories of final demand except net exports sharing the rise. The increase in federal defense purchases was particularly strong compared to past recoveries. However, the unemployment rate stayed just below its recession high (7.0 percent, reached in May) until October, with November and December 1961 providing the first significant signs of improvement. The unemployment rate by February 1962 was down to 5.6 percent (seasonally adjusted), but it appeared that further improvement might come rather slowly.

---

[22] Remarks of Secretary of the Treasury at Annual Meeting of American Society of Newspaper Editors, Washington, D.C., April 21, 1961, Treasury Department press release.

The depressed areas bill (Area Redevelopment Act, P.L. 87-27) was passed on May 1, 1961, and a week later the Area Redevelopment Administration was formed in the Department of Commerce. The bill authorized $395 million over four years, including loans for new factories, loans and grants to local governments to build water systems or other facilities needed by industry, and funds for job retraining and employment services.

Public Law 87-31 (May 8, 1961) extended federal grants to states for aid to dependent children of the unemployed (state participation optional) for a period of fourteen months beginning on May 1, 1961. Expenditures had been estimated at $28 million in fiscal 1961 and $215 million in fiscal 1962.

The administrative action taken in February which cut ceiling interest rates on FHA-insured mortgages from 5¾ to 5½ percent was followed by another cut from 5½ to 5¼ percent in May. Mortgage interest rates had been declining slowly until then, although FHA-insured mortgages—subject to the interest ceiling— were still trading at discounts. Average prices on mortgages started dropping after the May rate reduction, as buyers attempted first to maintain, and then to expand, their yield premiums.[23] Incidentally, if down payment and closing costs are more important than mortgage interest rates as determinants of the demand for new housing —a not unlikely proposition—the changes in interest rate ceilings on FHA mortgages were in the wrong direction so far as stimulating the economy. Undertaken in an effort to persuade the savings and loan associations—believed to be highly liquid at the time— that a general cut in mortgage interest rates was in order, the steps also had the effect of curtailing the supply of credit available for FHA-insured housing with low down payments. The administration later exhibited some embarrassment that these cuts did not have the desired effect of reducing market rates of interest, but saw no way to raise them again without tending to cause speculative increases in interest rates generally.

In May 1961, it became increasingly clear that GNP in the second quarter would show a large increase, and there was talk of the recovery exceeding the administration's earlier expectations. The recovery was still expected to stretch over a considerable

[23] *Wall Street Journal,* October 19, 1961.

period, however, and the unemployment rate still had not responded. As would be revealed in later statistics, a sharp rise in federal spending was a significant factor in the GNP increase during the second quarter.

The same month, Congress began to exhibit discontent with portions of the administration program. The tax credit for investment ran into stiff criticism from businessmen in House hearings, and Congress showed an interest in making substantial additions to the President's requests for defense appropriations.

Toward the end of May, a new round of budget increases and new program proposals were transmitted by the President. Substantial additional amounts were requested to accelerate space programs, to increase conventional warfare capability and step up army modernization, and for foreign military and economic aid. A message on "Urgent National Needs" on May 25 spoke of the need for legislation to provide for labor training and retraining and for youth fitness. And on June 7, the cost of administration proposals for retraining and relocating long-term unemployed, including a pilot program for youth training and employment, was placed at $700 million over the next four years. On June 13 a bill was transmitted to overhaul the federal-state unemployment compensation system. Proposed were uniform minimum federal standards, extended coverage, and standby federal supplements in periods of high unemployment. Financing would be provided by increasing the limit on taxable wages and increasing the federal share of the proceeds.

The Highway Act of 1961 (P.L. 87-61, June 29, 1961) gave the President the authorizations he had requested earlier. But it also provided, against his recommendations, for a diversion of $150 million of general fund revenues starting July 1, 1962. There would also be a $150 million increase in excise taxes on the truck and rubber industries starting July 1, 1961, and a cancellation of the cut scheduled for that time from 4 cents to 3 cents a gallon in the federal gas tax. The $2.4 billion in interstate highway authorizations that could now be apportioned in July represented a $200 million increase over the amount previously authorized, and a similar increase over the apportionment made in July 1960.

The Housing Act was signed the next day (P.L. 87-70, June 30, 1961). Although the voting was close, the bill as passed gave the President essentially what he had requested for FHA, and substantially more than he requested in FNMA special assistance and public facility loans. The provisions most immediately important to the construction industry were liberalization of terms concerning maturities, down payments, and maximum mortgage size under the FHA insurance program, which were placed in effect a few days later. The 1962 cost of the final bill was estimated at $250 million in expenditures, compared to $150 million for the administration proposals. However, the impact of advance commitments in 1962 under some of the new programs with long lead time would be somewhat greater than indicated by these expenditure figures.

The Social Security Amendments of 1961 (P.L. 87-64, June 30, 1961) covered practically the same OASDI liberalizations the President had recommended but with the amount of benefits cut in about half. The increase in benefits was estimated to come to an annual rate of approximately $800 million (effective August 1, and reflected in September benefit checks). The payroll tax increase was also cut from the President's request to ⅛ percent on employers and employees, or about $500 million annually (contrasted with $2 billion)—but the starting date was moved forward to January 1, 1962.[24] Also included in P.L. 87-64 was a temporary nine-month liberalization of the federal share of grants for public assistance payments, estimated to cost $15 million in fiscal 1962.[25]

Balancing the Budget Again

The last major revision by the administration to the 1962 budget came in response to the worsening Berlin situation in late July 1961. In a radio-television address on July 25, the President asked

[24] Under the administration proposals, the tax increase would not have taken place until January 1, 1963.

[25] An analysis of P.L. 87-64 appears in the *Social Security Bulletin,* September 1961.

for an increase in authorized military personnel strength and authority to call up reserves and extend tours of duty. An additional $3.4 billion in 1962 defense appropriations was requested to pay for these and for increases in air and sealift capability, tactical aircraft, and other nonnuclear weapons. It was revealed a little later that up to $2.75 billion of the requested funds would be expended within the current fiscal year. Added to previously released information on the 1962 budget, these plans took the prospective deficit to over $5 billion. The request had been widely anticipated.

Some of the advance speculation in the press assumed that, with recovery under way and several of the administration's nondefense expenditure proposals already starting to push up the level of spending, the President would now have to ask for a tax increase of $2 billion to $3 billion to finance increased defense.[26] When the President made known his decision to ask for the defense funds without a tax increase, he stated that he had been advised that, given the enormous revenue potential in the tax system, the economy could stand the increase without higher tax rates. By publicly weighing both sides, the President seemed to indicate some uncertainty as to whether this was really a sound course. He then went on to promise, emphatically, that the budget submitted in January 1962 for fiscal 1963 would be balanced. And that if this were not possible at current tax rates, because of unforeseen defense requirements, he would ask then for higher taxes.

With the new budget still six months away, a commitment to balance it might have seemed evidence of extraordinary confidence in the strength of the recovery. A critic of this move stated that, while there had been imprudent attempts before to balance the budget at the wrong time for the health of the economy, a commitment this far in advance was unprecedented and, in his opinion, "a most serious step backward" so far as responsible fiscal policy was concerned.[27] The field of fiscal politics, however, is more complicated than this view suggests. In the words of a kinder observer,

[26] See, for example, the *Washington Post,* July 22, 1961, and *Wall Street Journal,* July 24, 1961.

[27] Alvin H. Hansen, "Economic Policy for 1962: A Symposium," *Review of Economics and Statistics,* Vol. 44 (February 1962), p. 11.

"The notion that the fiscal 1963 budget could be balanced was a powerful one in quieting irrational opposition to needed fiscal expansion."[28]

The congressional response to the President's request for increased defense spending was overwhelmingly favorable.[29] However, a number of the President's proposals for new or enlarged federal nondefense programs were meeting opposition in the Congress. Former Vice President Nixon said the President should shelve all new spending programs not needed for defense, and the Republican Congressional Campaign Committee was critical of the President for not cutting domestic spending to offset the higher defense cost. Minority leaders Dirksen and Halleck also recommended curbs on domestic spending. One newspaper account said the announcement of possibly higher taxes in January had killed remaining hopes for the proposed investment tax credit (which had already been converted in the House Committee's version to a flat 8 percent credit for all new investment regardless of depreciation); and that the aid to education bill, also stalled, was another possible victim in the expected economy drive. The postal rate increase, on the other hand, was now given a slightly better chance of passage.[30]

In early August, Treasury Secretary Dillon, in a letter, told Chairman Wilbur D. Mills of the House Ways and Means Committee the defense increases did not mean the administration was no longer interested in the investment tax credit. Dillon said that the 1963 budget could be balanced without an increase in taxes. Later in the month, in testimony before the Senate Committee on Appropriations, Dillon undertook to rescue the administration's foreign aid requests, which then seemed to be bearing the brunt of the congressional economy drive.

Some competition between budgetary aims and the desire to re-

[28] Samuelson, *ibid.*, p. 6. Samuelson went on to say: "If private spending had boomed, that notion [that the 1963 budget could be balanced] would today do us no harm. But facts are facts . . . it would be tragic if a premature budget balance were to weaken the momentum of the present recovery long before we have come close to healthy employment and growth levels."

[29] For example, *Wall Street Journal,* July 27, 1961.

[30] See *New York Times,* July 27 and 28, 1961, and *Wall Street Journal,* July 25, 1961.

duce the still high level of unemployment could be seen in this period. According to the *Wall Street Journal* of August 23, the President said in a letter to Senator Joseph S. Clark—who had been pushing for a $1 billion public works bill to combat unemployment, and was reportedly disappointed at lack of administration support —he would consider asking for a standby, public works authorization in 1962 which could be used against unemployment and recessions. The President also said he could not support a public works bill at the time, primarily because of mounting budget deficits, and in addition, because unemployment might decrease at a faster rate than had previously been expected. In response to a question at the August 30 press conference, the President said the administration was still concerned because unemployment was too high. "But we have a large deficit and it is difficult to think that we could usefully increase that in order to affect unemployment without adversely affecting the cost of living. That is our difficulty."

By the time Congress adjourned on September 26, the administration's fiscal proposals had met with mixed success. Congress had acted promptly, and much along the lines recommended by the administration, on area redevelopment, temporary extended unemployment compensation, aid to dependent children, and housing. The President had received all he requested for defense, and an additional $500 million for strategic bombers which the Secretary of Defense said he did not need and would not use. Foreign aid authorizations, however, were a billion dollars below the requested amount.

Congress had scaled down the requested social security liberalization, had dealt harshly with the administration's tax and postal rate proposals, and had shown little enthusiasm for retraining and relocating workers in depressed areas. Medical care for the aged, aid to education, and permanent changes in the unemployment compensation system were all held over for the next session. In a last-minute maneuver, the House blocked "back-door" financing (that is, authority to spend funds borrowed from the Treasury without the need for annual appropriations), and substituted regular appropriations, at least for the coming year, for a number of loan programs that had already been set up earlier in the session with "back-door" authorizations. Affected by the move were the program for aid to depressed areas, the mass transit program, grants and loans for purchase of open space to avoid urban blight, and grants for experimental development of low-income housing. The revised appropriations were for less than the amount of commitments that had already been planned for the coming year for all but the depressed areas program.

Treasury Secretary Dillon, addressing the Governors of the International Monetary Fund in Vienna on September 21, 1961, said the recovery was well under way and moving strongly. Forecasting a GNP rate of $540 billion in the fourth quarter (up from $500 billion in the first), the Secretary said he was encouraged by the fact that the rise had not been accompanied by speculative buying, abnormal inventory accumulation, or price inflation. Pointing out that the 1962 budget deficit mainly represented reduced revenue because of the recession, and was considerably smaller than the deficit at the comparable stage of the 1958-59 recovery, he said planned expenditures were still "well within our capacity." He repeated that the administration planned to submit a balanced budget in January 1962 which, unless further increase in defense outlays became necessary, would not entail tax increases. However, should additional defense expenditures become necessary, the President had stated clearly and unequivocally that he was prepared to request such additional taxes as might be required to balance the budget.

At his October 11 news conference, the President was asked if increased defense expenditures would curtail his legislative program, particularly for tax revision. The President replied that the July decision on defense increases had killed his hope for a tax reduction of about $3 billion to be proposed if business recovered. However, whether tax increases would be proposed would depend on how much defense had to be increased, on how much could be cut from nondefense expenditures, and on how much of a tax burden could be sustained without strangling the recovery. The President said taxes were heavy and would bring in "tremendous receipts at full employment," and he did not want to add to the burden if it would result in waste of resources and manpower.

Also in October, Secretary of the Treasury Dillon indicated, in an address before the American Bankers Association in San Francisco, that the prospective deficit for 1962 had been raised to something over $6.75 billion, with most of the increase from the July estimate of a deficit of $5.3 billion a result of the "lamentable failure" of Congress to raise postal rates, and to farm price support costs that were heavier than expected. The Secretary called the deficit "uncomfortably large" but not of itself inflationary. He said there was substantial unused capacity of both plant and labor force, and that any renewal of inflationary dangers would reflect wage-price pressures rather than excess demand. And he expressed confidence that monetary stringency of the severity of 1959 could be avoided during the current recovery. He then revealed that the President had ordered federal agencies to practice the strictest economy and to defer expenditures wherever possible, and that the administration had achieved "substantial economies" by this means. He again pointed out that the administration planned to submit a balanced budget for fiscal 1963.[31]

Thus, by the fall of 1961, government policy appeared to be caught in a fiscal bind reminiscent in some respects of 1958-59, with budgetary goals and an adverse balance of international payments competing for attention with the rate of unemployment. Major differences were a more widespread awareness in 1961 of the dilemma posed by this competition, and the likelihood that, while the increase initiated in federal spending might be slowed, it would not be reversed. So far as the administration was concerned, counterrecession proposals were at an end—any further increases would have to be justified on their own merits, or perhaps to accelerate the rate of growth.

The review of the 1962 budget published in October revealed an expenditure estimate of approximately $89 billion—an increase of over $8 billion compared to the budget transmitted in January by the Eisenhower administration. Of the $8 billion, about half was for defense. Another $2.5 billion could be ascribed primarily to revisions of January estimates for program changes which were not made deliberately—such as public debt interest, farm price supports, and the absence of a postal rate increase. The remaining $2 billion covered all other program revisions and antirecession actions, including temporary extended unemployment compensation and any lingering 1962 cost (except for defense) of antirecession speed-ups.

In January 1962, the President's *Economic Report* described

[31] *Wall Street Journal,* October 18, 1961.

the reversal of the downtrend and the sharp gains in GNP and industrial production that had occurred since the first quarter of 1961.[32] The *Report* estimated that half the plant capacity which had been idle at the beginning of the year had been brought into productive use (p. 5). However, it said that actual output at the end of 1961 was still well below potential and unemployment "far too high." The administration's goal was to reduce the unemployment rate to 4 per cent in calendar year 1963, a target the *Report* said could be achieved if appropriate policies were followed (p. 8).

The budget for fiscal 1963 transmitted by the President at this time lived up to his earlier promise that it would be balanced.[33] While expenditures in the administrative budget were estimated $3.4 billion higher than for 1962, "more than three-quarters of the increase is accounted for by national security and space activities, and the bulk of the remainder by fixed interest charges" (p. 7). The President's budget message said that, because of increasing requirements for national security, strict standards had been applied to expenditure proposals and many new projects and activities had been deferred (p. 7).

Continued strong recovery during calendar 1962 and beyond was projected. As a result, revenues were expected to rise by enough more than expenditures to cause the estimated $7.0 billion deficit in fiscal 1962 (administrative budget) to be followed by a surplus of $0.5 billion in fiscal 1963. The President's budget message said that to plan a deficit under existing prospects for the economy "would increase the risk of inflationary pressures," but that a surplus larger than that proposed "would risk choking off economic recovery and contributing to a premature downturn" (pp. 8-9).

The *Economic Report* acknowledged that, under the administration's proposals, the budget would provide a smaller stimulus to the economy in the coming year. But it argued that "the disappointing 1959-60 experience" which showed that "an abrupt and excessively large swing in the budget can drain the vigor from the private economy and halt its progress" would not be repeated because the proposed shift would be "moderate and gradual" (p. 12).

[32] *Economic Report of the President, January 1962.* Page numbers in the text in this and the following paragraphs refer to this document.

[33] *Budget of the United States Government for the Fiscal Year Ending June 30, 1963* (January 1962).

Budget Director David Bell, in testimony before the Joint Economic Committee, pointed out that the swing in the budget surplus would be smaller in 1962-63 than in 1959-60 and mentioned the prospect for easier monetary policies. He added that the "administration remains alert to developing economic trends, and stands ready to change its policies when the evidence shows this is appropriate."[34]

The swing toward budget surplus contemplated by the administration was not merely a passive change to be induced by rising levels of economic activity (although this was the major part); it also reflected an increase in the implicit high-employment surplus as well. The CEA's annual report,[35] which made extensive use of the concept of the "full employment surplus," contained a chart (p. 82) showing a small further drop in that surplus in the first half of calendar 1962, but a rise thereafter. While the full employment surplus calculated by CEA would still, by the end of fiscal 1963, be below the level of 1960, it would be considerably higher than had prevailed (according to CEA calculations) in 1959.[36] This led some observers to question whether the administration's budget policies were fully appropriate in the light of its diagnosis that the problem was "to recover not from one but from two recessions," that is, "not only the setback of 1960-61, but the incomplete recovery from the recession of 1957-58" (*Economic Report*, p. 4).

Starting with the State of the Union message, three presidential messages in January 1962 recommended legislation giving the President discretionary authority to cut income tax rates and to expand federal and federally aided public works programs as temporary antirecession devices. However, the administration took pains to defend these proposals on general grounds, and to avoid the appearance that it thought they might actually be needed any time soon.[37]

[34] *Hearings on the Economic Report of the President,* Joint Economic Committee, 87 Cong. 2 Sess. (1962), pp. 80, 81.

[35] Printed with the President's *Economic Report, 1962.*

[36] The CEA's estimates of the full employment surplus differ considerably from the estimates of the implicit high employment surplus shown in Table 30 below. For a statement of conceptual differences, see Chapter I (footnote 13, p. 14). The high employment benchmarks used in this study are explained in Chapter I and Appendix A.

[37] The State of the Union message, for example, explained that "the time to repair the roof is when the sun is shining."

Effects of Antirecession Actions

The list of actions taken in 1961, administrative and legislative, to foster economic recovery and growth runs to ten pages in the 1962 *Economic Report*. Because the administration deliberately combined its attack on the recession with its attempt to permanently change the federal budget—and, in fact, described many of its proposals as aimed at both objectives simultaneously—there are no satisfactory guides for distinguishing "counterrecession" proposals and actions from others. The discussion which follows, and actions labeled "antirecession" in Table 30, are confined to those actions which, because they were essentially temporary in intent, might be viewed as directed more to the goal of quickly counteracting recession and initiating recovery than toward permanently lifting the level of federal expenditures.

Federal payments for temporary extended unemployment compensation began in April, and by the end of fiscal 1961 totaled $481 million. In the national income accounts (which lagged slightly behind the budget accounts) the payments reached an annual rate of about $900 million in the April-June quarter of 1961, and tapered off thereafter. Because the recipients can be presumed to spend a large fraction of the benefits, the economic stimulus was probably prompt and sizable. The 1962 increase in federal tax, however, came at a time when increases were also expected in state tax rates. The average effective state payroll tax has risen steadily since 1958, and was expected to increase further in 1962,[38] because of continued high insured unemployment, the effects of experience rating, and discretionary increases in some states to offset declining reserves and to anticipate repayments to the federal government of advances made to the states during the 1958 program.

Aid to dependent children of the unemployed made a slow start. Expenditures in fiscal 1961 were virtually nil, and fiscal 1962 expenditures also appear likely to fall short of the original estimate. Recipients no doubt will spend the benefits promptly; however,

[38] *Wall Street Journal*, October 5, 1961, and *Budget, Fiscal 1963, Special Analysis A*, p. 274.

TABLE 30. Factors Affecting Federal Surplus, 1960-62 Recession and Recovery[a]

(In billions of current dollars at seasonally adjusted annual rates)

Item	1960 II-P	1960 III	1960 IV	1961 I-T	Change Peak to Trough	1961 II	1961 III	1961 IV	1962 I	1962[b] II-R	Change Trough to Terminal (R)
Surplus at prerecession peak	4.5	4.5	4.5	4.5	...	4.5	4.5	4.5	4.5	4.5	...
Factors not due to recession											
Increased receipts, high employment, constant prerecession tax rates	...	1.0	2.0	3.0	3.0	3.9	4.9	5.9	6.9	7.9	4.9
Plus: tax rates increases—											
Highway excise							0.1	0.2	0.2	0.2	0.2
OASDI payroll tax									0.5	0.5	0.5
Federal unemployment tax									0.4	0.4	0.4
Less: expenditure increase—											
Purchases, goods and services:											
National defense		−0.1	0.2	1.7	1.7	1.8	4.0	6.2	7.0	7.5	5.8
Other (less sales)		1.2	—	0.2	0.2	0.3	0.8	1.0	1.2	1.4	1.2
Transfer payments to persons		0.1	0.6	1.1	1.1	2.2	2.5	3.3	3.7	4.1	3.0
Transfer payments abroad		−0.1				−0.1	0.1	0.2	0.2	0.3	0.3
Grants to state and local governments		0.1	−0.1	1.0	1.0	0.7	0.3	0.3	1.0	1.5	0.5
Net interest paid			−0.1	−0.3	−0.3	−0.5	−0.7	−0.6	−0.5	−0.5	−0.2
Subsidies less current surplus of government enterprises								0.1			—
Subtotal = prerecession surplus adjusted for factors not due to recession	4.5	4.3	5.9	3.8	−0.7	4.0	2.5	0.1	−0.1	−0.8	−4.6
Less: discretionary antirecession expenditures[c]											
Temporary extended unemployment compensation						0.9	0.8	0.6	0.5	0.4	0.4
Special veterans insurance dividends				0.7	0.7	−0.2	0.5	−0.2	0.1		−0.7
Speed-up, defense procurement						1.5	0.5				
Speed-up, other procurement and construction						0.2	0.2				
Farm price supports, feed grains, surplus food				0.1	0.1	1.0	1.5	1.5	1.5	1.5	1.4
Subtotal = implicit high employment surplus	4.5	4.3	5.9	3.0	−1.5	0.6	−1.0	−1.8	−2.2	−2.7	−5.7
Less: effect, built-in stabilizers											
Corporate profits tax accruals		1.8	2.4	4.1	4.1	1.8	1.2	−0.9			
Excise taxes		0.5	0.6	1.2	1.2	1.0	0.9	0.5			
Employment taxes		0.2	0.5	0.8	0.8	0.5	0.3	0.2			
Individual income tax accruals		0.3	1.0	2.2	2.2	1.7	1.5	1.3			
Unemployment compensation		0.5	1.3	1.2	1.2	1.0	0.5	0.4			
Other adjustments		0.4	0.3	1.0	1.0	1.1	2.3	1.2			
Total = actual surplus (national income account basis)	4.5	1.4	0.4	−5.5	−10.0	−4.3	−3.1	−2.1	...	...	...

a See Appendix D for sources and methods.
b Actual figures available only through the fourth quarter of 1961. Figures for first and second quarters of 1962 are those implicit in the Budget for the United States Government for the Fiscal Year Ending June 30, 1963 (January 1962).
c See text for methods of estimation.

most of the persons in the program in the early stage had been transferred from general relief rolls[39] and were not necessarily receiving more than previously. Although the shift probably loosened up state and local spending for other purposes, the short-run impact on aggregate demand is less than the amount of federal outlay.

Accelerated procurement and construction ordered in February 1961, was estimated by agencies in early March to permit an increase of $660 million in obligations and $247 million in expenditures by the end of June, with the Department of Defense accounting for the largest increases. A preliminary examination of the figures suggests that, while obligations fell short of their target, expenditures increased by substantially more. The reason lies in the nature of defense procurement. At any time, outstanding contracts for future delivery allow a large expenditure increase if contractors are told to hurry production, delivery, and the submission of bills, and are given authority for overtime work or similar practices. Prior to January, the Department had been trying to keep delivery schedules within current budget estimates. After the speed-up, the Department of Defense wound up fiscal 1961 with $650 million higher expenditures than estimated in March. There is, however, less scope for stepping up the rate at which new defense orders are placed, while still adhering to long-range defense programs and congressional authorizations. The defense appropriation bill was a little slower than usual in being enacted in 1961, and was not available at the start of fiscal 1962. Defense expenditures fell back considerably more than seasonally on a budget or cash basis in July-September 1961 (the national income estimate shows deliveries unchanged from the second quarter). Orders for the new fiscal year began accelerating during that quarter, and their effect on expenditures starting in the October-December quarter was strongly reinforced by other costs associated with defense program modifications.

The results of the public works speed-up were slightly mixed but total public works, both civil and military, appear to have been little affected by the speed-up by the end of fiscal 1961. Figures for the end of the fiscal year indicated that the Atomic Energy Commission had stepped up construction even more than estimated in

[33] *Social Security Bulletin,* September and October 1961.

March, but the General Services Administration and the Corps of Engineers had run into construction and land acquisition delays and had fallen behind. Some of the public works agencies were lower even than the January estimates.

Special payments of dividends on National Service Life Insurance came to $150 million in March and $218 million in July—which, when multiplied by twelve, amount to $1.8 billion and $2.6 billion, respectively, at annual rates. The first of these was an acceleration of payments that otherwise would have been made over the calendar year; the second was altogether extra. An additional special dividend was authorized later by Congress, and was paid starting in December 1961.

The acceleration of income tax refunds was more successful than in the two previous recessions when this was tried (see Table 25 in Chapter VI). About $480 million appears to have been added to refunds in February and March 1961, with a roughly offsetting reduction in April and May compared to the pattern of the preceding year. This acceleration is not reflected in the national income tabulation of income tax, since refunds are there apportioned equally among the quarters of the year.

Two aspects of the highway program should be considered: early release of already apportioned state contract authority, and the effects of legislative changes on subsequent apportionments and highway user charges. To take the administrative action first, the April-June contract authority was released two months before the start of the quarter. But January-March contract authority had also been released prior to the start of that quarter, and the subsequent action served only to maintain about the same quarter-to-quarter availability as had been planned before the beginning of the fiscal year. The same is true of the subsequent release of October-December 1961 authority prior to the start of that quarter, etc. Restraint over quarter-to-quarter state contracting of already apportioned funds was an innovation in 1959 that was not generally supposed to become permanent.

The highway legislation lifted 1963 authorizations (apportioned in July 1961) by $200 million above the previously authorized amounts and $200 million above the previous year's apportionment. Expenditures, however, will probably increase in fiscal 1962 by more than this amount, since the 1962 apportionment (made in July 1960) represented an increase of $400 million over 1961. Part of the expenditure increase in fiscal 1962 (the amount was estimated as $60 million in June) would not have been possible, however, without the legislative change, and another part might not have occurred if the states had taken anticipatory action in 1962 in response to reduced 1963 apportionments. On the other hand, the legislation increased tax rates for fiscal 1962 by $150 million over the level prevailing prior to July 1, 1961, and by $750 million over the level scheduled under previous law. The net effect of the highway program, therefore, was expansionary in 1962 compared to 1961, but considerably less than it would have been under previous law.

While a clear distinction between the weather, the recession, and long-run program goals, as reasons for the unusually large expenditures for farm price support programs in 1961 is impossible, it is probable that the desire to spend money quickly was a major factor. Table 30 includes, as a tentative measure of the "antirecession" portion, the increase that took place after the first quarter of 1961 in the national income account measures of federal subsidies. Budget expenditures—which have a decidedly different timing from the national income accounts expenditures in this area—rose by considerably more than this.

Conclusions—1960-1962

Fiscal developments in the recession and the first three quarters of recovery are summarized in Table 30. The total change of $10.0 billion in the federal surplus from peak to trough is comparable in order of magnitude to that in the 1957-58 recession, but is considerably larger relative to the decline in GNP. It is more accurate to ascribe the large relative change in the budget to the shallowness of the 1960-61 recession than to attribute the mildness of the recession to fiscal policy. The built-in stabilizers accounted for all but a minor part of the change in the budget surplus from peak to trough, and, as explained in Chapter II, the automatic stabilizers usually produce a relatively larger change in the surplus in a shallow recession than in a deep one.

As in earlier recessions, no discretionary antirecession actions were in effect before the trough month; discretionary actions are therefore relevant to the speed of the recovery but not to the initiation of a turning point. In the view of one spokesman, who was a member of the Council of Economic Advisers in 1960, the election was a factor in delaying official recognition of the recession in that year.[40]

Fiscal policy was influenced by outside factors to a somewhat greater degree than in earlier recessions. The balance of payments problem, for example, represented a constraint not previously present. Working in the opposite direction was the problem of overcoming chronic slack and stimulating adequate growth. This problem had policy implications supporting, rather than opposing, the stabilization program. Some of the other constraints noticeable in 1961 also were present in earlier recessions—uncertainty about future defense needs and an independent weight for budgetary objectives. On the other hand, the Kennedy administration in 1961 was conspicuously free from a constraint that had inhibited counterrecession proposals in the three previous recessions—the fear that an admission that the economy was in need of a fiscal stimulus would produce a perverse effect by depressing private expenditures.

Government expenditures on a national income basis rose sharply during the early recovery stage, and were undoubtedly a factor in the strong rise in the economy in the latter half of 1961. Defense expenditures account for a large part of this increase, and the purely (or primarily) counterrecession actions were not vastly different from those attempted in the two previous recoveries (Tables 30, 28, and 24). The latest experience confirms that any short-run, administrative speed-up of expenditures must depend heavily on actions of the Department of Defense, which accounts for two-thirds of the budget and perhaps 90 percent of federal procurement of goods and services. But the 1961 experience does not resolve doubts about how much flexibility in defense expenditures can be achieved on a sustained basis without revision of long-run program goals.

[40] Henry Wallich, in "Economic Policy for 1962: A Symposium," *Review of Economics and Statistics,* Vol. 44 (February 1962), p. 12.

The importance of budgetary goals, and the negative reaction of Congress and the public to a cash deficit coming after a recovery is clearly under way—but well before it is satisfactorily completed —suggest, as had the 1958-59 experience, the merit of concentrating attention on an accrual budget which shows its largest deficit close to the trough of the recession.

Progress can be discerned over the postwar period, from one recession to the next, in the public and political acceptance of unbalanced budgets as an appropriate means of combating recession. It remains true, however, that balanced budgets and "fiscal responsibility" are powerful ideas. Only for brief periods near the cyclical troughs has opposition been relaxed to deliberate additions to the passive budget deficits that inevitably accompany recession.

APPENDIX A

Calculation of High Employment
Benchmark Statistics

AT VARIOUS POINTS in this study, fiscal or economic statistics of actual developments during recession and recovery periods were compared with hypothetical high employment benchmark statistics. These benchmarks were constructed, in essence, by linear interpolation from the prerecession peak to the terminal quarter of recovery.

As explained more fully in Chapter I, peaks and troughs of recession periods, for purposes of this study, represent peaks and troughs in real deflated gross national product (GNP); terminal quarters of recovery periods represent the approximate points in time when the economy returned to its prerecession rate of activity or failed to recover further. (For dates of peaks, troughs, and terminal quarters, see Table A-1.)

Since the percentage of the labor force unemployed in each of the three terminal quarters of 1950, 1955, and 1959, was higher—and in 1962 was expected to be higher—than had prevailed at the prerecession peaks, data for these quarters were adjusted for the difference. "Terminal quarter adjustment factors"—the ratio of the prerecession

TABLE A-1. Actual and Hypothetical High Employment Measures of Gross National Product, Postwar Recessions and Recoveries[a]

(In billions of current dollars at seasonally adjusted annual rates)

Calendar Year Quarters		Actual[b]	Hypothetical High Employment	Shortfall
1948—IV	P	265.9	265.9	—
1949—I		259.8	268.2	−8.4
II	T	256.4	270.5	−14.1
III		258.8	272.9	−14.1
IV		257.0	275.2	−18.2
1950—I		265.8	277.5	−11.7
II	R	274.4	279.8	−5.4
1953—II	P	368.8	368.8	—
III		367.1	372.7	−5.6
IV		361.0	376.6	−15.6
1954—I		360.0	380.5	−20.5
II	T	358.9	384.4	−25.5
III		362.0	388.3	−26.3
IV		370.8	392.2	−21.4
1955—I		384.3	396.1	−11.8
II	R	393.0	400.0	−7.0
1957—III	P	448.3	448.3	—
IV		442.3	454.6	−12.3
1958—I	T	432.9	461.0	−28.1
II		437.2	467.3	−30.1
III		447.0	473.6	−26.6
IV		460.6	479.9	−19.3
1959—I		472.2	486.3	−14.1
II	R	488.5	492.6	−4.1
1960—II	P	506.4	506.4	—
III		505.1	513.4	−8.3
IV		504.5	520.3	−15.8
1961—I	T	500.8	527.2	−26.4
II		516.1	534.2	−18.1
III		525.8	541.2	−15.4
IV		542.2	548.1	−5.9
1962—I		550.0	555.0	−5.0
II	R	560.0	562.0	−2.0

[a] P, T, and R stand for peak, trough, and terminal quarter of recovery. The terminal quarter of the 1961-62 recovery (1962-II) was selected on the basis of projections made in March 1962.

[b] U. S. Department of Commerce, except for first and second quarters of 1962 which were projected on the basis of preliminary information in March 1962.

278

peak rate of employment to the terminal quarter rate of employment—
were calculated as follows:[1]

	Civilian Employment Percent of Civilian Labor Force		Terminal Quarter Adjustment Factor
Recession and Recovery	Prerecession Peak	Terminal Quarter	
1948-50	96.2	94.3	102.0
1953-55	97.4	95.7	101.8
1957-59	95.7	94.9	100.8
1960-62	94.8	94.5	100.3

All series for which hypothetical high employment values were required were constructed in one or the other of two ways:

Method 1: For the gross national product and most other series,
the actual value in the terminal quarter was raised by multiplying it by
the "terminal quarter adjustment factor" described above, and making
a linear interpolation from the actual value at the prerecession peak to
the adjusted value in the terminal quarter.

Method 2: For corporate profits, corporate gross saving, and corporate profits tax, it was felt that Method 1 gave unreliable results because of the tendency of profits, for largely cyclical reasons, to have a
temporarily higher value relative to GNP at the terminal quarter than
they would under conditions of stable growth. For these items, the
series in question was held at its prerecession ratio to GNP, with GNP
interpolated by Method 1.

For reference purposes, actual and high employment GNP are given
in Table A-1.

[1] Figures from U.S. Department of Labor, *Monthly Report on the Labor Force,*
February 1960 (for 1948-50) and January 1962 (for 1953-61). Figure for terminal
quarter (second quarter of 1962) was projected in March 1962.

Measurement of Individual Income Tax Accruals, 1946-1959

THE QUARTERLY SERIES used to measure the built-in flexibility of the individual income tax was constructed by adjusting for (discretionary) changes in tax rates, by eliminating estimated capital gains tax from collections which were not withheld, by converting collections to estimates of accrued liabilities, and by adjusting for seasonality.

Declaration and Final Payments

Published statistics on the individual income tax are not in a form which allows separation of the effects of discretionary changes in tax rates from the automatic built-in stabilizer effects. Aside from annual data in *Statistics of Income,* published Treasury Department statistics on nonwithheld individual income tax make no distinction between declarations of estimated tax and final payments on the preceding year's liabilities. Similarly, the Commerce Department estimates included in the national income accounts combine nonwithheld collections regardless of year of liability. It was necessary to make use of unpublished monthly estimates of the break between declarations on the current year's tax, declarations on the previous year's tax, and final payments. These data, which were made available by the Treasury Department, are summarized quarterly by year of liability in Table B-1, along with figures on unadjusted collections of withheld tax and payments of refunds. The final results of adjustments described below are given in Table B-4.

Capital Gains

Published statistics on the individual income tax make no distinction between the tax on ordinary income and the tax on capital gains. For many purposes, a distinction is unnecessary, since the tax on capital gains is an integral part of the tax system and as much a tax on individuals as the tax attributable to ordinary income. However, in a national income accounting framework, capital gains income is excluded conceptually and statistically from aggregate income and from the incomes of particular sectors of the economy. It is misleading to compare tax figures which include the tax on capital gains with tax base figures which exclude that source of income. This is particularly true for comparisons of change in tax with change in income over the cycle, since capital gains have tended toward a roughly contracyclical pattern in the postwar period. In the absence of a reliable method of adjusting national income account statistics to include capital gains income, it was considered advisable to adjust the tax statistics to exclude the estimated liability attributable to capital gains.

Statistics of Income data include annual figures on reported capital gains subject to the alternative rate of tax optional for such gains, and capital gains taxed at normal plus surtax rates. For capital gains taxed at normal plus surtax rates, the tax was estimated by calculating the average marginal rate for 1949, 1953, and 1956 on short-term capital gains plus 50 percent of long-term gains, less allowable capital losses on taxable returns. For each taxable income bracket, a weighted average of marginal tax rates on taxable joint returns and returns for single taxpayers was computed. For brackets where the resulting rate was below 50 percent in 1949 and 1955 and below 52 percent in 1953, this calculated rate was applied to capital gains in that bracket. For higher brackets, the limiting rate for long-term capital gains (set by the optional alternative rate of tax) of 50 percent (or 52 percent in 1953) was used. Although using the upper limit slightly overstates the effective tax rate, the inclusion in the figures of (relatively minor amounts of) short-term gains, to which the limit does not apply, works in the opposite direction.

The average marginal rate of tax on capital gains so calculated was remarkably similar for the three years, although each of the years featured different rate schedules under different tax codes and each was at a different stage of the business cycle. The average marginal rate of

TABLE B-1. Individual Income Tax by Type: Cash Collections, Unadjusted for Seasonality or Change in Tax Rates

(In millions of dollars)

Calendar Year and Quarter	Withheld Tax[a]	Nonwithheld Tax[b] Current-Year Income[c]	Nonwithheld Tax[b] Previous-Year Income[d]	Less Refunds[e]	Total[f]	Estimated Capital Gains Tax[g]
1945—I	2,748	906	3,617	280	6,991	212
II	2,708	1,328	918	215	4,739	90
III	2,638	1,229	349	255	3,961	35
IV	2,355	504	411	65	3,205	39
Year	10,449	3,967	5,295	815	18,896	376
1946—I	2,298	1,079	3,538	520	6,395	474
II	2,101	1,098	639	1,390	2,448	164
III	2,289	1,335	329	125	3,828	72
IV	2,435	446	306	44	3,143	56
Year	9,123	3,958	4,812	2,079	15,814	766
1947—I	2,708	863	4,382	522	7,431	760
II	2,581	1,202	671	1,003	3,451	189
III	2,676	1,164	324	78	4,086	76
IV	2,839	435	286	35	3,525	47
Year	10,804	3,664	5,663	1,638	18,493	1,072
1948—I	3,184	993	4,382	611	7,948	579
II	2,737	1,013	867	958	3,659	165
III	2,394	1,059	287	129	3,611	41
IV	2,449	302	282	38	2,995	30
Year	10,764	3,367	5,818	1,736	18,213	815
1949—I	2,643	843	3,822	918	6,390	576
II	2,356	914	488	1,293	2,465	97
III	2,371	976	281	56	3,572	43
IV	2,392	241	263	38	2,858	32
Year	9,762	2,974	4,854	2,305	15,285	748
1950—I	2,672	843	3,157	761	5,911	378
II	2,638	892	611	800	3,341	97
III	2,676	1,031	307	60	3,954	35
IV	3,123	316	227	36	3,630	14
Year	11,109	3,082	4,302	1,657	16,836	524
1951—I	3,997	1,013	4,636	613	9,033	638
II	3,740	1,263	1,115	1,040	5,078	259
III	3,984	1,348	364	76	5,620	69
IV	4,317	416	206	36	4,903	18
Year	16,038	4,040	6,321	1,765	24,634	984
1952—I	4,920	1,146	4,782	632	10,216	605
II	5,100	1,705	1,577	1,208	7,174	326
III	4,823	1,617	559	213	6,786	97
IV	5,029	439	220	46	5,642	19
Year	19,872	4,907	7,138	2,099	29,818	1,047
1953—I	5,790	1,242	5,001	1,254	10,779	621
II	5,709	1,480	859	1,179	6,869	168
III	5,473	1,750	264	93	7,394	52
IV	5,605	358	221	54	6,130	15
Year	22,577	4,830	6,345	2,580	31,172	856
1954—I	5,576	1,259	4,605	1,415	10,025	538
II	4,982	1,326	964	1,317	5,955	149
III	5,035	1,455	319	120	6,689	48
IV	5,194	471	78	29	5,714	1
Year	20,787	4,511	5,966	2,881	28,383	736

TABLE B-1. Individual Income Tax by Type (continued)

Calendar Year and Quarter	Withheld Tax[a]	Nonwithheld Tax[b] Current-Year Income[c]	Nonwithheld Tax[b] Previous-Year Income[d]	Less Refunds[e]	Total[f]	Estimated Capital Gains Tax[g]
1955—I 5,521	280	3,585	871	8,515		479
II 5,503	2,515	1,694	1,928	7,784		629
III 5,492	1,811	265	195	7,373		61
IV 5,819	393	230	72	6,370		40
Year 22,335	4,999	5,774	3,066	30,042		1,209
1956—I 6,565	268	3,448	796	9,485		610
II 6,136	2,767	2,140	2,144	8,899		979
III 6,338	2,024	310	194	8,478		106
IV 6,682	418	253	24	7,329		54
Year 25,721	5,477	6,151	3,158	34,191		1,749
1957—I 6,946	269	3,487	752	9,950		569
II 6,762	3,100	2,442	2,440	9,864		912
III 6,888	1,898	322	207	8,901		88
IV 6,872	398	256	85	7,441		47
Year 27,468	5,665	6,507	3,484	36,156		1,616
1958—I 6,934	232	3,266	944	9,488		424
II 6,346	2,956	2,199	2,609	8,892		687
III 6,764	1,883	314	182	8,779		71
IV 7,005	367	263	66	7,569		37
Year 27,049	5,438	6,042	3,801	34,728		1,219
1959—I 7,517	229	3,338	1,408	9,676		518
II 7,716	2,975	2,364	2,361	10,694		874
III 7,725	1,977	347	222	9,827		89
IV 7,927	447	271	72	8,573		49
Year 30,885	5,628	6,320	4,063	38,770		1,530
1960—I 8,236	248	3,570	1,650	10,404		672
II 7,787	3,196	3,216	2,386	11,813		1,438
III 8,431	2,097	354	248	10,634		122
IV 8,185	446	287	94	8,824		68
Year 32,639	5,987	7,427	4,378	41,675		2,300
1961—I 8,243	251	3,443	2,195	9,742		...
II 8,119	3,276	3,021	2,278	12,138		...
III 8,551	2,071	352	222	10,752		...
IV 9,101	486	281	70	9,798		...
Year 34,014	6,084	7,097	4,765	42,430		...

a Figures on withheld tax for period 1945–I to 1952–II are from Daily Treasury Statement based mainly on telegraphic reports on deposits at Federal Reserve Banks. Figures from 1953–II on are based on Internal Revenue Service collections reported in the Monthly Treasury Statement, reflecting a change in the Treasury reporting method starting with data for February 1953. Figures for the period 1952–II to 1953–I are derived from unpublished Treasury Department estimates to agree with the Monthly Treasury Statement basis. All figures on withholdings are gross of any refunds that may subsequently be made, and exclude amounts estimated by the Treasury for old-age and survivors insurance payroll taxes.

b Figures on current-year declarations of estimated tax are from unpublished Internal Revenue Service tabulations. Figures on total nonwithheld tax for the period 1946–I to 1952–II are also from Internal Revenue Service tabulations and do not agree with the Daily Treasury Statement. Excludes amounts estimated by the Treasury for self-employment taxes.

c $1,771.5 million classified in Internal Revenue Service tabulations as a final declaration on 1945 tax was reclassified as part of initial declarations on 1946 tax to eliminate what otherwise would be a negative entry.

d Includes (relatively minor) amount of back taxes, in addition to final declarations and final payments on income of the immediately previous year.

e Figures on individual income tax refunds in the first and second quarters of 1946 were estimated consistent with annual total of refunds by source and quarterly totals for combined refunds. All other figures are from Internal Revenue Service tabulations.

f Includes tax paid on capital gains.

g See text of Appendix B for method of estimation.

tax on reported capital gains taxed at normal plus surtax tax rates was as follows:

1949	32.4%
1953	31.2
1955	32.8

It was therefore assumed that 32 percent would represent a reasonable rate to use for all years, at least since 1948. The rate for 1949 was also computed on the assumption of no income-splitting to see what effect this provision of the Revenue Act of 1948 might have had. For 1949, income-splitting reduced the average rate of tax attributable to capital gains by approximately one-tenth. It appears therefore that 35 percent would be an appropriate estimate of the rate on capital gains prior to the 1948 act. Table B-2 gives calendar-year estimates of capital gains and capital gains tax.

To estimate the timing of capital gains payments, it was necessary to allocate estimated capital gains tax between declarations and final pay-

TABLE B-2. Capital Gains in Taxable Individual Income Tax Returns and Tax Attributable to Capital Gains[a]

(Dollar amounts in millions of dollars)

TAX YEAR	RETURNS TAXED AT NORMAL PLUS SURTAX TAX RATES			RETURNS USING ALTERNATIVE RATES[b]			ALL TAXABLE RETURNS	
	Net Capital Gains[c]	Assumed Tax Rate[d] Percent	Tax Attributable	Net Capital Gains	Alternative Tax Rate Percent	Tax Attributable	Net Capital Gains[c]	Total Tax Attributable
1945	964	35	338	836	50	418	1,801	756
1946	1,667	35	584	942	50	471	2,609	1,055
1947	1,362	35	477	690	50	345	2,053	822
1948	1,474	32	472	556	50	278	2,030	750
1949	1,029	32	329	413	50	206	1,442	536
1950	1,515	32	485	964	50	482	2,479	967
1951	1,675	32	536	1,010	50	505	2,686	1,041
1952	1,362	32	436	870	52	452	2,232	861
1953	1,125	32	360	733	52	381	1,858	741
1954	1,893	32	606	1,167	50	584	3,060	1,189
1955	2,688	32	860	1,728	50	864	4,416	1,724
1956	2,617	32	838	1,563	50	782	4,180	1,619
1957	1,956	32	626	1,221	50	611	3,178	1,237
1958	2,517	32	806	1,427	50	714	3,944	1,519
1959	3,621	32	1,159	2,133	50	1,066	5,754	2,225

a See *The Federal Revenue System: Facts and Problems, 1961*, Joint Economic Committee, 87 Cong. 1 sess. (1961), Table 53, p. 236, for alternative estimates yielding rather similar results.
b Internal Revenue Service, *Statistics of Income: Individual Income Tax Returns*, annually.
c Source same as b. Net short-term gains plus 50 percent of net long-term gains, less allowable losses.
d See text of Appendix B.

ments. Several correlations were run associating declarations and final payment in various forms with changes in tax rates, changes in income other than capital gains, capital gains in the current year, and capital gains in the previous year. While the results were not identical, they all pointed to the conclusions that changes in capital gains from one year to the next have little effect on declarations of estimated tax, and that declarations, insofar as they include capital gains at all, are more significantly affected by capital gains of the preceding year than by the current year's capital gains. A correlation of declarations with income other than capital gains and capital gains of the current and preceding years gave coefficients of .034 and .056 on capital gains of the current and preceding years respectively, and these were the percentages finally used. To spread the annual amounts for capital gains included in declarations by quarters, 5.6 percent of capital gains in the preceding year was allocated to the four declarations in proportion to tax paid at each of these times, and 3.4 percent of capital gains of the current year was allocated entirely to the fourth declaration. The remainder of capital gains tax was assumed to be paid with final payments.

Estimation of Accrued Tax Liabilities

Apart from annual data in *Statistics of Income,* Treasury Department reports on the individual income tax show collections on a cash flow rather than on an accrued liability basis. The national income account estimates for this tax are also on a collection rather than an accrual basis, with the exception that an adjustment is made to the withheld portion of the tax to eliminate the lag between withholding by the employers and payment by employers to the Treasury.

Whether accrued liabilities or cash payments represent the better measure of economic impact of the nonwithheld individual income tax may be debated. But in any event, it seems appropriate in analyzing the built-in stabilizer effects of the tax to distinguish between the change in liability associated with a change in income, and the logically separable effects of a lag between liability and cash payment.

To take the withheld tax first, informal Treasury Department estimates are that about 90 percent of taxes withheld by employers in the first two months of each quarter, and 10 percent of taxes withheld in the third month, are deposited to Treasury accounts by the end of the calendar quarter. The remainder is not paid until the following quarter. To test the implied 60-40 break between payment in the current quarter and following quarter, quarterly withheld collections (seasonally adjusted) were correlated with Commerce Department estimates of wages and salaries for the current quarter and the previous quarter. The correlation of absolute magnitudes yielded coefficients suggesting a longer time lag than 60-40, but a correlation of increments yielded a coefficient for the current quarter almost exactly 50 percent larger than the coefficient for the preceding quarter. The 60-40 distribution was consequently accepted as a basis for placing withheld tax on an accrual basis (with the percentages modified for those quarters in which a change in tax rates took place).

To place declarations of estimated tax on an accrual basis, a rearrangement of the data summarized in Table B-1 was necessary. Monthly reports of the Internal Revenue Service on estimated tax were not specifically labeled "first declaration," "second declaration," etc. However, satisfactory estimates of these were possible using the following plan:

> First declaration: current-year declarations for January, February, March, April, and one-half of May.
> Second declaration: current-year declarations for one-half of May, all of June and July, and one-half of August.
> Third declaration: current-year declarations for one-half of August, and all of September, October, and November.
> Fourth declaration: current-year declarations for December, and all of the declarations not paid until the following year.

It was then assumed that the first, second, third, and fourth declarations, so computed (and after seasonal adjustment, because the fourth declaration is considerably larger than the others), represented in effect liabilities accrued in the first, second, third, and fourth calendar-year quarters, respectively. Accrual of final payments and of refunds was accomplished in one step along with their seasonal adjustment.

Seasonal Adjustment

Seasonal adjustment of withheld collections and of the four quarterly declarations was accomplished by electronic computer, using the Univac II method for moving seasonal indexes. Seasonal adjustment of final payments and refunds was accomplished (simultaneously with transforming the estimates to an accrued liability basis) by spreading final payments in proportion to the sum of seasonally adjusted accrued withholdings and seasonally adjusted accrued declarations, and refunds in proportion to seasonally adjusted accrued withholdings.

In passing, the method of seasonal adjustment employed in the national income account estimates of nonwithheld individual income tax and refunds makes these data unsatisfactory for studying built-in flexibility on a quarter-by-quarter basis (aside from the impossibility of making adjustments for changes in tax rates). The procedure there used is to take the calendar year total (on a cash flow basis) and to enter this amount as the constant seasonally adjusted annual rate for each quarter of the calendar year. This gives rise to discontinuities between the fourth quarter of each calendar year and the first quarter of the next, reflecting a change from one annual level of tax to another.

Tax Rate Adjustments

Adjustments for changes in tax rates were accomplished by multiplying in proportion to change in first-bracket rates plus an additional adjustment for the estimated reduction of 2.5 percent in effective tax rates consequent to the Revenue Act of 1954. (See Table B-3.)

TABLE B-3. Tax Rate Adjustment Factors for Individual Income Tax Accruals

Calendar-Year Quarters	Adjustment for Changes in First Bracket Rate		Adjustment for Effect 1954 Code[a]	Combined Index	
	First Bracket Rate Percent	Index, 1960 = 100	Index, 1960 = 100	1960 = 100	Pre-recession Peak = 100
1948-III through 1950-II	16.6	83.0	102.5	85.1	100.0
1950-III	18.9[b]	94.5	102.5	96.9	...
1950-IV through 1951-III	20.0	100.0	102.5	102.5	...
1951-IV	21.5[c]	107.5	102.5	110.2	...
1952-I through 1953-I	22.2	111.0	102.5	113.8	...
1953-II through 1953-IV	22.2	111.0	102.5	113.8	100.0
1954-I through 1954-II	20.0	100.0	101.0	101.0	88.8
1954-III through 1955-II	20.0	100.0	100.0	100.0	87.9
1955-III through 1959-IV	20.0	100.0	100.0	100.0	...

[a] Estimated revenue effect of $570 million on calendar 1954 liabilities and $685 million on a full year basis (the 4 percent dividend credit applied to only the second half of 1954).
[b] First bracket rate increased to 20.0 percent effective August 1, 1950 (Revenue Act of 1950).
[c] First bracket rate increased to 22.2 percent effective Nov. 1, 1951 (Revenue Act of 1951).

TABLE B-4. Individual Income Tax by Type: Seasonally Adjusted Accruals, Excluding Estimated Capital Gains Tax

(In millions of dollars)

Calendar Year Quarters	Individual Income Tax Components (Quarterly Totals, Actual Tax Rates)					Total Individual Income Tax (Annual Rates)	
	Withheld Tax	Declarations Estimated Tax	Final Payments and Other	Less Refunds	Total Individual Income Tax	At Constant 1960 Tax Rates[a]	At Constant Prerecession Tax Rates[b]
1946—I	2,017	1,565	624	358	3,848	...	...
II	2,251	1,371	631	400	3,853	...	...
III	2,459	1,435	679	437	4,136	...	...
IV	2,494	1,519	700	443	4,270	...	...
1947—I	2,536	1,299	745	400	4,180	...	...
II	2,707	1,416	801	426	4,498	...	...
III	2,872	1,328	816	452	4,564	...	...
IV	2,921	1,398	839	459	4,699	...	...
1948—I	2,956	1,436	718	645	4,465	...	...
II	2,587	1,134	609	564	3,766	...	...
III	2,530	1,159	604	552	3,741	17,584	...
IV	2,489	1,221	607	543	3,774	17,739 P	15,096
1949—I	2,421	1,114	624	409	3,750	17,626	15,000
II	2,428	1,083	620	410	3,721	17,490 T	14,884
III	2,479	1,074	628	419	3,762	17,683	15,048
IV	2,474	1,017	617	418	3,690	17,344	14,760
1950—I	2,559	1,125	730	387	4,027	18,929	16,108
II	2,629	1,086	736	397	4,054	19,055 R	16,216
III	3,010	1,175	829	455	4,559	18,820	...
IV	3,477	1,568	999	525	5,519	21,537	...
1951—I	3,755	1,445	913	480	5,633	21,982	...
II	3,908	1,461	943	500	5,812	22,681	...
III	4,187	1,483	996	536	6,130	23,922	...
IV	4,565	1,649	1,091	584	6,721	24,396	...
1952—I	4,866	1,798	840	618	6,886	24,204	...
II	5,058	1,782	862	643	7,059	24,812	...
III	5,073	1,684	852	645	6,964	24,478	...
IV	5,294	1,711	883	673	7,215	25,360	...
1953—I	5,589	1,668	815	711	7,361	25,873	...
II	5,693	1,723	833	724	7,525	26,450 P	30,100
III	5,687	1,739	834	723	7,537	26,492	30,148
IV	5,686	1,642	823	723	7,428	26,109	29,712
1954—I	5,066	1,582	618	752	6,514	25,798	29,342
II	5,085	1,570	618	755	6,518	25,814 T	29,360
III	5,219	1,633	636	775	6,713	26,852	30,548
IV	5,264	1,734	650	782	6,866	27,464	31,244
1955—I	5,402	1,618	631	750	6,901	27,604	31,404
II	5,602	1,590	647	777	7,062	28,248 R	32,136
III	5,722	1,703	668	794	7,299	29,196	...
IV	6,030	1,830	707	837	7,730	30,920	...
1956—I	6,286	1,777	770	846	7,987	31,948	...
II	6,348	1,814	779	854	8,087	32,348	...
III	6,558	1,801	798	882	8,275	33,100	...
IV	6,700	1,809	812	902	8,419	33,676	...
1957—I	6,787	1,871	791	939	8,511	34,044	...
II	6,945	1,858	805	960	8,648	34,592	...
III	6,941	1,828	802	960	8,611	34,444 P	34,444
IV	6,820	1,750	783	943	8,410	33,640	33,640
1958—I	6,629	1,772	768	987	8,182	32,728 T	32,728
II	6,627	1,762	768	986	8,171	32,684	32,684
III	6,900	1,773	793	1,027	8,439	33,756	33,756
IV	7,135	1,786	816	1,062	8,675	34,700	34,700
1959—I	7,531	1,798	808	1,033	9,104	36,416	36,416
II	7,824	1,838	838	1,074	9,426	37,704 R	37,704
III	7,849	1,874	843	1,077	9,489	37,956	...
IV	7,974	1,918	857	1,095	9,654	38,616	...

[a] See Table B-3; adjustment factors for change in tax rates in Revenue Act of 1948 not available. P, T, and R refer to peaks, troughs, and terminal periods of recovery.
[b] See Table B-3.

Measurement of Fiscal Effects of Built-in Stabilizers

THIS APPENDIX discusses some of the more technical aspects of the measurement of the fiscal effects of the built-in stabilizers and includes statistical data and estimates in addition to those given in Chapter II.

Corporation Income Tax

In order to relate the changes in corporate tax to trends in the economy, it is best to deal with the national income estimates of the tax rather than Treasury statistics of tax liabilities or collections. Further, the national income accounts provide the only quarterly estimate of the tax on a seasonally adjusted accrual basis. However, isolation of the sources of cyclical change is helped by also considering the income and tax liability data reported by corporations to the Internal Revenue Service and recorded in *Statistics of Income*. Both the tax and the base differ in the national income framework from the amounts reported by the Internal Revenue Service. A detailed reconciliation of the statistics is given in Table C-1, and the major summary items, and their year-to-year changes, are given in the top part of Table C-2.[1]

[1] The sources of cyclical change in yield can be isolated in the following fashion. Let T_c and T_r represent federal corporate profits tax as measured in the national income accounts and in *Statistics of Income* respectively. Let π represent corporate profits before tax, national income basis, and R stand for "taxable profits" on a *Statistics of Income* basis. Then the ratio of tax to profits $\dfrac{T_c}{\pi}$ can be decomposed as follows:

$$\frac{T_c}{\pi} = \frac{T_c}{T_r} \cdot \frac{T_r}{R} \cdot \frac{R}{\pi}$$

Values for these ratios are shown in the second half of Table C-2.

TABLE C-1. Corporate Profits and Profits Taxes: National Income Account Accruals Compared to Tax Returns[a]

(In millions of dollars)

Item	1948	1949	1950	1951	1952	1953	1954	1955	1956	1957	1958
Profits before tax, national income account basis	33,000	26,370	40,628	42,153	36,691	38,311	34,061	44,862	44,683	43,208	37,410
Plus: Profits of mutual financial intermediaries	1,440	1,583	1,707	1,763	2,095	2,383	2,560	2,819	3,123	3,403	725
Gains, net of losses, from sale of property	796	667	1,083	1,294	1,216	978	1,997	1,977	2,004	1,851	3,175
Domestic dividends received	2,194	2,162	2,460	2,377	2,350	2,389	2,332	2,572	2,688	2,681	2,829
Corporation income from foreign equities	1,147	1,174	1,504	1,920	1,841	1,901	1,827	2,393	2,487	2,667	2,694
Less: Resident income from foreign equities (net)	836	832	1,000	1,215	1,121	1,126	1,413	1,558	1,757	1,925	1,799
Depletion	1,711	1,476	1,709	2,085	2,126	2,302	2,359	2,806	3,084	3,347	3,148
State corporation income taxes	670	602	767	878	820	803	765	958	1,032	1,006	989
Profits of Federal Reserve banks	232	239	195	299	351	400	329	302	474	632	604
Post-tabulation amendments	540	420	880	1,230	1,040	1,530	1,190	1,050	1,225	1,827	1,069
Compiled net profit or loss, IRS	34,588	28,387	42,831	43,800	38,735	39,801	36,721	47,949	47,413	45,073	39,224
Less: Wholly tax-exempt interest	163	192	218	254	279	316	393	471	528	597	701
Net income or deficit, IRS	34,425	28,195	42,613	43,546	38,456	39,485	36,328	47,478	46,885	44,476	38,523
Plus: Deficit, returns with no net income	1,848	2,382	1,528	1,787	1,976	2,334	3,245	2,851	3,299	4,188	4,967
Net income, returns with net income, IRS	36,273	30,577	44,141	45,333	40,432	41,819	39,573	50,329	50,184	48,664	43,490
Less: Net operating loss deduction	204	196	345	402	396	413	438	836	918	963	1,074
Net income, small business returns (1120-S)											288
85 percent of domestic dividends	1,847	1,818	2,074	1,995	1,976	2,010	1,915	2,154	2,210	2,144	2,315
Special credits, life insurance companies	1,450	1,470	1,550	1,640	1,830	2,000	2,220	2,480	2,710	2,950	...
Special credits, Western Hemisphere Trade Corporations	...	...	140	146	140	135	141	196	222	238	201
"Taxable income," IRS basis	32,772	27,093	40,032	41,150	36,090	37,261	34,859	44,663	44,124	42,369	39,612
Income tax if alternative tax not used	12,006	9,883	16,069	19,870	17,820	18,470	17,170	22,126	21,790	20,992	19,384
Less: Tax saving from alternative tax	86	66	140	247	223	214	347	385	426	410	570
Corporation income tax, IRS	11,920	9,817	15,929	19,623	17,597	18,256	16,823	21,741	21,364	20,582	18,814
Plus: Excess profits tax	...	...	1,387	2,459	1,551	1,613	38	...	...	...	...
Income and excess profits tax, IRS	11,920	9,817	17,317	22,082	19,148	19,869	16,861	21,741	21,364	20,582	18,814
Plus: Post-tabulation amendments	18	80	125	−23	−69	11	220	64	−323	115	−326
Income taxes of Federal Reserve Banks	167	193	197	255	292	343	276	252	402	543	524
Less: Taxes on mutual financial intermediaries	14	47	74	120	145	162	176	229	250	271	285
U.S. credits for foreign taxes paid	278	270	467	625	587	642	726	959	998	1,053	1,070
Federal profits tax liability, national income account basis	11,813	9,773	17,098	21,569	18,639	19,419	16,455	20,869	20,195	19,916	17,657

[a] From U. S. Department of Commerce, Internal Revenue Service (IRS) tabulations, and Treasury Department estimates.

TABLE C-2. Relation of Federal Corporate Profits Tax to Profits Before Taxes[a]

(Amounts in billions of current dollars)

A. AMOUNTS

Calendar Year	T_c = Corporate Profits Tax Accruals, National Income Account Basis		T_r = Corporation Income Tax Liability, IRS		R = Taxable Income, IRS Basis		π = Corporate Profits Before Tax, National Income Account Basis	
	Amount	Increment	Amount	Increment	Amount	Increment	Amount	Increment
1948	11.8	1.1	11.9	...	32.8	...	33.0	3.5
1949 (T)	9.8	—2.0	9.8	—2.1	27.1	—5.7	26.4	—6.6
1950	15.7	5.9	15.9	6.1	40.0	12.9	40.6	14.3
1951	19.1	3.4	19.6	3.7	41.2	1.1	42.2	1.5
1952	17.1	—2.0	17.6	—2.0	36.1	—5.1	36.7	—5.5
1953	17.8	0.7	18.3	0.7	37.3	1.2	38.3	1.6
1954 (T)	16.4	—1.4	16.8	—1.4	34.9	—2.4	34.1	—4.2
1955	20.9	4.5	21.7	4.9	44.7	9.8	44.9	10.8
1956	20.2	—0.7	21.4	—0.4	44.1	—0.5	44.7	—0.2
1957	19.9	—0.3	20.6	—0.8	42.4	—1.8	43.2	—1.5
1958 (T)	17.7	—2.3	18.8	—1.8	39.6	—2.8	37.4	—5.8

B. COMPOSITION OF CHANGE IN RATIO OF TAX TO PROFITS, NATIONAL INCOME ACCOUNT BASIS

Calendar Year	$\dfrac{T_c}{\pi}$	$=$	$\dfrac{T_c}{T_r}$	$\cdot$	$\dfrac{T_r}{R}$	$\cdot$	$\dfrac{R}{\pi}$
1948	.358		.991		.364		.993
1949 (T)	.371		.996		.362		1.027
1950	.387		.986		.398		.985
1951	.453		.974		.477		.976
1952	.466		.971		.488		.984
1953	.465		.975		.490		.972
1954 (T)	.482		.976		.483		1.023
1955	.465		.960		.487		.996
1956	.452		.945		.484		.988
1957	.461		.968		.486		.980
1958 (T)	.472		.938		.475		1.059

[a] See Table C-1. Data adjusted to exclude excess profits tax accruals for the years 1950-54. No adjustment made for the different tax rates in effect prior to 1952; however, the comparability of data for each recession year with that of the year preceding it is not affected by tax rate change. T stands for trough year of recession.

As seen from the ratios in the second half of Table C-2, national income taxes are smaller than taxes reported in *Statistics of Income* (see Table C-1 for the differences). However, the ratio shows no particular cyclical pattern.

At given tax rates,[2] the cyclical changes in yield due to any progressivity of the tax would show up in the ratio of tax to income on a *Statistics of Income* basis. Values for this ratio do decline slightly in recession years (column headed T_r/R), but this ratio is better described as very nearly constant. The major cyclical volatility is apparent in the ratio of profits for tax purposes to national income profits (the column marked R/π). Ignoring differences between these two measures of profits which do not appear to exhibit regular cyclical patterns, sensitivity to cycles appears to be the result of the following:

1) Profits of mutual financial intermediaries (stock as well as mutual life insurance companies): Such profits are included in taxable income, but treated in the national income accounts as part of the household rather than the corporate sector. In the first two postwar recessions, profits of mutual financial intermediaries rose, causing a smaller drop in taxable than in national income profits. But in 1958 the profits of mutual financial intermediaries declined sharply.

2) Capital gains (net of losses): These are included in taxable profits but excluded from national income profits. Realized capital gains rose sharply in the recession years 1954 and 1958, causing taxable profits to decline less than national income profits, but there was no such influence in 1949.

3) Deficits of loss corporations: In the national income account figures on total profits, losses of one corporation are offset against the income of another, although corporations experiencing losses do not have negative taxes. This item is probably the major and most consistent reason for a smaller drop in tax than in aggregate profits during recession. The increase in average effective rate because of loss corporations is partially offset by the loss carryback provisions of the law, which allow a loss corporation to file for reimbursement of taxes paid

---

[2] Excess profits taxes (in effect 1950 through 1953, with a minor residual effect in 1954) are excluded from the figures in Table C-2. Aside from excess profits taxes, the rates in effect for the postwar period are as follows:

Calendar Year		Tax Rate (% of income)
1946-49	First $25,000	21-25
	$25,000 to $50,000	53
	Over $50,000	38
1950	Normal tax	23
	Surtax (over $25,000)	19
1951	Normal tax	28¾
	Surtax (over $25,000)	22
1952-present	Normal tax	30
	Surtax (over $25,000)	22

TABLE C-3. Federal Corporation Income Tax Loss Carrybacks, Fiscal 1957-60[a]

(In millions of dollars)

Fiscal Year	Claims Allowed for Operating Loss Carryback
1957	237
1958	297
1959	600
1960	479

^a U.S. Treasury Department.

[a] U.S. Treasury Department.

in the three years previous.[3] If loss carrybacks were fully effective, there would be no rise in average rate of tax in recession. But some losses cannot be absorbed by the carryback and are carried forward to future years. For example, deficits of loss corporations rose $779 million in the recession year 1958 (Table C-1) but loss carrybacks in the corresponding fiscal year (1959) rose only $303 million (Table C-3).

4) Net operating loss deduction: Losses not covered by profits in the tax year or during the loss carryback period may be carried forward against profits in subsequent years for up to five years. This factor also reduces the cycle sensitivity of the tax. Operating loss deductions carried forward (again, see Table C-1) rise sharply the year following recession, reducing the responsiveness of the tax to increasing income during recovery.

Individual Income Tax

Taxable income is compared to personal income in Table C-4. As before, a convenient method of isolating influences on the cyclical behavior of the tax base consists of separating the aggregate ratio into its components, which is done in the bottom part of the table.[4]

[3] Two years for losses incurred 1954-57 and one year for losses prior to 1954.
[4] Let: *PI* = Personal income
      PI' = Personal income less transfer payments
      AGI' = Adjusted gross income reported on taxable returns, excluding capital gains
      TI = Taxable income (adjusted gross income less personal exemptions and deductions)
      TI' = Taxable income, excluding capital gains
Then the ratio of taxable to personal income can be represented by,

$$\frac{TI}{PI} = \frac{TI}{TI'} \cdot \frac{TI'}{AGI'} \cdot \frac{AGI'}{PI'} \cdot \frac{PI'}{PI}$$

TABLE C-4. Personal, Taxable, and Adjusted Gross Income, 1948-59[a]

(Amounts in billions of current dollars)

A. AMOUNTS

Calendar Year	TI = Taxable Income[b]		TI' = Taxable Income Excluding Capital Gains		AGI' = Adjusted Gross Income on Taxable Returns Excluding Capital Gains		PI' = Personal Income Less Transfer Payments	
	Amount	Increment	Amount	Increment	Amount	Increment	Amount	Increment
1948	74.7	...[c]	72.7	...[c]	140.0	6.8	199.2	19.4
1949 (T)	71.6	−3.0	70.2	−2.5	137.1	−2.9	195.9	−3.2
1950	84.3	12.6	81.8	11.6	156.1	18.9	213.3	17.4
1951	99.3	15.0	96.6	14.8	182.5	26.4	244.1	30.8
1952	107.5	8.1	105.2	8.6	196.3	13.8	259.9	15.7
1953	115.6	8.1	113.7	8.5	210.6	14.3	274.0	14.1
1954 (T)	115.2	−0.3	112.2	−1.5	206.6	−4.0	273.6	−0.4
1955	127.9	12.7	123.5	11.3	225.2	18.6	292.7	19.1
1956	141.4	13.5	137.2	13.8	245.4	20.2	314.1	21.4
1957	149.2	7.8	146.0	8.8	259.0	13.6	329.5	15.4
1958 (T)	149.2	—	145.2	−0.8	258.2	−0.7	333.9	4.4
1959	166.4	17.2	160.6	15.4	282.0	23.8	356.1	22.2

B. COMPOSITION OF RATIO OF TAXABLE TO PERSONAL INCOME[d]

Calendar Year	$\dfrac{TI}{PI}$ =	$\dfrac{TI}{TI'}$.	$\dfrac{TI'}{AGI'}$.	$\dfrac{AGI'}{PI'}$.	$\dfrac{PI'}{PI}$
1948	.355	1.028	.519	.703	.946
1949 (T)	.344	1.021	.512	.700	.940
1950	.369	1.030	.524	.732	.934
1951	.387	1.028	.529	.748	.951
1952	.393	1.021	.536	.755	.952
1953	.401	1.016	.540	.768	.951
1954 (T)	.398	1.027	.543	.755	.944
1955	.412	1.036	.548	.769	.944
1956	.425	1.030	.559	.781	.944
1957	.425	1.022	.564	.786	.938
1958 (T)	.414	1.027	.562	.773	.927
1959	.434	1.036	.570	.792	.929

[a] Taxable income for 1954-59 and adjusted gross income from *Statistics of Income*. Taxable income for 1948-53 from Leo Cohen, "A More Recent Measurement of the Built-in Flexibility of the Individual Income Tax," *National Tax Journal*, Vol. 13 (June 1960), p. 122. Taxable income for 1948 from Joseph Pechman, "What Would a Comprehensive Individual Income Tax Yield?", *Tax Revision Compendium*, House Ways and Means Committee; 86 Cong. 1 sess. (1959), p. 257. Personal income and transfer payments are from U.S. Department of Commerce. T stands for trough year of recession.

[b] Taxable income on returns with tax; excludes taxable income of persons whose income was completely offset by tax credits. Not corrected for certain minor redefinitions of the tax base in the Revenue Code of 1954.

[c] Increase in taxable income from 1947 to 1948 not comparable to other years, because of increases in personal exemptions in the Revenue Act of 1948.

[d] PI = total personal income, including transfer payments.

The rise in the ratio of taxable to personal income over the period 1948-59 is due to an increase in the ratio of adjusted gross (on taxable returns) to total personal income, and of taxable to adjusted gross income. The rise in the ratio of adjusted gross to total personal income, reflecting a decline in the proportion of income received by nontaxable families in low income brackets, is not a surprising development during a period of generally rising incomes.[5] The rise in the ratio of taxable to adjusted gross income reflects the role that personal exemptions play in the built-in flexibility of the tax.

Although built-in flexibility (measured by the percentage of the total change in income which is taxable) has been in excess of the average ratio of tax base to total income, this does not by itself mean that built-in flexibility of the tax base has increased. In fact, Pechman, using annual data for the period 1946-53, found the marginal ratio rather stable and concluded that built-in flexibility for that period was fairly constant.[6] Brown and Kruizenga, using annual data for 1929 to 1953, estimated that the ratio of taxable to personal income, as would be expected, responds positively to changes in per capita income and negatively to changes in per capita exemptions. But the preferred version of their equation implies little increase in built-in flexibility over a fairly extended period.[7]

A comparison of individual income tax withholdings against wages and salaries (see Table C-5) suggests an income elasticity substantially greater than unity for periods of rising income. Withholdings climbed distinctly more rapidly than wages and salaries in all three recovery periods shown in Table C-5. Progressivity is less pronounced in the re-

[5] See Joseph A. Pechman, "What Would a Comprehensive Individual Income Tax Yield?," *Tax Revision Compendium*, Vol. 1, House Ways and Means Committee, 86 Cong. 1 sess. (1959), Tables 2 and 4, pp. 256 and 257. His estimates of total adjusted gross income, reported and nonreported, show a stable relation to personal income. While total personal income almost doubled since 1948, nonreported adjusted gross income increased by only about one-third.

[6] Joseph A. Pechman, "Yield of the Individual Income Tax During a Recession," *Policies to Combat Depression*, Conference of the Universities-National Bureau Committee for Economic Research (Princeton University Press, 1956), pp. 123-45. The figures he gives imply built-in flexibility of taxable income equal to about 55 percent of changes in personal income.

[7] E. Cary Brown and Richard J. Kruizenga, "Income Sensitivity of a Simple Personal Income Tax," *Review of Economics and Statistics*, Vol. 41 (August 1959), pp. 260-69. Their measurement of built-in flexibility ranged narrowly between 51 and 54 percent (taxable income compared to personal income) for the period 1948-53.

TABLE C-5. Relation of Individual Income Tax to Selected Income Measures in Three Recessions and Recoveries[a]

Item	Recession Percent Change Peak to Trough			Recovery Percent Change Trough to Terminal Quarter		
	1948-49	1953-54	1957-58	1949-50	1954-55	1958-59
Income						
Wages and salaries	—2.6	—1.8	—2.5	5.2	6.9	10.8
Proprietors and property income[b]	—6.0	0.8	0.9	4.8	6.5	4.7
Total personal income less transfers ..	—3.6	—1.1	—1.5	5.1	6.8	8.9
Tax[c]						
Withheld tax (gross)	—2.5	0.6	—4.5	8.3	11.3	18.0
Nonwithheld tax (gross)	—6.8	—3.6	—3.4	7.0	3.3	5.4
Total (net of refunds)	—1.7	—2.5	—5.0	8.9	9.4	15.2

[a] From Appendix B and U.S. Department of Commerce. All data seasonally adjusted. Peaks and troughs are GNP peaks and troughs, as in Table I, which are usually, but not necessarily, the peaks and troughs for personal income. Terminal quarters of recovery are identified in Table 3.

[b] Consists of proprietor's income, rent, interest, and dividends.

[c] Measured at constant (prerecession) tax rates, excluding tax attributable to realized capital gains and losses.

cession stages, elasticity rising distinctly above unity only in 1957-58 and falling distinctly below unity in 1953-54.[8]

There is also some evidence of growing elasticity of the withheld tax with the passage of time (aside from tax rate changes), which agrees with (and could be due to the same reasons as) the earlier observation made with respect to annual data for the total individual income tax. If a drop in income represents a fall from a higher to a lower level of taxable income, the drop in tax as a percentage of the drop in income is larger than if the same drop carries income below the taxable level set by deductions and exemptions, in which case some of the taxpayer's potential exemptions go "unused." This "unused exemption" offset to progressivity may be presumed to be a relatively less important factor the higher the average level of income and the smaller the proportion of taxpayers on the margin between having taxable income and not having taxable income. For similar reasons, the built-in flexibility of the tax will be affected by the extent to which the drop in aggregate income represents shorter hours, loss of overtime work, or reduced wage rates—

[8] It may be that the drop in tax rates on January 1, 1954, has partially obscured the measurement for the 1953-54 decline, although adjustments were made to all series in an attempt to correct for tax rate changes.

that is, reductions from a higher to a lower level of taxable income—rather than unemployment, which is more likely to give rise to unused exemptions.

Turning to the nonwithheld tax, quarterly declarations of estimated tax and final payments on a calendar year's liability are due at the following times:

	Present	*Prior to January 1955*
1st declaration	...April	March
2nd declaration	..June	June
3rd declaration	..September	September
4th declaration	..January, following year	January, following year
Final payment	...April, following year	March, following year

The law intends that a fourth of estimated liability for the year (in excess of amounts paid through withholding) be paid with each declaration. However, there is no penalty for underestimation on the first three declarations if total declarations for the year come to 70 percent of final liability (or the preceding year's final liability). Generally, taxpayers prefer to hold their money as long as possible, and, as a result, fourth declarations are considerably higher than the first three, and substantial additional amounts are not paid until filing the final return. This means a substantial lag of unadjusted cash payments behind accrued liability in recession years. But part of the lag is purely "seasonal" in the sense that deferrals to the fourth declaration occur every year. Seasonally adjusted declarations, in fact, respond with a rather short lag to changes in income levels. Calculations in Appendix B go one step further and assume that first, second, third, and fourth declarations represent liabilities accruing in the first, second, third, and fourth calendar-year quarters respectively.

While seasonally adjusted declarations, whether measured by accruals or cash payments, respond quickly to recessions, they lag behind in recovery. This is probably attributable to the rule allowing estimated tax to be based on the preceding year's liability. To that extent, the lag will be offset by higher final payments if these are recorded on an accrual basis.

Total nonwithheld accruals are shown in Table C-5. Nonwithheld tax is frequently assumed to represent principally the tax on self-employed and property incomes which are not subject to withholding. The inadequacy of changes in income from these sources as an explanation of cyclical changes in nonwithheld tax, however, is illustrated by the contrast between the sharp fall in nonwithheld tax in 1953-54 and 1957-

58 in the face of increased proprietor's and property income. Although the possibility of downward redistribution of income by tax bracket may partially explain the discrepancy, as might the inclusion in the income estimates of certain imputed items not subject to tax, it appears that changes in liability on wages and salaries in excess of withholdings are a more significant factor. However, the large drop in proprietor's and property income in 1948-49 was undoubtedly a factor in the particularly large decrease in nonwithheld tax that year.

With respect to total tax liabilities (net of refunds), also shown in Table C-5, the percentage change in tax is considerably greater than the percentage change in income in both recession and recovery. Lower tax rates in 1948 are part of the explanation of lower income elasticity at that time than subsequently, although it has already been argued above that, aside from rate changes, an increase in average income should increase the cycle sensitivity of tax. Starting tax rates were lower in 1957-59 than in 1953-55. Income elasticity, nevertheless, was somewhat greater in 1957-59.

Employment Taxes

The estimates of employment taxes at constant rates during recession and recovery which are presented in Chapter II were derived by applying the computed effective rate in prerecession peak years to total private wages and salaries. The effective rates for the prerecession peak years are shown in Table C-6.

The method may somewhat overstate the marginal changes in employment taxes inasmuch as the employment taxes do not apply to the part of wages of covered persons that is in excess of an upper limit (now $4,800). For individuals whose income was below the taxable limit at the prerecession peak, average and marginal rates of tax are equal and there is no distortion. For others, overstatement involved in letting the average rate represent the marginal rate depends on the amount of income earned in excess of the taxable limit in relation to the size of the recession-induced drop in income. For example, if the payroll tax rate is 6 per cent of the first $4,800 of income, an individual whose income falls from $6,000 to $3,000 has a ratio of change in tax to change in income of 3.6 per cent compared to an average rate of tax of 4.8 per cent. However, an individual making $5,000 also experiencing a $3,000 drop in income has a marginal rate of 5.6 per cent, only slightly less than his average rate of 5.8 per cent.

TABLE C-6. Federal Employment Taxes in Prerecession Peak Years[a]

(Amounts in millions of dollars)

Item	1948	1953	1957	1960
Contributions				
Employer:				
Old-age and survivors insurance	839	1,882	3,673	5,671
State unemployment insurance	965	1,288	1,507	2,344
Federal unemployment tax	228	298	337	358
Railroad retirement insurance	283	312	304	295
Railroad unemployment insurance	25	25	97	165
Employee:				
Old-age and survivors insurance	839	1,882	3,673	5,671
Railroad retirement insurance	283	312	304	295
Self-employed persons:				
Old-age and survivors insurance	. . .	219	522	708
Total contributions	3,462	6,218	10,417	15,507
Private wages and salaries	116,443	164,157	198,379	222,953
Total contributions as percent of private wages and salaries	2.97	3.79	5.25	6.96
Employer contributions as percent of total	67.6	61.2	56.8	57.0

[a] Data from U.S. Department of Commerce, *U.S. Income and Output (1958)* and *Survey of Current Business*, July 1961. Contributions for social insurance on a national income account basis, excluding those contributions presumed not to be sensitive to cycles (such as contributions to federal employee retirement systems).

299

APPENDIX D

Notes on Sources and Data

General

MOST of the basic economic and fiscal data used in this study are drawn from the national income accounts as published by the U.S. Department of Commerce. Future revisions of the data used for the first three recessions[1] will probably be minor. For the 1960-61 recession, preliminary Commerce Department estimates for the first quarter of 1962 were the latest official figures available for this study. The July 1962 *Survey of Current Business* will, if the past is a guide, make wholesale revisions in the data for the calendar year 1961. These may slightly change the perspective from the one available at the time of this writing (March 1962) in several minor respects, but probably will not alter the overall picture significantly. For certain benchmark calculations, the author made tentative projections for the second quarter of 1962 of the gross national product (GNP), unemployment rate, and a few other statistical measures. However, the use to which these calculations is put is such that conclusions based on them would not be significantly affected by moderate forecasting errors.

Perhaps the next most significant body of statistical data used consists of monthly labor force data now published by the U.S. Department of Labor. The reader should be alerted to the fact that seasonally adjusted labor force data for most of the postwar period were revised in early 1962,[2] which gives rise to some revisions in the dating of cyclical

[1] U.S. Department of Commerce, *U.S. Income and Output* (1958), and *Survey of Current Business,* July 1961.

[2] U.S. Department of Labor, *Monthly Report on the Labor Force,* January 1962.

300

peaks and troughs in unemployment. In this study, the recent data were used except for the period 1948-50, for which they were discarded in favor of the earlier data[3] since the new series covers only part of 1948. In all cases, seasonally adjusted quarterly labor force figures used in the study are simple arithmetic averages of the seasonally adjusted monthly figures published by the Department of Labor.

The principal sources of information used for the chronological discussion of fiscal policy developments are the ordinary published sources for which footnotes are included at appropriate places. On some points, the study drew on information which cannot be documented in the ordinary fashion, such as conversations with some of the government officials involved.

In tables, the insertion of three dots (. . .) means "not available" or "not applicable"; the insertion of a dash (—) means "zero" or a figure less than the smallest unit shown. Also, since figures have been rounded, many do not add to totals.

On Charts

In Charts 2, 3, 4, and 5, gross national product represents seasonally adjusted annual rates in billions of constant prerecession dollars. The actual rates were derived from Department of Commerce estimates in constant dollars; the high employment estimates from Table A-1. Both series were converted to prerecession prices by applying the implicit price deflator for GNP with the base shifted (prerecession peak quarter = 100).[4]

Unemployment is the seasonally adjusted rate, as a percentage of the civilian labor force. For 1948-50, the estimates are those used by the Department of Labor in 1960, since—as noted above—the more recent series includes data only for the period since mid-1948. (The estimates shown in Table 15 are from the revised series and differ somewhat from those underlying Chart 2.) For later periods, the revised series was used. Quarterly figures were derived by averaging monthly estimates.[5]

Federal receipts, expenditures, and actual surplus or deficit represent seasonally adjusted quarterly totals at annual rates, in current prices, on the national income account basis.[6]

[3] *Ibid.,* February 1960.

[4] Sources were *U.S. Income and Output* (1958); *Survey of Current Business,* various issues; and *Economic Indicators,* March 1962.

[5] Source: Department of Labor, *Monthly Report on the Labor Force,* January 1962.

[6] Sources: *U.S. Income and Output* (1958); *Survey of Current Business,* July 1961; and preliminary estimates for 1961.

The implicit federal surplus or deficit represents seasonally adjusted annual rates, in current prices, on the national income account basis, as shown in Tables 20, 24, 28, and 30.

Summary Tables on Factors Affecting
the Federal Surplus

Text Tables 20, 24, 28, and 30 summarize factors affecting the federal surplus for each of the postwar recessions and recoveries. They are based, as much of the data in this study are, on the U. S. Department of Commerce national income and product accounts, and are at seasonally adjusted annual rates. Peaks (P), troughs (T), and terminal quarters of recovery (R) are as in Table 1.

High employment receipts at constant precession tax rates were calculated as described in Appendix A. Method 1 was used for excise, individual income, and employment taxes. Method 2 was used for corporate profits taxes. Individual income taxes were computed on a "full accrual" basis, described in Appendix B, except in Table 30, where the national income account basis had to be used because data were not available to allow full accrual estimates. Other receipts are on a national income account basis. Adjustments for changes in tax rates were calculated at presumed high employment yields.

The expenditure items listed under "factors not due to the recession" include all changes in expenditures, as shown in the national income accounts, except for items classified as discretionary antirecession actions, and so listed in the tables, and unemployment compensation. Temporary extended unemployment compensation payments in 1957-59 and 1960-62 are classified as discretionary expenditures. The item for unemployment compensation under built-in stabilizers represents the increase in payments, under the regular program, attributable to the departure of the economy from high employment.

The effect of built-in fiscal stabilizers represents the shortfall of actual from hypothetical high employment, both adjusted to constant prerecession tax rates. "Other adjustments" (which enter into the total actual surplus or deficit) include adjustments for (1) the exclusion of capital gains tax from individual income tax accruals; and (2) the differences in timing between the "full accrual" basis of individual income tax and the national income account basis. Also, in Tables 20 and 24, additional adjustments were required; these are indicated in notes to the tables.

Index

Sem.

40 hrs. × 40 = 1600 hrs.
$$\frac{\times\ 20}{32\ 000}$$